GREENLAND

ASIA

EUROPE

AFRICA

SOUTH
AMERICA

Cape Town

Kerguelen

SMILLIE

Credit: Author's Private Collection

Voyage to the Pacific Ocean

Seventy North to Fifty South

PORTRAIT OF CAPTAIN JAMES COOK

Credit: Engraving, Author's Private Collection

Seventy North to Fifty South

The Story of Captain Cook's Last Voyage

Wherein Are Discovered

Numerous South Pacific Islands, The Hawaiian Islands, The Coast of North America, and Alaska

---

Condensed, Edited, and Annotated

by

Paul W. Dale

❦

Prentice-Hall, Inc., Englewood Cliffs, N.J.

Seventy North to Fifty South: Captain Cook's Last Voyage
by Paul W. Dale

Library of Congress Catalog Card Number: 69-11969
Printed in the United States of America · T
Prentice-Hall International, Inc., London
Prentice-Hall of Australia, Pty. Ltd., Sydney
Prentice-Hall of Canada, Ltd., Toronto
Prentice-Hall of India Private Ltd., New Delhi
Prentice-Hall of Japan, Inc., Tokyo

This book is dedicated to all small boys and girls
in small boats, and grown men and women in large boats, who
sail on intrepid voyages . . . not to gain in wealth, but
to enrich their lives, and to enlarge their
knowledge of the world

Contents

List of Illustrations

Introduction ੨~

My little daughter once asked me, "Daddy, who are you writing that book for?"

I replied, "It is for someone who has to take an airplane from New York to Los Angeles and wants something interesting to read."

My answer to her was correct, but not the whole answer; for I had in mind, as I was working, all those who love the sea and collect accounts of cruises and voyages. My own voyaging has been confined to sailing small boats in spare moments—and some not so easily spared—off the coasts of both extremes of the continent. Much of this book was written in the cabin of my little ship.

As any Corinthian sailor would be, I was immeasurably pleased and excited when, almost by chance, I came into possession of Captain Cook's account of his third voyage. I had in my hands the daily record of the master sailor of all times. Of special interest was the fact that in this voyage Cook discovered territories that later became part of the United States. I thought that most every sailor I knew would be interested in this account, but the three books were too old and fragile to lend out. Furthermore, the type, spelling, and language of two hundred years ago limited its usefulness for recreational reading. (No one would want to take the original volumes on an airplane to Los Angeles.) Yet I dearly wished to share my find with all fellow-sailors without having to send them to the rare-book section of some large library.

My enjoyment in the first reading was so great that I readily began again at the first page preparing a modernized and somewhat con-

densed rendition of these historic volumes. Along the way, it seemed
to me that some explanation might be in order to make the whole
account more intelligible and to connect events that Cook recorded
with occurrences that both preceded and followed his voyage. Scholars
and pedants alike are cautioned that in order to condense the three
volumes of the 1784 manuscript into a single volume of pleasurable
reading, some liberties have been taken with the original text. All
spelling, including that of geographical place names, has been changed
to modern American English. Punctuation has been altered to con-
form with current practice; paragraphs have become sentences; dele-
tions have been made (but not indicated) and connective words and
phrases have been inserted where necessary to make the meaning
clear, also not indicated. In all instances the original meaning has been
preserved, and because I believe no one could tell it better than Cook,
there has been no significant paraphrasing.

Footnotes have their place, but not here. Anyone curious enough
to read the book in the first place would surely want to read the footnotes. Therefore, what might be considered footnote material is intro-
mitted into the body of the Cook account. The same technique is used
for more lengthy annotations, explanations, and historical references.
All passages preceded by ✍ and followed by ☙ are entries from the
journals; author's comments included in these entries are in italics
within parentheses.

A

VOYAGE

TO THE

PACIFIC OCEAN.

UNDERTAKEN,

BY THE COMMAND OF HIS MAJESTY,

FOR MAKING

Diſcoveries in the Northern Hemiſphere.

TO DETERMINE

The POSITION and EXTENT of the WEST SIDE of NORTH AMERICA ;
its DISTANCE from ASIA ; and the PRACTICABILITY of a
NORTHERN PASSAGE to EUROPE.

PERFORMED UNDER THE DIRECTION OF

Captains COOK, CLERKE, and GORE,

In his MAJESTY's Ships the RESOLUTION and DISCOVERY.

In the Years 1776, 1777, 1778, 1779, and 1780.

IN THREE VOLUMES.

VOL. I. and II. written by Captain JAMES COOK, F.R.S.
VOL. III. by Captain JAMES KING, LL.D. and F.R.S.

Illuſtrated with MAPS and CHARTS, from the Original Drawings made by Lieut.
HENRY ROBERTS, under the Direction of Captain COOK.

Publiſhed by Order of the Lords Commiſſioners of the Admiralty.

VOL. I.

DUBLIN:

Printed for H. CHAMBERLAINE, W. WATSON, POTTS, WILLIAMS,
CROSS, JACKSON, MONCRIEFFE, WALKER, JENKIN, BURNET,
WILSON, WOGAN, EXSHAW, VALLANCE, BEATTY,
WHITE, WHITESTONE, BURTON, BYRNE,
MILLS, J. PORTER, STEWART,
WALLACE, HIGLY, CASH,
HEREY and Mc. KENZIE.

M,DCC,LXXXIV.

*TITLE PAGE OF FIRST EDITION
OF COOK'S JOURNALS*

Credit: Author's Private Collection

CHAPTER ONE

PREPARATIONS

February 9, 1776———July 14, 1776

ENGLAND, 1776 ⋖ᣠ Having, on the ninth day of February, 1776, received a commission to command His Majesty's sloop the *Resolution,*
I went on board the next day, hoisted the pennant, and began to enter
men. The *Discovery* was purchased into the service and command of
her given to Captain Clerke, who had been my second lieutenant on
board the *Resolution* in my second voyage around the world, from
which we had lately returned. ᣠᣔ

When Captain James Cook wrote these first words of his *Journal,*
he was forty-eight years of age. The son of a poor Yorkshire farm
laborer, he had been apprenticed at the age of sixteen to a haber-
dasher in the small, north-sea coastal town of Staithes. Within a year
and a half, he had left with his employer's blessing to go to sea in the
coastwise coal and merchant ships sailing out of the neighboring
harbor of Whitby. Over a period of ten years, he rose to the rank of
first mate. But, at the age of twenty-seven, he sought a more adventuresome life, joined the Royal Navy, and started over again at the lowly
rank of ordinary seaman.

Four years later, he commanded a succession of small vessels de-
ployed off Quebec, Newfoundland, the St. Lawrence, and New Bruns-
wick. England, at the time, was fighting the French and Indian Wars.
Both during the war, and especially after the English victory, he showed
his talent for surveying, charting, mathematics, astronomy and seamanship. These things he taught himself or learned from others at

1

sea, for he had no formal schooling beyond the elementary grades. He cruised his ships to unknown lands, where currents, fogs, tides, and the generally bad and inconstant weather of the North Atlantic make life miserable for the sailor.

His *Sailing Directions to the Coast of Newfoundland and Labrador,* published in 1767, and his astronomical observations of a solar eclipse, observed in Newfoundland on August 5, 1766, impressed the Royal Society, the leading scientific body of its day. The Society had received support from King George III to send a naval ship to observe a predicted transit of Venus. To accomplish this mission, the Royal Navy on May 25, 1768, commissioned Cook to sail the *Endeavour,* a converted Thames Coal ship (the same design of ship as he had started out in when a young man), to the South Pacific. Not only did he reach Tahiti on schedule to observe Venus cross the face of the sun on June 3, 1769, but he also sailed on to discover and explore New Zealand and the west coast of Australia. Continuing westerly, he went around the world and returned to England in June 1771—a voyage of three years.

The next summer he was sent to sea again to continue his explorations of the South Pacific Ocean. He sailed in the ship *Resolution,* with a companion vessel, the *Adventure,* under command of Captain Furneaux. This time he went from east to west. Between Africa and New Zealand, he sailed south all the way to the Antarctic Circle looking for new lands, but found none. (He was supposed to be looking for a theoretical southern continent needed to balance the land masses of the northern continents and keep the world from "tipping over"— a theory he took no stock in.) Beyond New Zealand, he sailed east across the polar seas of the Pacific, again sometimes south of the Antarctic Circle, then north and west again, back across the Pacific to visit Easter Island, the Marquesas, Tahiti, Tonga, New Hebrides, New Caledonia, and other islands of the South Pacific. Provisioning again in New Zealand, he waited in vain for the *Adventure,* which had been lost during a storm. Finally, he sailed alone east through the latitudes of the Roaring Forties and the violent winds, seas, and terrible cold of the fifties and sixties all the way to Tierra del Fuego and Cape Horn. Ice prevented his getting as far south as the Antarctic Continent. In a snaking path through the oceans of the southern part of the world, Cook made another circumnavigation. All told, he was away three years in hostile lands and Antarctic seas, twice going past the world's most distant point from land, and lost only four men of his crew of 118. Such a record was phenomenal in its time and would be hard to equal in the annals of modern exploration.

At the time the Captain was preparing for a third voyage, the British Navy suffered from the greatest corruption and incapacity of the fleet that the country had ever experienced—though there is no hint of it in the polite and subservient language of his *Journal*. Cook knew well what his needs would be. Before the Navy purchased his ships, they, like the *Endeavour,* were coal-carrying barks from Whitby, where his seafaring education had begun. The *Resolution* had returned from Cook's long second voyage the year before. As events proved, she was too old, tired, and rotten for another long voyage and required constant repairs during this cruise. She was 110 feet long, had a beam of 30 feet, and drew 13 feet. The *Discovery* was the smallest vessel ever to sail with Cook. She measured about 90 feet on deck, had a beam of 27 feet, and drew 11 feet. She was a newer boat and, although smaller, did not fall apart as much as the *Resolution*.

Cook chose vessels of the Whitby coal-shipping design not only because he was familiar with their sailing characteristics but also because these ships by reason of the job they were built for had the capacity for large, heavy loads and thus could carry all the supplies for a long expedition. At the same time they did not draw much water and could be taken into comparatively shallow and unexplored harbors and bays. Furthermore they had nearly flat bottoms and would not lie over on their sides if grounded and could be beached and hauled down for repairs, if needed, in some remote spot in the world.

◄§ With the benevolent view of conveying some permanent benefit to the inhabitants of Tahiti and of the other islands in the Pacific Ocean whom we might happen to visit, His Majesty commanded some useful animals to be carried out. We took on board, on the tenth (*June 1776*), a bull, two cows with their calves, and some sheep, with hay and corn for their subsistence; intending to add other useful animals, when I should arrive at the Cape of Good Hope.

I was also, from the same laudable motives, furnished with a sufficient quantity of such of our European garden seeds as could not fail to be a valuable present to our newly discovered islands by adding fresh supplies of food to their own vegetable productions. (*Starving England was sending seeds where want of food was never known.*)

Many other articles, calculated to improve the condition of our friends in the other hemisphere, were at the same time delivered to us by order of the Board of Admiralty. Both ships were provided with a proper assortment of iron tools and trinkets as the means of enabling us to traffic, and to cultivate a friendly intercourse, with the inhabitants of such new countries as we might be fortunate enough to meet with.

The same humane attention was extended to our own wants. Some additional clothing, adapted to a cold climate, was ordered for our crews. And nothing was denied to us that could be supposed in the least conducive to health or even to convenience. Both ships indeed were supplied with as much of every necessary article as we could conveniently stow and with the best of every kind that could be procured. And besides this, everything that had been found by the experience acquired during our former extensive voyage to be of any utility in preserving the health of seamen was supplied in abundance. ֍

There were few Navy commanders of his day who would look first to "preserving the health of seamen." Seamen were the lowest of the low and usually expendable. Cook not only knew that once he left England there would be no more seamen available, but, as we shall see, he was from first to last a humanitarian to all—savage and seaman alike—and genuinely interested in the welfare of his crew.

֍ Nor did the extraordinary care of those at the head of the Naval Department stop here. They were equally solicitous to afford every assistance toward rendering our voyage of public utility. Accordingly, we received on board the next day several astronomical and nautical instruments, which the Board of Longitude entrusted to me and to Mr. King, my second lieutenant; we having engaged to that Board to make all the necessary observations during the voyage for the improvement of astronomy and navigation; and, by our joint labors, to supply the place of a professed observer—such a person had originally intended to be sent out in my ship.

The board, likewise, put into our possession the same watch, or timekeeper, which I had carried out in my last voyage and which had performed its part so well. It was a copy of Mr. Harrison's, constructed by Mr. Kendall. This day, at noon, it was found to be too slow for mean time at Greenwich by 3 min., 31.890 sec.; and by its rate of going it lost, on mean time, 1.209 sec. per day.

Another timekeeper and the same number and sort of instruments for making observations were put on board the *Discovery* under the care of Mr. William Bayly, who, having already given satisfactory proofs of his skill and diligence as an observer while employed in Captain Furneaux's ship during the late voyage (*the ship* Adventure *on Cook's second voyage*), was engaged a second time in that capacity to embark with Captain Clerke. ॐ

John Harrison, the watchmaker, solved the plaguing question of longitude—how far a ship was east or west on the earth's surface—in the same way that it is solved today. A watch set to the time at Greenwich, English, is carried with the ship. The time for astronomical events at Greenwich is predetermined and tables constructed to record the time of these events. When the sun passes the meridian at Greenwich, it is noon at Greenwich and the clock, corrected for its error and rate of going, will read twelve hours exactly. When this clock is carried elsewhere on the earth's surface, east or west of Greenwich, the same event, such as the sun passing the meridian at noon, will occur too soon if you are east, and too late if you are west of Greenwich. One minute of time equals 15 minutes of longitude, or, at the equator, 15 nautical miles. To make a clock accurate enough to be serviceable on a long voyage with the ship pitching and rolling was quite a trick and still is. Cook's clock, it should be noted, is going to lose a minute every sixty days; not a problem if the rate of loss is constant; but if it changes, all determinations of longitude by this method will be erroneous. Every minute the clock is off will mean about 15 miles of error from the true position. The log of the voyage indicates this actually happened to Kendall's clocks and sets forth the measures Captain Cook took to prevent this error from creeping into his calculations.

Harrison solved many of the difficulties of accurate timekeeping by inventing devices to compensate for temperature, to keep the clock going unchanged when it was wound, and to keep friction to the minimum. The "Board of Longitude" referred to in the *Journal* was set up by the British government to stimulate work on the problem. It offered a prize to anyone who might discover a solution. Harrison was finally awarded the prize in 1773 and died in March 1776, just before Cook sailed on his third voyage.

◄§ Mr. Anderson, my surgeon, who, to skill in his immediate profession added great proficiency in natural history, was as willing as he was well qualified, to describe everything in that branch of science which should occur worthy of notice. As he had already visited the South Sea Islands in the same ship and had been of singular service by enabling me to enrich my relation of that voyage with various useful remarks on men and things, I reasonably expected to derive considerable assistance from him in recording our new proceedings.

I had several young men among my sea officers who, under my direction, could be usefully employed in constructing charts, in taking views of the coast and headlands near which we should pass, and in drawing plans of the bays and harbors in which we should anchor. A constant attention to this I knew to be highly requisite if we would render our discoveries profitable to future navigators.

And, that we might go out with every help that could serve to make the result of our voyage entertaining to the generality of readers, as well as instructive to the sailor and scholar, Mr. Webber was pitched upon and engaged to embark with me for the express purpose of supplying the unavoidable imperfections of written accounts by enabling us to preserve and to bring home such drawings of the most memorable scenes of our transactions as could be executed by a professed and skillful artist.

Every preparation now being completed, I received an order to proceed to Plymouth and to take the *Discovery* under my command. I accordingly gave Captain Clerke two orders: one to put himself under my command, and the other to carry his ship around to Plymouth.

On the fifteenth of June, 1776, the *Resolution* sailed from Long Reach, with the *Discovery* in company. The *Resolution* was ordered to remain at the Nore until I should join her, being at this time in London.

As we were to touch at Tahiti and the Society Islands, on our way to the intended scene of our fresh operations (*a search for the Northwest Passage*) it has been determined not to omit this opportunity (the only one ever likely to happen) of carrying Omai back to his native country. ◊►

Omai was the fourth Polynesian to sail with Captain Cook. On the first voyage, a minor chief and his grandson, also from Tahiti, sailed with Captain Cook when he left that island. The man and boy volunteered to go with Cook and proved invaluable when later they came

PORTRAIT OF OMAI

Credit: Engraving, Author's Private Collection

upon New Zealand. Here, 2,400 miles from Tahiti, Cook and his Polynesian friends made the amazing discovery that the language of the New Zealand Maori was so much the same as in Tahiti as to be easily understood. This meant that Polynesian, in geographic distance, was the most widely distributed language in the world. While the ships were refitting at Batavia, this brave Polynesian pair unfortunately succumbed to cholera along with many of the crew. About the only man not taken ill was the old sailmaker, who drank only rum.

In the second voyage, Cook stayed away from civilization and everyone remained free of contagious and fatal diseases. Very likely the death of his two Tahitian shipmates hurt him deeply, for he firmly declined the entreaties of other Polynesians to sail with him except for one man who went with him from Tahiti and stayed on board until they returned to Tahiti a second time to refit. He also permitted Furneaux, captain of the *Adventure,* to take Omai aboard his ship when they left Tahiti for the last time. Leaving Tahiti, the *Adventure* was blown off course in a heavy gale and parted company from the *Resolution.* Cook waited for them at the rendezvous anchorage in Queen Charlotte Sound in New Zealand, but when Furneaux finally arrived there, he found the *Resolution* had left six days earlier, so he sailed directly home to England, where he arrived with Omai aboard, a full year before Cook returned.

◄§ Omai left London with a mixture of regret and satisfaction. When he talked about England and about those who during his stay had honored him with their protection or friendship, I could observe that his spirits were sensibly affected and that it was with difficulty he could refrain from tears. But the instant the conversation turned to his own islands, his eyes began to sparkle with joy. (*The English, also living on an island, no doubt felt a kinship to this Pacific islander. By this time Omai had been in England for two years.*) He was deeply impressed with a sense of the good treatment he had met with in England and entertained the highest ideas of the country and of the people. But the pleasing prospect he now had before him of returning home, loaded with what he well knew would be esteemed invaluable treasures there, and the flattering hope which the possession of these gave him of attaining to a distinguished superiority among his countrymen, were considerations which operated by degrees to suppress every uneasy sensation; he seemed to be quite happy when he got on board the ship.

He was furnished by His Majesty with an ample provision of every article which, during our intercourse with his country, we had observed to be in any estimation there, either as useful or as ornamental. He had, besides, received many presents of the same nature from Lord Sandwich, Sir Joseph Banks, and several other gentlemen and ladies of his acquaintance. In short, every method had been employed, both during his abode in England and at his departure, to make him the instrument of carrying to the islands of the Pacific Ocean the most exalted opinion of the greatness and generosity of the British nation. ৯

We will see that when Omai returned to his island home he had in no sense developed, in his absence, the Western notion of private property. All of these "treasures" came to naught in a land where storing up treasure was unknown.

৯ While the *Resolution* lay at the Nore (*Lower Thames, below London*), Mr. King made several observations for finding the longitude by the watch. The mean of them all gave 0° 44′ 0″ for the longitude of the ship. This, reduced to Sheerness, by the bearing and estimated distance, will make the place to be 0° 37′ 0″ east of Greenwich; which is more by 7 miles than Mr. Lyons made it, by the watch which Lord Mulgrave had with him on his voyage toward the North Pole. Whoever knows anything of the distance between Sheerness and Greenwich will be a judge which of these two observations is nearer the truth.

The variation of the needle here, by a mean of different sets, taken by different compasses, was 30° 37′ west.

On the twenty-sixth, about noon, we weighed anchor and made sail for the Downs (*mouth of the Thames*) through the Queen's Channel, with a gentle breeze at northwest by west. ৯

The careful navigator, at the start of a voyage, works his sights and makes his calculations when his position is still known, so as to check the accuracy of his instruments, sighting, and mathematics. But even in familiar England, mapping was not so precise that the distance from Greenwich to a point at Sheerness, about 40 land miles away, was reliably known. Pinning down the exact locations of geographical points continues in our age of missiles. Navigational data from the manmade satellites have enabled geographers to locate, with precision, places on the earth's surface where measurements have previously been at fault by several miles.

The variation of the compass was determined by measuring the angular distance of the compass needle from true north, as determined by celestial observations such as observing the North Star or the Sun at the time of its meridian passage.

᪥ Sunday, June 30, 1776: On the thirtieth, at three o'clock in the afternoon, we anchored in Plymouth Sound, where the *Discovery* had arrived only three days before. I saluted Admiral Amherst, whose flag was flying on board the *Ocean,* with thirteen guns and he returned the compliment with eleven.

It could not but occur to us as a singular and affecting circumstance that at the very instant of our departure upon a voyage, the object of which was to benefit Europe by making fresh discoveries in North America, there should be the necessity of employing others of His Majesty's ships, and of conveying numerous bodies of land forces, to secure the obedience of those parts of that continent which had been discovered and settled by our countrymen in the last century. On the sixth, His Majesty's ships *Diamond, Ambuscade* and *Unicorn,* with a fleet of transports consisting of sixty-two sail bound to America, with the last division of Hessian troops and some horses, were forced into the Sound by a strong northwest wind.

On the eighth I received, by express, my instructions for the voyage and an order to proceed to the Cape of Good Hope with the *Resolution.*

SECRET INSTRUCTIONS FOR CAPTAIN JAMES COOK, COMMANDER OF HIS MAJESTY'S SLOOP THE *Resolution*:

Whereas the Earl of Sandwich has signified to us His Majesty's pleasure (*King George III*), that an attempt should be made to find out a northern passage by sea from the Pacific to the Atlantic Ocean; and whereas we have in pursuance thereof, caused His Majesty's sloops *Resolution* and *Discovery* to be fitted, in all respects, proper to proceed upon a voyage for the purpose above mentioned, and, from the experience we have had of your abilities and good conduct in your late voyages, have thought fit to entrust you with the conduct of the present intended voyage and with that view appointed you to command the first-mentioned sloop and directed Captain Clerke, who commands the other, to follow your orders for his further proceedings. You are hereby required and directed to proceed with the said two sloops directly to the Cape of Good Hope, unless you shall judge it necessary to stop at Madeira, the Cape de Verdi, or Canary Islands to take in wine for the use of their companies; in which case you are at liberty to do so, taking care to remain there no longer than may be necessary for that purpose.

On your arrival at the Cape of Good Hope, you are to refresh the sloop's companies and to cause the sloops to be supplied with as much provisions and water as they can conveniently stow.

You are, if possible, to leave the Cape of Good Hope by the end of October, or the beginning of November next, and proceed to the southward in search of some islands said to have been lately seen by the French, in the latitude of 48° 0′ south, and about the meridian of Mauritius. In case you find those islands, you are to examine them thoroughly for a good harbor and upon discovering one, make the necessary observations to facilitate the finding it again; as a good port in that situation may hereafter prove very useful, although it should afford little or nothing more than shelter, wood, and water. You are not, however, to spend too much time in looking out for those islands or in the examinations of them, if found, but proceed to Tahiti or the Society of Isles (touching at New Zealand on your way thither, if you should judge it necessary and convenient), and taking care to arrive there time enough to admit of your giving the sloops' companies the refreshment they may stand in need of, before you prosecute the further object of these instructions.

Upon your arrival at Tahiti or the Society of Isles you are to land Omai at such of them as he may choose, and to leave him there.

You are to distribute among the chiefs of those islands such part of the presents with which you have been supplied as you shall judge proper, reserving the remainder to distribute among the natives of the countries you may discover in the Northern Hemisphere. And having refreshed the people belonging to the sloops under your command and taken on board such wood and water as they may respectively stand in need of, you are to leave those islands in the beginning of February, or sooner if you shall judge it necessary, and then proceed in as direct a course as you can to the coast of North America, endeavoring to fall in with it in the latitude of 45° 0′ north; and taking care, in your way thither, not to lose any time in search of new lands, or to stop at any you may fall in with, unless you find it necessary to recruit your wood and water.

You are also, in your way thither, strictly enjoined not to touch upon any part of the Spanish dominions on the western continent of America, unless driven thither by some unavoidable accident; in which case you are to stay no longer there than shall be absolutely necessary, and to be very careful not to give any umbrage or offense to any of the inhabitants or subjects of His Catholic Majesty. And if in your progress to the northward, as hereafter directed, you find any subjects of any European Prince or State upon any part of the coast you may think proper to visit, you are not to disturb them or give them any just cause of offense, but, on the contrary, to treat them with civility and friendship.

Upon your arrival on the Coast of North America, you are to put into the first convenient port to recruit your wood and water and procure refreshments, and then to proceed northward along the coast, as far as the latitude of 65°, or farther if you are not obstructed by lands or ice; taking care not to lose any time in exploring rivers or inlets, or upon any other account, until you get into the beforementioned latitude of 65°, where we could wish you to arrive in the month of June next. When you get that length, you are very carefully to search for and to explore such rivers or inlets as may appear to be of a considerable extent, and pointing toward Hudson's or Baffin's bays; and if from your own observations or from any information you may receive from the native (who, there is reason to believe, are the same race of people and speak the same language, of which you are furnished with a vocabulary, as the Eskimo), there shall appear to be a certainty or even a probability of a water passage into the aforementioned bays, or either of them, you are in such case to use your utmost endeavors to pass through with one or both of the sloops, unless you shall be of opinion that the passage may be effected with more certainty or with greater probability by smaller vessels; in which case you are to set up the frames of one or both the small vessels, with which you are provided, and, when they are put together and are properly fitted, stored, and victualled, you are to dispatch one or both of them under the care of proper officers, with a sufficient number of petty officers, men and boats, in order to attempt the same passage; with such instructions for their rejoining you, if they should fail, or for their further proceedings if they should succeed in the attempt, as you shall judge most proper. But, nevertheless, if you shall find it more eligible to pursue any other measures than those above pointed out in order to make a discovery of the before-mentioned passage (if any such there be) you are at liberty, and we leave it to your discretion, to pursue such measures accordingly.

In case you shall be satisfied that there is no passage through to the above-mentioned bays sufficient for the purpose of navigation, you are, at the proper season of the year, to repair to the port of St. Peter and St. Paul in Kamchatka, or wherever else you shall judge more proper, in order to refresh your people and pass the winter; and, in the spring of the ensuing year 1778, to proceed from thence to the northward as far as in your prudence you may think proper in further search of a northeast or northwest passage from the Pacific Ocean into the Atlantic Ocean, or the North Sea; and if, from your own observation or any information you may receive, there shall appear to be a probability of such passage, you are to proceed as above directed; and having discovered such passage or failed in the attempt, make the best of your way back to England as you may think best for the improvement of geography and navigation, repairing to Spithead with both sloops, where they are to remain 'til further order.

At whatever places you may touch in the course of your voyage where accurate observations of the nature hereafter mentioned have not already been made, you are, as far as your time will allow, very carefully to observe the true situation of such places, both in latitude and longitude, the variation of the needle, bearing of head lands, height, direction and course of the tides and currents, depths and soundings of the sea, shoals, rocks, etc; and also to survey, make charts and take views of such bays, harbors, and different parts of the coast and to make such notations thereon as may be useful either to navigation or commerce. You are also carefully to observe the nature of the soil and produce thereof, the animals and fowls that inhabit or frequent it, the fishes that are to be found in the rivers or upon the coast and in what plenty, and, in case there are any peculiar to such places, to describe them as minutely and make as accurate drawings of them as you can; and, if you find any metals, minerals or valuable stones or any extraneous fossils, you are to bring home specimens of each; as also of the seeds of such trees, shrubs, plants, fruits and grains peculiar to those places as you may be able to collect and to transmit them to our Secretary that proper examination and experiments may be made of them. You are likewise to observe the genius, temper, disposition, and number of the natives and inhabitants where you find any and to endeavor by all proper means to cultivate a friendship with them, making them

presents of such trinkets as you may have on board and they may
like best, inviting them to traffic and showing them every kind of
civility and regard, but taking care, nevertheless, not to suffer
yourself to be surprised by them, but to be always on your guard
against any accidents.

You are also, with the consent of the natives, to take possession in the name of the King of Great Britain, of convenient
situations in such countries as you may discover, that have not
already been discovered or visited by any other European power,
and to distribute among the inhabitants such things as will remain
as traces and testimonies of your having been there; but if you find
the countries so discovered are uninhabited, you are to take possession of them for His Majesty by setting up proper marks and
inscriptions as first discoverers and possessors.

But forasmuch as in undertakings of this nature several emer-
gencies may arise not to be foreseen and therefore not particularly to be provided for by instructions beforehand, you are in
all such cases to proceed as you shall judge most advantageous
to the service on which you are employed.

You are by all opportunities to send to our Secretary for our
information accounts of your proceedings and copies of the sur-
veys and drawings you shall have made; and upon your arrival
in England, you are immediately to repair to this office in order
to lay before us a full account of your proceedings in the whole
course of your voyage, taking care before you leave the sloop to
demand from the officers and petty officers the log books and
journals they may have kept and to seal them up for our inspection and enjoining them and the whole crew not to divulge where
they have been until they shall have permission so to do; and you
are to direct Captain Clerke to do the same with respect to the
officers, petty officers, and crew of the *Discovery*.

If any accident should happen to the *Resolution* in the course
of the voyage so to disable her from proceeding any farther, you
are in such case to remove yourself and her crew into the *Discovery* and to prosecute your voyage in her; her commander
being hereby strictly required to receive you on board and to
obey your orders the same in every respect as when you were
actually on board the *Resolution*. And in case of your inability
by sickness or otherwise to carry these instructions into execution, you are to be careful to leave them with the next officer in
command, who is hereby required to execute them in the best
manner he can.

Given under our hands the sixth day of July, 1776.

Sandwich
C. Spencer
H. Palliser

By command of their Lordships.

PH. Stephens ຂ້ອຍ

Cook reports some of his thoughts just before his departure; but thoughts of wife and children he does not include, as having no place here.

ຂ້ອຍ The first discoverers of the New World, and navigators of the Indian and Pacific oceans, were justly thought to have exerted such uncommon abilities and to have accomplished such perilous enterprises that their names have been handed down to posterity as so many Argonauts. Nay, even the hulks of the ships that carried them, though not converted into constellations in the Heavens, used to be honored and visited as sacred relics upon earth. We, in the present age of improved navigation, who have been instructed by their labors and have followed them as our guides, have no such claim to fame. Some merit, however, being still in the public opinion considered as due to those who sail to unexplored quarters of the globe, in conformity to this favorable judgment, I prefixed to the account of my last voyage the names of the officers of both my ships and a table of the number of their respective crews. The like information will be expected from me at present.

The *Resolution* was fitted out with the same complement of officers and men she had before; and the *Discovery*'s establishment varied from that of the *Adventure* in the single instance of her having no marine officer on board. This arrangement was to be finally completed at Plymouth and on the ninth we received the party of marines allotted for our voyage. ຂ້ອຍ

In the listing of officers and men was included the name of William Bligh, master of the *Resolution*. The "master" of a ship was equivalent to first mate, and was the chief officer in command of the day-by-day navigation and sailing. His position was one of great responsibility and required accomplished skill in seamanship. The master of the *Resolution* was the same William Bligh who later, in command of the

Officers and Men.	Nº	RESOLUTION. Officers Names.	Nº	DISCOVERY. Officers Names.
Captain, - -	1	James Cook. -	1	Charles Clerke.
Lieutenants, -	3	John Gore. -	2	James Burney.
		James King. -		John Rickman.
		John Williamson.		
Master, - -	1	William Bligh. -	1	Thomas Edgar.
Boatswain, - -	1	William Ewin. -	1	Eneas Atkins.
Carpenter, - -	1	James Clevely. -	1	Peter Reynolds.
Gunner, - -	1	Robert Anderson. -	1	WilliamPeckover.
Surgeon, - -	1	William Anderson. -	1	John Law.
Master's Mates, -	3	- - -	2	
Midshipmen, - -	6	- - -	4	
Surgeon's Mates, -	2	- - -	2	
Captain's Clerk, -	1	- - -	1	
Master at Arms, -	1	- - -	1	
Corporal, - -	1			
Armourer, - -	1	- - -	1	
Ditto Mate, - -	1	- - -	1	
Sail Maker, - -	1	- - -	1	
Ditto Mate, - -	1	- - -	1	
Boatswain's Mates,	3	- - -	2	
Carpenter's Ditto,	3	- - -	2	
Gunner's Ditto, -	2	- - -	1	
Carpenter's Crew,	4	- - -	4	
Cook, - -	1	- - -	1	
Ditto Mate, - -	1			
Quarter Masters, -	6	- - -	4	
Able Seamen, -	45	- - -	33	
		Marines.		
Lieutenant, - -	1	MolesworthPhilips.		
Serjeant, - -	1	- - -	1	
Corporals, - -	2	- - -	1	
Drummer, - -	1	- - -	1	
Private, - -	15	- - -	8	
Total,	112		80	

TABLE OF OFFICERS AND MEN ABOARD THE RESOLUTION *AND* DISCOVERY

Credit: Author's Private Collection

Bounty, lost his ship by mutiny while in the same seas where he had sailed with Cook. From his Captain he did not learn, or chose to ignore, how to care for his crew with thoughtfulness and humanity. Moreover, after the *Bounty* fiasco, he was made Governor of New South Wales, in Australia, where his soldiers mutinied and kept him prisoner for several years. Seamanship, even when faultless, is not enough to successfully complete a voyage into remote parts of the world; a discernment into the ways of men, and the ability to direct all on board to the common task, are equally essential.

⋖§ On the tenth, the commissioner and pay clerks came on board and paid the officers and crew up to the thirtieth of last month. The petty officers and seamen had, besides, two months wages in advance. Such indulgence to the latter is no more than what is customary in the Navy. But the payment of what was due to the superior officers was humanely ordered by the Admiralty in consideration of our peculiar situation, that we might be better able to defray the very great expense of furnishing ourselves with a stock of necessities for a voyage which probably would be of unusual duration and to regions where no supply could be expected.

Nothing now obstructing my departure but a contrary wind which blew at southwest, in the morning of the eleventh I delivered into the hands of Mr. Burney, first lieutenant of the *Discovery,* Captain Clerke's sailing orders. In the afternoon, the wind moderating, we weighed with the ebb and got farther out beyond all shipping in the Sound, where, after making an unsuccessful attempt to get to sea, we were detained most of the following day, which was employed in receiving on board a supply of water; and, by the same vessel that brought it, all the empty casks were returned.

As I did not imagine my stay at Plymouth would have been so long as it proved, we did not get our instruments on shore to make the necessary observations for ascertaining the longitude by the watch. For the same reason, Mr. Bayly did not set about this till he found that the *Discovery* would probably be detained some days after us. He then placed his quadrant upon Drake's Island and had time before the *Resolution* sailed to make observations sufficient for the purpose we had in view. Our watch made the island to be 4° 14′, and his 4° 13½′, west of Greenwich. Its latitude as found by Messrs. Wales and Bayly on the last voyage is 50° 21′ 20″ north.

We weighed again at eight in the evening and stood out of the Sound with a gentle breeze at northwest by west. We had not been long out of Plymouth Sound before the wind came more westerly and blew fresh, so that we were obliged to ply (*tack*) down the Channel; and it was not till the fourteenth of July at eight in the evening that we were off the Lizard. ॐ

The Declaration of Independence had been signed ten days before this date. The battles of Concord and Ticonderoga had occurred the year before. England had had twelve years of peace since the Seven Years War with France, but by the time the voyagers returned, England was at war with France, Spain, Holland, and the American colonies. It was not an auspicious time to send an exploring party to the Pacific.

The fastest communication was no swifter than a sailing ship, and Cook could not know of the American colonies' declaration; although, as he left the bay at Plymouth, he saluted the fleet and soldiers that would be fighting in the American Revolution. Furthermore, he could not know that England would soon be at war with most of Europe; but past experience led him to be more wary of his fellow Europeans than the native inhabitants of the Pacific islands and shores. It must be said in favor of our ancestors of the day, that through their ambassadors, and especially at the request of Benjamin Franklin, who was in England at the time the ships sailed, an attempt was made to get the warring nations to agree not to molest Cook's expedition. His fame as seaman, navigator, astronomer, explorer, geographer, and humanist, from two previous voyages on the Pacific Ocean, had spread to all the Western world. Unlike the secretive Spanish, his charts and findings were published and available to all. In the opinion of the scientists and statesmen of the world, to sink him with a cannonball would have been unthinkable. To that end, Benjamin Franklin dispatched the following letter.

To all Captains and Commanders of armed Ships acting by Commission from the Congress of the United States of America, now in war with Great Britain.

Gentlemen,
A ship having been fitted out from England before the commencement of this war, to make discoveries of new countries in

unknown seas, under the conduct of that most celebrated navigator and discoverer, Captain Cook, an undertaking truly laudable
in itself, as the increase of geographical knowledge facilitates the
communication between distant nations in the exchange of useful
products and manufactures, and the extension of arts whereby
the common enjoyments of human life are multiplied and aug-
mented, and science of other kinds increased to the benefit of
mankind in general.—This is therefore most earnestly to recommend to every one of you, that in case the said ship which is now
expected to be soon in the European seas on her return, should
happen to fall into your hands, you would not consider her as an
enemy, nor suffer any plunder to be made of the effects contained
in her, nor obstruct her immediate return to England by detain-
ing her, or sending her into any other part of Europe or to America; but that you would treat the said Captain Cook and his
people with all civility and kindness, affording them, as common
friends to mankind, all the assistance in your power which they
may happen to stand in need of. In so doing, you will not only
gratify the generosity of your own dispositions, but there is no
doubt of your obtaining the approbation of the Congress and
your own American owners.

I have the honor to be, Gentlemen

Your most obedient, humble servant,

B. Franklin

At Passy, near Paris,   Minister Plenipotentiary
this 10th day of March,   from the Congress of the
1779.   United States, at the
                                            Court of France.

Congress did not agree with Mr. Franklin. Believing that English
explorations on the West Coast of America could be injurious to the
United States, Congress reversed the order of Benjamin Franklin and
furthermore directed that Cook's ships be seized if any American
vessel fell in with them. Señor de Belluga, a Spanish officer and also
a member of the Royal Society of London, met resistance in the Court
of Spain similar to that which Franklin met in Congress. Only France,
among the warring nations, granted Cook a safe passage.

CHAPTER TWO

TO THE CANARY ISLANDS

July 19, 1776——August 3, 1776

⋖§ With a strong gale at south, on the nineteenth of July we stood to the westward till eight o'clock in the morning; when, the wind shifting to the west and northwest, we tacked and stretched to the southward. At this time, we saw nine sail of large ships which we judged to be French men-of-war. They took no particular notice of us, nor we of them.

The ship was smoked between decks with gunpowder (*a measure thought to aid in preserving the health of the crew*) and the spare sails also were then well aired (*to prevent mildew and rot*).

After two days of calm weather, on the afternoon of the twenty-fourth, with a fine gale at north-northeast, we passed Cape Finisterre, (*the northwest cape of the Spanish coast*). The longitude of this Cape by the watch is 9° 29′ west; and by the mean of forty-one lunar observations, made before and after we passed it and reduced to it by the watch, the result was 9° 12′ 12″. ৯

Modern geographers locate the Cape at 9° 16′ west. Lunar observations are yet another way of determining time at sea to find the longitude. The moon, the fastest-moving of celestial objects in the sky, appears to move against a background of slower-moving sun, stars, and planets. The distance the moon has moved from a point of reference, like the distance the minute hand was moved from the 12 on the face of a clock, can be used to tell the time. The calculations are lengthy and not too accurate at best. "The mean of forty-one lunar observations" would take the navigator most of the day to work out.

◄§ On the thirtieth at six minutes and thirty-eight seconds past ten o'clock at night, apparent time, I observed with a night telescope the moon totally eclipsed. By the ephemeris the same happened at Greenwich at nine minutes past eleven o'clock; the difference being one hour, two minutes, and twenty-two seconds, or 15° 35' 30" of longitude. The watch for the same time gave 15° 20' 45" longitude west, and latitude 31° 10' north. (*This unusual astronomical event gave the Captain an excellent opportunity to check his chronometers and position.*)

Finding that we had not hay and corn sufficient for the subsistence of the stock of animals on board till our arrival at the Cape of Good Hope, I determined to touch at Tenerife to get a supply of these and of the usual refreshments for ourselves, thinking that island for such purposes better adapted than Madeira. At four in the afternoon of the thirty-first, we saw Tenerife and steered for the eastern part. At nine, being near it, we hauled up and stood off and on during the night. ε►

TENERIFE ◄§ At daylight, on the morning of the first of August, we sailed around the east point of the island and about eight o'clock anchored on the southeast side of it, in the Road of Santa Cruz, in 23 fathoms of water, the bottom sand and ooze. We found riding in the Road, *La Boussole,* a French frigate, commanded by the Chevalier de Borda; two brigantines of the same nation; an English brigantine from London bound to Senegal; and fourteen sail of Spanish vessels.

In the afternoon I waited upon the Governor in person, accompanied by some of my officers, and before I returned to my ship bespoke some corn and straw for the livestock, ordered a quantity of wine from Mr. McCarrick, the contractor, and made an agreement with the master of a Spanish boat to supply us with water, as I found that we could not do it ourselves.

At the southwest part of the road a stone pier runs out into the sea from the town for the convenience of loading and landing goods. To this pier the water that supplies the shipping is conveyed. This, and also what the inhabitants of Santa Cruz use, is derived from a rivulet that runs from the hills, the greatest part of which comes into town in wooden spouts on troughs that are supported by slender posts.

Were we to judge from the appearance of the country in the neighborhood of Santa Cruz, it might be concluded that Tenerife is a barren spot, insufficient to maintain even its own inhabitants. The ample supplies, however, which we received, convinced us that they had enough to spare for visitors. Besides wine, which is the chief produce of the island, beef may be had at moderate price. The oxen are small and bony. The meat is lean, and is at present sold for half a bit (*a Spanish bit, from whence came our "two-bits," meaning a quarter-dollar*) a pound. Hogs, sheep, goats, and poultry are likewise to be bought at the same moderate rate; and fruits are in great plenty. At this time we had grapes, figs, pears, mulberries, plantains (*bananas*) and muskmelons. Their pumpkins, onions, and potatoes are exceedingly good of their kind and keep better at sea than any I ever before met with.

The Indian corn (*from America*) cost me about three shillings and sixpence a bushel; and the fruits and roots were, in general, very cheap. Upon the whole, I found Tenerife to be a more eligible place than Madeira for ships bound on long voyages to touch at; though the wine of the latter, according to my taste, is as much superior to that of the former, as strong beer is to small (*a brew containing little malt, no hops, and much water*).

The three days comparisons which we made assured us that the watch had not materially, if at all, altered her rate of going and gave us the same longitude, within a very few seconds, that was obtained by finding the time from observations of the sun's altitude from the horizon of the sea. The watch, from a mean of these observations, made the longitude 16° 31' west and in a like manner, the latitude was found to be 28° 30' 11" north. (*Modern geographers place Santa Cruz at 16° 14' west longitude and 28° 28' north latitude. His longitude error, then, was 17', or about 17 nautical miles.*) ❧

Mr. Anderson, the ship's surgeon on board the *Resolution,* who also served as the naturalist, recorded some of his observations:

❧ Behind the city of Santa Cruz the country rises gradually. To the southwestward it becomes higher and continues to rise toward a central mountain peak known as the Pico de Teyde. From a supposition that we should not stay above one day, I was obliged to contract my excursions into the country; otherwise, I had proposed to visit the top of this mountain. (*Our surgeon would have found the central mountains of Tenerife high—12,000 feet, cold, snow-covered, and not easy to climb.*)

To the eastward of Santa Cruz the island appears perfectly barren. Ridges of hills run toward the sea. The moldering state of these hills is, doubtless, owing to the perpetual action of the sun, which calcines their surface.

In the afternoon of the second, four of us hired mules to ride to the city of Laguna, so called from an adjoining lake, about 4 miles from Santa Cruz. We found the sight of it unable to compensate for our trouble, as the road was very bad and the mules most indifferent.

I had an opportunity of conversing with a sensible and well-informed gentleman residing here and whose veracity I have not the least reason to doubt. From him I learned that a certain sort of grape growing here is reckoned an excellent remedy in phthisical complaints. (*These are diseases of the chest and lungs corresponding in modern diagnosis to tuberculosis, probably also asthma, and other less common pulmonary diseases.*) And the air and climate, in general, are remarkably healthful and particularly adapted to give relief in such diseases. This he endeavored to account for by its being always in one's power to procure a different temperature of the air by residing at different heights in the island; and he expressed his surprise that the English physicians should never have thought of sending their consumptive (*tubercular*) patients to Tenerife instead of Nice or Lisbon. How much the temperature of the air varies here, I myself could sensibly perceive only in riding from Santa Cruz to Laguna; and you may ascend till the cold becomes intolerable. I was assured that no person can live comfortably within a mile of the perpendicular height of the summit after the month of August.

Although some smoke constantly issues from near the top of the peak, they have had no earthquake or eruption of a volcano since 1704, when the Port of Garachico, where much of the trade was formerly carried on, was destroyed.

Their trade must be considered as very considerable, for they reckon that forty thousand pipes of wine are annually made. (*A "pipe" is equivalent to a little more than thirteen U.S. gallons.*) About six thousand pipes were exported every year to North America while the trade with it was uninterrupted; at present, they think not above half the quantity. The corn they raise is in general insufficient to maintain the inhabitants; but the deficiency used to be supplied by importation from the North Americans, who took their wine in return. (*The interruption was due to the American Revolution.*)

None of the race of inhabitants found here when the Spaniard discovered the Canaries now remain a distinct people, having intermarried with the Spanish settlers; but their descendants are known for being remarkably tall, large-boned, and strong. The men are of a tawny color and the women have a pale complexion, destitute of that bloom which distinguishes our northern beauties. We found the inhabitants of Tenerife to be a decent and very civil people, retaining that grave cast which distinguishes those of their country from European nations. Although we think that there is not a great similarity between our manners and those of the Spaniards, it is worth observing that Omai did not think there was much difference. He only said that they seemed not so friendly as the English; and that, in their persons, they approached those of his countrymen. &

CHAPTER THREE

TO CAPE TOWN

August 4, 1776———November 30, 1776

⌐§ Having completed our water and got on board everything we wanted at Tenerife, we weighed anchor on the fourth of August and proceeded on our voyage with a fine gale at northeast. §~

Between the fourth and tenth of August, the Captain twice exercised his men at great guns and small arms and cleared and smoked the ship below. Both measures were intended to improve the morale and health of the crew.

CAPE VERDE ISLANDS ⌐§ At nine o'clock in the evening of the tenth, we saw the Island of Boa Vista (*one of the Cape Verde Islands*) bearing south, distant little more than a league; though, at this time, we thought ourselves much farther off; but this proved a mistake. For, after hauling to the eastward till twelve o'clock to clear the sunken rocks that lie about a league from the southeast point of the island, we found ourselves at that time close upon them and did but just weather the breakers. Our situation for a few minutes was very alarming. I did not choose to sound, as that might have heightened the danger without any probability of lessening it. As soon as we were clear of the rocks, we steered south-southwest till daybreak next morning and then hardened to the westward to go between Boa Vista and the Isle of Maio, intending to look into Port Praia for the *Discovery,* as I had told Captain Clerke that I should touch there and did not know how soon he might sail after me. At one in the afternoon, we saw the rocks that lie on the southwest side of Boa Vista.

Next morning at six o'clock the Isle of Maio bore south-southeast. At the distance we now saw this island, which was 3 or 4 miles, there was not the least appearance of vegetation, nor any relief to the eye from the lifeless brown which prevails in countries under the Torrid Zone that are unwooded. While we were among these islands we had light breezes of wind varying from the southeast to east and some calms. This shows that the Cape Verde Islands are either extensive enough to break the current of the trade winds, or that they are situated just beyond its verge and in that space where variable winds are found on getting near the line (*near the equator*). The weather was hot and sultry with some rain; and for the most part a dull whiteness prevailed in the sky that seems a medium between fog and clouds. In general the tropical regions seldom enjoy that clear atmosphere observable where variable winds blow; nor does the sun shine with such brightness. This circumstance, however, seems an advantage; for otherwise, perhaps, the rays of the sun, being uninterrupted, would render the heat quite unsupportable. The nights are, nevertheless, often clear and serene. ❧

THE SOUTH ATLANTIC OCEAN ❧ Between the latitude of 12° and of 7° north, the weather was generally dark and gloomy, with frequent rains, which enabled us to save as much water as filled most of our empty casks. These rains and the close sultry weather accompanying them, too often bring on sickness in this passage. Every bad consequence, at least, is to be apprehended from them; and commanders of ships cannot be too much on their guard by purifying the air between decks with fires and smoke and by obliging their people to dry their clothes at every opportunity. These precautions were constantly observed on board the *Resolution;* and we certainly profited by them, for we had now fewer sick than on either of my former voyages. We had, however, the mortification to find our ship extremely leaky in all her upper works. The hot and sultry weather we had just passed through had opened her seams, which had been badly caulked, so wide that they admitted the rain water through as it fell. There was hardly a man that could lie dry in his bed, and the officers in the gun-room were all driven out of their cabins by the water that came through the sides. The sails in the sail-room got wet and before we had weather to dry them, many of them were much damaged and a great expense of canvas and time became necessary to make them in some degree

serviceable. Having experienced the same defect in our sail-rooms on
my late voyage, it had been represented to the yard officers, who
undertook to remove it. But it did not appear to me that anything had
been done to remedy the complaint.

On the first of September, we crossed the equator. The afternoon
was spent in performing the old and ridiculous ceremony of ducking
those who had not crossed the line before.

With a fine gale at southeast by south and notwithstanding my
apprehensions of falling in with the coast of Brazil in stretching to the
southwest, I kept the ship a full point from the wind. However, I
found my fears were ill-grounded, for on drawing near that coast we
met with the wind more and more easterly, so that by the time we
were in the latitude of 10° south, we could make good a southeasterly
course. ೪ఴ

The coast of Brazil is a long way west of the direct course from
England to Cape Town. The square-rigged, round-bilged ships of the
day sailed well only with the wind abaft the beam. The Captain made
full use of his knowledge of the prevailing trade winds, so called
because trading vessels used these winds to make ocean crossings. He
sailed southwest in the easterly trades north of the equator, crossed
through the area of squalls and doldrums at the equator, then picked
up the easterly winds on the other side of the line. He continued to
go southwest until 40° west, where he expected westerly winds to blow
him back across the Atlantic, east to Cape Town.

ఴఇ We proceeded on our voyage without meeting with anything of
note till the sixth of October, being in the latitude of 35° 15′ south.
We had, for some days before, seen albatrosses, pintados and other
petrels, and here we saw three penguins. We put a boat in the water
and shot a few birds, one of which was a black petrel about the size
of a crow and, except as to the bill and feet, very like one. It had a
few white feathers under the throat, and the underside of the quill
feathers was of an ash color. All the other feathers were jet black, as
were the bill and legs. In the evening one of those birds which sailors
call noddies (*a kind of tern*) settled on our rigging and was caught.
It was somewhat larger than an English blackbird and nearly as black,
except for the upper part of the head, which was white, looking as if
it were powdered; the whitest feathers growing out of the base of the

upper bill, from which they gradually assumed a darker color, to about the middle of the upper part of the neck, where the white shade soon was lost in the black without being divided by any line. It was web-footed, had black legs, and a black bill, which was long and not unlike that of a curlew. It is said these birds never fly far from land, though we know of none near the station we are in.

The calm weather was succeeded by a fresh gale from the north-west, which lasted two days. (*He was now south enough to begin to pick up the westerly trade winds.*) Then we again had variable light airs for about twenty-four hours; when the northwest wind returned and blew with such strength that on the seventeenth we had sight of the Cape of Good Hope and the next day anchored in Table Bay, in four fathoms of water. I sent an officer to wait on Baron Plettenberg, the Governor. ঌ

CAPE TOWN ঌ The Governor promised me every assistance that the place afforded. I obtained leave to set up our observatory on any spot I should think most convenient, to pitch tents for the sailmakers and coopers, and to bring the cattle on shore to graze near our encampment. I ordered soft bread, fresh meat, and greens to be provided every day for the ship's company.

The next day we began to observe equal altitudes of the sun in order to ascertain the rate of the watch or, which is the same thing, to find whether it had altered its rate. The watch, by means of the results of fifteen days' observation, was found to be losing 2.261 seconds each day, which is 1.052 seconds more than at Greenwich. From this 18° 32' 10" will be the longitude of Cape Town by the watch. Its longitude as found by Messrs. Mason and Dixon is 18° 23' 15". ঌ

Charles Mason and Jeremiah Dixon, surveyors, astronomers, and mathematicians, had been sent out from England in 1761 to the Island of Sumatra to observe a transit of Venus across the disk of the sun. Because of a slow passage they found themselves unable to reach Sumatra in time, and instead set up their observatory in Cape Town. In cooperation with other observers scattered over the earth's surface, this was an effort to measure more accurately the distance from the earth to the sun. Also, matters of longitude could be determined by this astronomical event and maps of the world thereby made more precise. It so happened that two transits of Venus occurred close together in those years: one in 1762, which Messrs. Mason and Dixon observed, and the other in 1769, which Cook observed in Tahiti on his first voyage. The next transit did not occur until more than a hundred years later in 1874. In 1680 the English astronomer Edmund Halley had calculated the date and time of these events.

Mason and Dixon were the same surveying team who struck the boundary between Maryland and Pennsylvania, which was thereafter called "The Mason-Dixon line." Their work was accurate, more accurate than Cook's watch. Cape Town is located at 18° 26′ east.

∽§ The error of the watch in longitude is no more than 8′ 55″. Hence we have reason to conclude that she had gone well all the way from England.

Nothing remarkable happened till the evening of the thirty-first, when it came on to blow excessively hard at southwest and continued for three days. During this time there was no communication between the ship and the shore. The *Resolution* was the only ship in the bay that rode out the gale without dragging her anchors. We felt its effects as sensibly on shore: our tents and observatory were torn to pieces, and our astronomical quadrant narrowly escaped irreparable damage.

On the sixth a Hampshire India ship sailed for England. In her I sent home an invalid, whom Captain Trimble was so obliging as to receive on board. I was afterward sorry that I did not avail myself of this opportunity to part with two or three more of my crew who were troubled with different complaints.

On the morning of the tenth, the *Discovery* arrived in the bay. Captain Clerke informed me that he had sailed from Plymouth on the first of August and should have been with us here a week sooner if the late gale of wind had not blown him off the coast. He was seven days longer in his passage from England than we had been. He had the misfortune to lose one of his marines by falling overboard; but there had been no other mortality among his people and they now arrived well and healthy.

I have before made mention of our getting our cattle on shore. The bull and two cows, with their calves, were sent to graze along with some other cattle; but I was advised to keep our sixteen sheep close to our tents, where they were penned up every night. During the night some dogs got in among them, forced them out of the pen, killed four and dispersed the rest. The Dutch, we know, boast that the policing of the Cape is so carefully executed that it is hardly possible for a slave, with all his cunning and knowledge of the country, to effectuate his escape. Yet my sheep evaded all the vigilance of the Fescal's officers and people. After much trouble and expense, by employing some of the meanest and lowest scoundrels in the place (who, to use the phrase of the person who recommended this method to me, would, for a ducatoon, cut their master's throat, burn the house over his head, and bury him and the whole family in the ashes), I recovered them all but two ewes. Of these I never could hear the least tidings. After the disaster which happened to our sheep, it may be well supposed I did not trust those that remained on shore; but got them and the other cattle on board as fast as possible. I also added to my original stock by purchasing two young bulls, two heifers, two ewes, and goats and some rabbits and poultry. All of them were intended for New Zealand, Tahiti, and the neighboring islands, or any other places in the course of our voyage where there might be a prospect that the leaving of them would be useful to posterity. ໑

All of this livestock must have had an uncomfortable time of it on board a heeling and pitching sailing ship, no less than the sailors, who had to tend them and clean up the mess. The stumbling about of hoofs, and the bleating, neighing, mooing, and general complaints of the animals must have been heard all over the ship. The ship lacked only a few females of the human species to be a veritable Noah's Ark. The rabbits may have been the first of the species that were later to overrun Australia and so drastically destroy the balance of nature on that continent.

໑ Toward the latter end of November (*midsummer in the Southern Hemisphere*) the caulkers had finished their work on board the *Discovery*. Both ships had a supply of provisions to last for two years and upwards. Every article we could think of necessary for such a voyage that could be had at the Cape was procured; neither knowing when or where we might come to a place where we could furnish ourselves so well.

Having given Captain Clerke a copy of my instructions and an order directing him how to proceed in case of separation, on the morning of the thirtieth we repaired on board. At five in the afternoon a breeze sprang up at southeast with which we weighed and stood out at the bay. ໑

CHAPTER FOUR

ANTARCTIC ISLANDS

December 5, 1776——December 29, 1776

∾ On the fifth of December, a sudden squall of wind carried away the *Resolution*'s mizzen top-mast. Having another to replace it, the loss was not felt, especially as it was a bad stick and had often complained. On the sixth we passed through several small spots of water of reddish color. Some of this was taken up and it was found to abound with a small animal which the microscope discovered to be like a crayfish of reddish hue (*a species of brine shrimp*).

We continued our course to the southeast with a very strong gale from the westward, followed by a mountainous sea which made the ship roll and tumble exceedingly. ∾

The *Resolution* was now in the Roaring Forties, where the ever-prevailing westerly wind continually circles the globe, building up high winds and great rolling seas, round and round, with no continent to break its strength.

∾ Notwithstanding all our care, several goats, especially the males, died, and also some sheep. This misfortune was in a great measure owing to the cold, which we now began sensibly to feel. ∾

The ship was still as far from the South Pole as New York is from the North Pole, and the time was midsummer! The great cold, even in summer at these low southern latitudes, equivalent to New England in the north, is due to the northward-flowing cold antarctic water, which reaches nearly to the 40th Parallel before it sinks below the lighter, warmer waters of the South Atlantic and South Pacific; and a cold wind blows northward off the icy Antarctic continent. Coming from comparatively warm England at 55° north latitude, and knowing of the existence of an ice pack below 70° south latitude seen on his previous voyage, Captain Cook may have guessed that there must be a great mass of ice south of him.

◄§ On the twelfth, at noon we saw land. Upon a nearer approach we found it to be two islands. That which lies to the south and is the largest I judged to be in the latitude of 45° 53′ south and in the longitude of 37° 46′ east. The most northerly one is about nine leagues in circuit. The distance from the one to the other is about five leagues. We passed through this channel at equal distance from both islands and could not discover, with the assistance of our best glasses, either tree or shrub on either of them. They seemed to have a rocky and bold shore, and, excepting the southeast parts, where the land is rather low and flat, they have a surface composed of barren mountains which rise to considerable height. The summits and sides were covered with snow, which in many places seemed to be of considerable depth. There was no appearance of an inlet and no promise of a good anchoring-place. These two islands, as also four others which lie from 9 to 12 degrees of longitude more to the east and nearly in the same latitude, were discovered by captains Marion du Fresne and Crozet, French navigators, in January 1772 on their passage from the Cape of Good Hope to the Philippines. As they have no names in the French chart of the Southern Hemisphere which Captain Crozet communicated to me in 1775, I shall distinguish the two we now see by calling them Prince Edward's Islands, after His Majesty's fourth son (*the name still stands on modern charts and the islands are part of the territory of South Africa*); the other four by the name of Marion's and Crozet's islands to commemorate their discoverers. (*Now called simply Isles Crozet. These Islands are French territory.*)

We had now, for the most part, strong gales between the north and west and but very indifferent weather; not better, indeed, than we generally have in England in the very depth of winter though it was now the middle of summer in this hemisphere. Not discouraged, however, by this, I shaped our course to the southward that I might get into the latitude of the land discovered by Monsieur de Kerguelen. My instructions directing me to examine it, with a view to discovering a good harbor, I proceeded in the search and on the sixteenth, being in the longitude of 52° east, we saw penguins and rockweed floating in the sea. We proceeded eastward and on the twenty-first, in the longitude of 65° east, a very large seal was seen. We had now much foggy weather and, as we expected to fall in with the land every hour, our navigation became both tedious and dangerous. At length on the twenty-fourth, at six o'clock in the morning, as we were steering east-ward, the fog clearing away a little, we saw land. At times, as the fog broke away, we had the appearance of land beyond small islands; and I had thought of steering for it by running in between them. But, on drawing nearer, I found this would be a dangerous attempt while the weather continued foggy. As it was, we did just weather the island last mentioned. It is a high round rock, which I named Bligh's Cap. (*Cook must have thought well of his sailing master to give his name to this landmark.*) &

KERGUELEN'S ISLAND ⌊ At eleven o'clock the weather began to clear up and we immediately tacked and steered in for the land. At noon we had a pretty good observation, which enabled us to deter-mine the latitude of Bligh's Cap, which is the northern-most island, to be 48° 29′ south and its longitude 68° 40′ east. (Kerguelen himself only says it is about 68° of east longitude.) Soon after we saw the land of which we had a faint view in the morning. From this point the coast seemed to turn around to the southward. We had no sooner got off the Cape than we observed the coast to be much indented by project-ing points and bays; so we now made sure of soon finding a good harbor. Accordingly we had not run a mile farther before we dis-covered one behind the Cape into which we began to ply; but after making one board it fell calm and we anchored at the entrance in 45 fathoms (*270 feet*), the bottom being black sand. I immediately dispatched Mr. Bligh, the master, in a boat to sound the harbor; he, on his return, reported it to be safe and commodious with good an-chorage in every part and great plenty of fresh water, seals, penguins, and other birds on the shore, but not a stick of wood.

At daybreak, in the morning of the twenty-fifth (*Christmas*) we weighed with a gentle breeze at west; and having wrought into the harbor to within a quarter mile of the sandy beach at its head, we anchored in 8 fathoms of water, the bottom of fine dark sand. The *Discovery* did not get in till two o'clock in the afternoon. Captain

Clerke informed me that he narrowly escaped being driven on the south point of the harbor. His anchor started before they had time to shorten the cable. This obliged them to set sail and drag the anchor after them till they had room to heave it up. Then they found that one of its palms was broken off.

As soon as we had anchored, I ordered all the boats hoisted out, the ship moored with a kedge anchor and the water-casks sent on shore. I found the shore covered with penguins and other birds and seals. The latter were not numerous, but so insensible of fear—which seemed to indicate that they were unaccustomed to human visitors—that we killed as many as we chose for the sake of their fat or blubber to make oil for our lamps and other uses. Fresh water was no less plenty than the birds, for every gully afforded a large stream. But not a single tree or shrub, nor the least sign of any was to be discovered, and but very little herbage of any sort. Before I returned to my ship, I ascended the first ridge or rocks which rise in a kind of amphitheater above one another. I was in hope by this means of obtaining a view of the country; but before I reached the top there came in so thick a fog that I could hardly find my way down again.

We went to work to fill the water-casks and to cut grass for our cattle which we found in small spots near the head of the harbor. The rain which fell swelled all the rivulets to such a degree that the sides of the hills seemed to be covered with a sheet of water that precipitated down their sides in prodigious torrents.

The people, having wrought hard the two preceding days, I allowed them the twenty-seventh day as a day of rest to celebrate Christmas. Upon this indulgence many of them went on shore and made excursions in different directions into the country. In the evening one of them brought to me a quart bottle which he had found fastened with some wire to a projecting rock on the north side of the harbor. The bottle contained a piece of parchment on which was written the following inscription:

LUDOVICO XV GALLIARUM
REGE, ET D. DE BOYNES
REGI A SECRETIS AD RES
MARITIMAS ANNIS 1772 ET
1773.

From this inscription it is clear that we were not the first Europeans who had been in this harbor. I supposed it to be left by Monsieur de Boisguehenneu. ❦

The translated Latin would be:

> Louis XV, King of Gaul [France]
> and Lord de Boynes, His Majesty's
> Secretary of the Marine
> years 1772 and 1773.

Boisguehenneu was in the party of the French navigator Kerguelen, who discovered these islands in February 1772. However, the bottle was left on a second voyage of Kerguelen, who again sighted this harbor in December 1773—thereby explaining the two dates. It was not Boisguehenneu, as Cook thought, who left the bottle, but a Monsieur de Rochegude. Cook did not know when he left England that Kerguelen had departed on a second voyage, and had preceded him here.

❧ As a memorial of our having been in this harbor, I wrote on the other side of the parchment:

> NAVES *Resolution*
> ET *Discovery*
> DE REGE MAGNAE BRITAINNIAE
> DECEMBRIS 1776.

I then put it again into a bottle, together with a silver two-penny piece of 1772; and having covered the mouth with a leaden cap, I placed it, the next morning, in a pile of stones erected for the purpose on the north shore of the harbor. ❦

The bottle remained in this pile of stones until 1792, when it was picked up by the men from the United States brig *Ino* under command of Captain Simon Metcalf and taken on board for inspection. They found in the bottle another note from Captain Durgin of the *Phoenix,* who had preceded them here. An attempt was made to put the bottle back, but the *Ino* was driven off shore by a gale and had to take the

THE RESOLUTION
ANCHORED IN CHRISTMAS

Credit: Engraving, Author's Private Collection

AND DISCOVERY
HARBOR, KERGUELEN ISLAND

bottle with her. In what manner Captain Metcalf ultimately disposed of the bottle, I have not been able to discover.

◄§ Here I displayed the British flag and named the place Christmas Harbor, from our having arrived in it on that festival. The head of the harbor lies open only to two points of the compass; and even these are covered by islands in the offing, so that no sea can fall in to hurt a ship. The appearance on shore confirmed this; for we found grass growing close to the high-water mark, which is a sure sign of a pacific harbor. (*This might be a valuable hint for skippers of modern yachts.*)

After I had finished the business of the inscriptions, I went in my boat around the harbor and landed in several places to look for driftwood. Although the land was totally destitute of trees, this might not be the case in other parts, and if there were any, the torrents would force some branches into the sea, which would afterward throw them upon the shore, as in all countries where there is wood and in many where there is none; but throughout the whole extent of the harbor, I found not a single piece.

When I got on board, I found the launch hoisted, the ships unmoored and ready to put to sea. §►

Cook continued southward along the east coast of the island, making several more landings. He successfully skirted the rocks by frequent soundings with the leadline, by sending Mr. Bligh ahead in a boat to sound out the harbor, and by using the growth of rockweeds, a kind of seaweed that fastens to submerged rocks, as a guide to the location of shoals. There were near misses but, by his care and diligence, he avoided grounding. Mr. Anderson, the ship's surgeon and naturalist, went ashore and was struck by the desolation of these islands at only 49° south latitude, while all of England is more than 50° north. Mr. Anderson reports:

◄§ Perhaps no place, hitherto discovered in either hemisphere under the same parallel of latitude, affords so scanty a field for the naturalist as this barren spot. There is a plant, plentifully enough scattered about the boggy declivities which grows to near the height of 2 feet and not unlike a small cabbage. It has not only the appearance, but the watery, acrid taste of the antiscorbutic plants and yet differs materially from the whole tribe so that I looked upon it as a production entirely

"KERGUELEN ISLAND CABBAGE"

Credit: Author's Private Collection

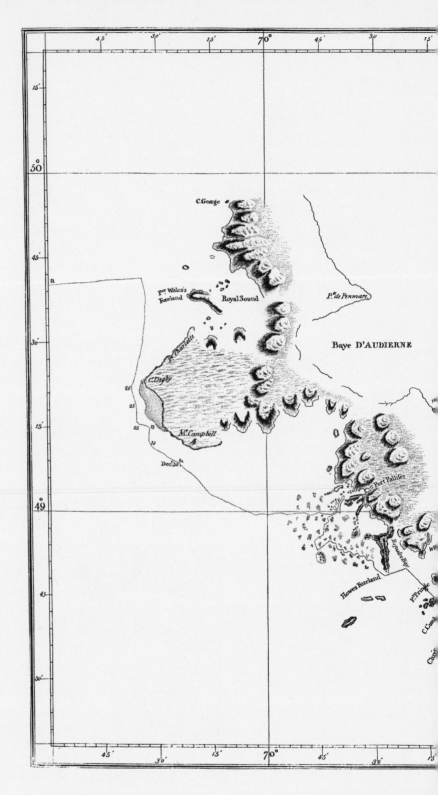

CHART OF

OBSERVE THE NUMEROUS OUTLYING ROCKS AND SHOALS THAT COOK'S

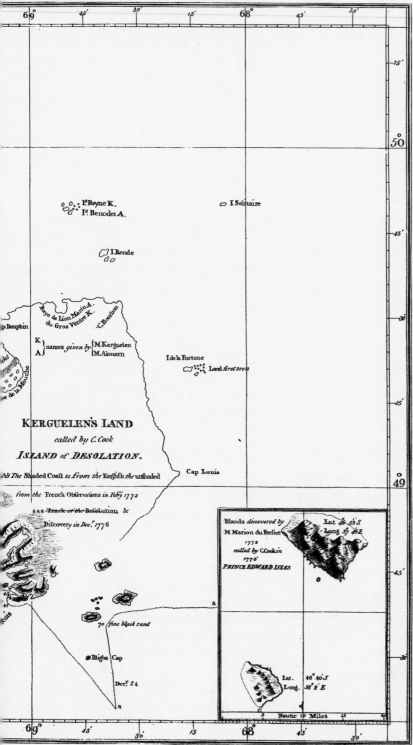

KERGUELEN ISLAND

HIPS THREADED BETWEEN CHRISTMAS HARBOR AND PORT PALLISER.

peculiar to the place. We ate it raw and found it almost like New
Zealand scurvy-grass. It seemed to acquire a rank flavor by being
boiled, which, however, some of our people did not perceive and
esteemed it good. If it could be introduced into our gardens, it would
in all probability be an excellent pot-herb; at this time, some of its
seeds were ripe enough to be preserved and brought home to try the
experiment. ॐ

To preserve the health of the crew and prevent scurvy the Captain
insisted upon everyone eating such fresh meats and vegetables as could
be obtained from islands and lands along the way. Apparently no one
was poisoned by eating these unknown plants. Perhaps someone at
this date should bring home some "Kerguelen Island Cabbage" and
try Mr. Anderson's suggested experiment.

Cook knew, and rightly so, that scurvy could be prevented by eating fresh fruits and vegetables, that almost any green plant would do,
and ordered these plants to be boiled and served to his crew. He could
prevail upon his ship's officers and crew to eat the greens, but in his
first voyage could not so command the gentlemen scientists. Those
men who stuck to their civilized ship's fare sickened, and the astronomer died, even in the presence of crewmen, sick like himself, who
steadily gained in health and recovered as soon as they were fed the
"scurvy-grass."

The Captain induced the crew to eat these unfamiliar foods by first
serving them to the ship's officers as if they were something special
and reserved for men of rank only, and soon the crew desired these
specialties too. But the gentlemen would not be psychologically tricked
in this way.

ॐ Nature has been more bountiful in furnishing it with animals,
though, strictly speaking, they are not inhabitants of the place, being
all of the marine kind and using the land for a breeding and resting
place. The most considerable are seals; and so tame that we killed
what number we chose. No other quadruped either of the sea or land
was seen, only a great number of birds, viz: ducks, petrels, albatrosses,
shags, gulls, and sea-swallows. The Cape petrel, or Pintado bird, the
small blue one which is always seen at sea, and the small black one,
or Mother Carey's chicken, are not here in great number. Another
sort, which is the largest of all the petrels, and called by seamen

Mother Carey's goose is in great numbers and so tame that at first we could kill them with a stick. Their color is a sooty brown with a greenish bill and feet. Penguins form by far the greatest number of birds. All the penguins were so tame that we took as many as we pleased with our hands. Ducks were in tolerable plenty and were good without the least fishy taste. The shags are of two sorts, the lesser cormorant or water crow, and another which is black above with a white belly. We also met with the common seagull, sea-swallow, tern, and Port Egmont hen. Another sort of white bird is very singular, having the base of the bill covered with a horny crust. It is larger than a pigeon with a black bill and white feet, like those of a curlew. Some of our people put it in competition with the duck as food. ॐ

Here in this remote island, Captain Cook not only takes an interest in the birds and animals of the land as native creatures but sets his crew to gathering them for food. He knows that fresh meat and vegetables will make for a healthy crew. Even when he finds a bird not seen before, they eat it. We learn here that they are eating seal, ducks, Mother Carey's goose, penguins, and the birds with the horny-crusted bill.

ॐ The rocks are composed chiefly of a dark blue and very hard stone intermixed with small particles of glimmer or quartz (*granite*). This seems to be one of the most universal productions of nature, as it constitutes whole mountains in Sweden, Scotland, the Canary Islands, the Cape of Good Hope, and this place. (*Widely traveled, Mr. Anderson almost guessed that this island is part of the same geologic formation and north-south mountain ridge that extends through the places that he names.*) ॐ

CHAPTER FIVE

ACROSS THE SOUTH INDIAN OCEAN
AND ON TO NEW ZEALAND

December 30, 1776——February 6, 1777

ACROSS THE SOUTH INDIAN OCEAN *◄§* After leaving Kerguelen Island, I steered east by north, intending, in obedience to my instructions, to touch next at New Zealand to recruit our water, to take in wood, and to make hay for the cattle—their number by this time having been considerably diminished while we were employed in exploring that desolate coast.

Tuesday, December 31, 1776, the day after we stood out to sea, we had several observations of the sun and moon. Their results gave the longitude 72° 33′ 36″ east, the timekeeper in this situation gave 72° 38′ 15″. These observations served to assure us that no material error had crept into the timekeeper.

January 3, 1777. The wind veered to the north, where it continued for eight days (*the summer monsoon*) and was attended with a thick fog. During this time we ran above 300 leagues in the dark (*in the "dark" as to their position*). Only now and then the weather would clear up and give us a sight of the sun. On the seventh I hoisted out a boat and sent an order to Captain Clerke appointing Adventure Bay in Van Diemen's Land (*now called Tasmania*) as our place of rendezvous in case of separation before we arrived in the meridian of that land. But we were fortunate enough, amid all this foggy weather, by frequently firing guns as signals, though we seldom saw each other, not to lose company. (*Throughout the entire voyage, in spite of storm, fog, ice, or darkness, these two sailing ships succeeded in keeping together.*)

At four o'clock on the morning of the nineteenth, in a sudden squall of wind, our fore-top-mast went by the board and carried the main-top-gallant-mast with it. This occasioned some delay, as it took the whole day to clear the wreck and fit another top-mast. This was accomplished without losing any part of it. Not having a spare main-top-gallant-mast on board, the fore-top-gallant-mast was converted into one for our immediate use. ॐ

TASMANIA ॐ On the twenty-fourth, at three o'clock in the morning, we discovered Van Diemen's Land. At six o'clock the next afternoon we sounded and found 60 fathoms of water on a bottom of broken coral and shells. The South Cape then bore north 75° west two or three leagues distant, Tasman's Head northeast, and Swilly Rock south by west ½ west. About a league to the eastward of Swilly is another elevated rock. I called it the Eddystone from its great resemblance to that lighthouse. Nature seems to have left these two rocks here for the same purpose that the Eddystone lighthouse was built by man, viz., to give navigators notice of the dangers around them. They are conspicuous summits of a ledge of underwater rocks on which the sea in many places breaks very high. Their surface is white with the dung of seafowls so that they may be seen at some distance even in the night.

I carried the ships into Adventure Bay, where I might expect to get a supply of wood, and of grass for the cattle; both of which articles we should be in great want of if I had waited till our arrival in New Zealand. (*The supplies of wood so often needed were for heating and cooking.*) We therefore stood for the bay and anchored in it at four o'clock in the afternoon, in 12 fathoms water over a bottom of sand and ooze. (*The lead, at the end of the leadline, was, as they say, "armed" with a sticky tallow placed in a depression at the bottom of the lead made for that purpose. This permitted the heaver of the lead to determine the nature of the bottoms from the material that stuck to the tallow.*)

As soon as we had anchored, I ordered the boats to be hoisted out. In one of them I went myself to look for the most commodious place for furnishing ourselves with the necessary supplies. Wood and water we found in plenty, but grass, which we stood most in need of, was scarce and very coarse. Although as yet none of the natives had appeared, there could be no doubt that some were in our neighborhood, as we had seen columns of smoke from the time of our approaching the coast. In the afternoon we were agreeably surprised at the place where we were cutting wood with a visit from some of the natives: eight men and a boy. (*Cook was always happy to meet with the natives of the land and surely would have been disappointed to have had to sail away without a visit with these people. Their wild appearance caused him no panic and no unwarranted defensive hostility. He could see past their unfamiliar, devilish appearance into the common human nature that he shared with them.*) They approached us from the woods, without betraying any marks of fear, with the greatest confidence imaginable. None of them had weapons except one who held in his hand a stick about 2 feet long and pointed at one end. They were naked and wore no ornaments except some large punctures or ridges raised on different parts of their bodies, some in straight, and others in curved lines. They were of common stature and rather slender. Their skin was black and also their hair, which was as wooly as that of any native of Guinea (*Africa*). Their features were far from disagreeable. They had good eyes, and their teeth were even, but very dirty. Most of them had their hair and beards smeared with a red ointment and some of their faces were painted with the same composition. They received every present we made without the least appearance of satisfaction. When some bread was given, as soon as they understood that it was to be eaten, they either returned it or threw it away without even tasting it. They also refused some fish, both raw and dressed, which we offered them. But upon giving some birds to them, they did not return these and easily made us comprehend that they were fond of such foods. Being desirous of knowing the use of the stick which one of our visitors carried in his hand, I made signs to them to show me, and so far succeeded that one of them set up a piece of wood as a mark and threw it at it, at a distance of about 20 yards. We had little reason to commend his dexterity, for after repeated throws he was still very wide from the object. Omai, to show them how much superior our weapons were to theirs, fired his musket at it, which alarmed them so much they ran instantly into the woods. From us, however, they went to the place where the *Discovery*'s crew was taking water into their boat. The officer of that party, not knowing that they had paid us so friendly a visit, fired a musket into the air, which sent them off with the greatest precipitation. ॐ

Cook constantly had difficulty in getting his crew and officers to adapt his attitude of friendliness, scientific interest, and above all, lack of hostility toward the natives of the lands they visited. The crew's

response was perhaps the more natural one. Who of us would extend
a friendly greeting to naked, black, mud-smeared, spear-carrying men
stalking out of a dark, unknown forest? Our fear and suspicion would
lead us to defend ourselves and, at the very least, fire guns in the air,
to frighten the wild men away. Cook was cautious but curious. He
was genuinely disappointed that he could communicate so little with
them and thus lose an opportunity to learn more about them. Captains, both before and long after him, shot first and asked questions
afterward.

⤳ Immediately after their final retreat, judging that their fears would
prevent their remaining near enough to observe what was passing,
I ordered the two pigs, being a boar and sow, to be carried about a
mile within the woods at the head of the bay. I saw them left there
by the side of a freshwater brook. A young bull and a cow, some sheep
and goats, were also intended to have been left by me as an additional
present to Van Diemen's Land, but I soon laid aside all thoughts of
this, from a persuasion that the natives, incapable of entering into my
views of improving their country, would destroy them. If ever they
should meet with the pigs, I have no doubt this will be their fate. But
as these animals soon become wild and are fond of the thickest cover
of the woods, there is great probability of their being preserved. An
open place must have been chosen for the accommodation of the
cattle; and in such a situation they would not possibly have remained
concealed many days.

Wednesday, January 29, 1777. The morning was ushered in with
a dead calm which continued all day and effectually prevented our
sailing. (*A good excuse to get ashore again and explore some more.*)
A party to cut wood was ordered to go to the usual place, and I
accompanied them myself. We had observed several of the natives
this morning sauntering along the shore, which assured us that though
their consternation had made them leave us so abruptly the day before,
they were convinced that we intended them no mischief and were
desirous of renewing the intercourse. It was natural that I should wish
to be present on the occasion.

We had not long landed before about twenty of them, men and
boys, joined us without expressing the least sign of fear or distrust.
There was one of this company conspicuously deformed and who was
not more distinguishable by the hump upon his back than by the

drollery of his gestures and the seeming humor of his speeches, which he was fond of exhibiting, as we supposed, for our entertainment. ෫

The usual cause of "humpback," Pott's Disease, is tuberculosis. Tuberculosis was common in Europe at the time and probably Captain Clerke, infected before he left England, was suffering from this disease throughout the voyage. It is not known that the bacterium of tuberculosis existed in remote Tasmania, before the coming of white men; it is possible. More likely this man's humpback was due to other causes.

෫ The language spoken here was wholly unintelligible to us. It appeared to me to be different from that spoken by the inhabitants of the more northern parts of the country whom I met with on my first voyage. (*Cook did not know that "Adventure Bay" was on an island [Tasmania] and not part of the Australian continent, where he had been before.*) Some of our present group wore loose around their necks, three or four folds of small cord made of the fur of some animal; and others of them had a narrow slip of kangaroo skin tied around their ankles. They seemed to set no value on iron or iron tools, and they were even ignorant of the use of fish hooks. There were no canoes or vessels in which they could go upon the water. It was evident from the many heaps of mussel shells we saw near the shore that shellfish made a part of their food. For shelter, little sheds were built of sticks and covered with bark, and we could also see signs of their taking up abode in the trunks of large trees which had been hollowed out by fire for this purpose.

Several women and children made their appearance. These females wore a kangaroo skin (in the same shape as it came from the animal) tied over the shoulder and round the waist. But its only use seemed to be to support their children when carried on their backs. It did not cover those parts which most nations covered, the women being otherwise as naked as the men, and as black. Their bodies were marked with scars. Some of them had their heads completely shorn or shaved, in others this operation was performed only on one side. Many of the children had fine features and were thought pretty, but of the persons of the women, especially those advanced in years, a less favorable report was made.

Some of the gentlemen belonging to the *Discovery,* I was told, paid their addresses to some women, which were rejected with great disdain, whether from a sense of virtue, or fear of displeasing their own men, I shall not pretend to determine. That this gallantry was not very agreeable to their men is certain: for an elderly man, as soon as he observed it, ordered all the women and children to retire, which they did, though some of the women showed a little reluctance.

The conduct of Europeans among savage women is highly blamable. It creates a jealousy in their men that may be attended with consequences ill-fated to the success of the common enterprise and to the whole body of adventurers without advancing the private purpose of the individual or enabling him to gain the object of his wishes. I believe it has been generally found among uncivilized people that where the women are easy of access the men are the first to offer them to strangers; and that where this is not the case, neither the allurement of presents nor the opportunity of privacy will be likely to have the desired effect. This observation, I am sure, will hold good throughout all parts of the South Seas where I have been. Why then should men act so absurd a part as to risk their own safety, and that of their companions, in pursuit of a gratification which they have no probability of obtaining? ε∾

Evidently, Cook did not or, more likely, could not prevent his men from having sexual relations with the native women. His disapproval is clear. These advances in Tasmania were made, without his prior knowledge, by men from the other ship. Though they did not succeed here, Cook knew from previous experience that at other places they would be nearly swamped in women.

∾§ Van Diemen's Land has been visited twice before. It was so named by Tasman, who discovered it in November 1642. (*Abel Janszoon Tasman, a Dutch navigator, sailed from the Dutch settlement of Batavia on the island of Java on several voyages of exploration into the Pacific. He succeeded in sailing around the continent of Australia, touching on several points along the coast, including Van Diemen's Land, which he named, and discovering the islands of New Zealand, Fiji, and Tonga. Although more than a hundred years before the time of Cook, Van Diemen's explorations provided a rough chart of that portion of the Pacific.*) From that time, it had escaped all further notice of European navigators till Captain Furneaux touched at it in March 1773. (*In the preceding voyage, Furneaux, Captain of the companion ship, the* Adventure, *had put in here on his way to a rendezvous at New Zealand after his ship had become separated from Cook in a South Atlantic fog.*) I hardly need say that it is the southern point of New Holland (*Australia*), which, if it does not deserve the name of "continent," is by far the largest island in the world. (*As seen before, Cook did not know that he was really on an island off the southern coast of Australia, and not on the continent itself.*)

The land is for the most part of a good height, diversified with hills and valleys and everywhere of a greenish hue. It is well wooded, and from what we met with in Adventure Bay, not ill-supplied with water. We found plenty of it in three or four places in this bay. The only wind to which this bay is exposed is the northeast, but as this wind blows from Maria's Islands, it brings no great sea along with it. Therefore, upon the whole, this may be accounted a very safe road. The bottom is clean, good holding ground, and the depth of the water from 12 to 54 fathoms. The rise of the tide was 18 inches and there was no appearance of its having ever exceeded 2½ feet. The tall straight trees are of a different sort from those which are found in the more northern parts of the coast. The wood is very long, close-grained, extremely tough; fit for spars, oars, and many other uses; and would on occasion make good masts (perhaps none better) if a method could be found to lighten it. These are all the memorials useful to navigators which my short stay enabled me to record.

At eight o'clock in the morning of the thirtieth of January, a light breeze springing up at west, we weighed anchor and put to sea from Adventure Bay. Soon after the wind increased to a perfect storm. The fury abated in the evening, when it veered to the east and northeast. This gale was indicated by the barometer, for the wind no sooner began to blow than the mercury in the tube began to fall. Another remarkable thing attended the coming of the wind, which was very faint at first; it brought with it a degree of heat that was almost intolerable. The mercury in the thermometer rose, as it were, instantaneously, from about 70° to near 90°. This heat was of so short a continuance that it seemed to be wafted away before the breeze that brought it.

We pursued our course to the eastward, without meeting with anything worthy of note, till the night of the sixth of February, when a marine belonging to the *Discovery* fell overboard and was never seen afterward. This was the second misfortune of the kind that had happened to Captain Clerke since he left England. ॐ

CHAPTER SIX

NEW ZEALAND

February 10, 1777——February 24, 1777

NEW ZEALAND ⋖ On the tenth, at four in the afternoon, we discovered the land of New Zealand. After making the land, I steered for Cape Farewell, which at daybreak the next morning bore south by west, distance about 4 leagues. I then steered for Stephen's Island, which we came up with at nine o'clock at night, and at ten the next morning anchored at our old station in Queen Charlotte's Sound.

We had not been long at anchor before several canoes, filled with natives, came alongside the ships; but very few of them would venture on board, which appeared the more extraordinary, as I was well known to them all. There was one man in particular among them whom I had treated with remarkable kindness during the whole of my stay when I was last here. Yet now, neither professions of friendship nor presents could prevail upon him to come onto the ship. His shyness was to be accounted for only upon this supposition: that they were apprehensive we had revisited their country in order to revenge the deaths of Captain Furneaux's people. ⋗

When in the course of the second voyage, Cook and Furneaux had again become separated, Cook left this rendezvous point at Queen Charlotte's Sound only four days before Furneaux was able to put in there in the *Adventure*. Furneaux, the more typical European, used force rather than friendliness in his relations with the Maoris, and probably behaved in a fearful, self-protective, and aggressive way toward these natives and was unable to see them as people whom it would be rewarding to have as friends. One day all the men in a boat

55

crew were killed and very likely eaten. Furneaux returned directly to England after leaving Queen Charlotte's Sound. What had caused the deadly fight, in the familiar anchorage, Cook was now trying to piece together.

◄§ Seeing Omai on board my ship, whom they must have remembered seeing on board the *Adventure* when that melancholy affair happened, and whose conversations with them, as they approached, generally turned to that subject, they must have been well assured that I was no longer a stranger to it. I thought it necessary, therefore, to use every endeavor to assure them of the continuance of my friendship and that I should not disturb them on that account. I do not know whether this carried any weight with them; but they very soon laid aside all manner of restraint and distrust.

We set up two tents, one from each ship, on the same spot where we had pitched them formerly. The observatories were at the same time erected to find the rate of the timekeeper and make other observations.

A boat was never sent any considerable distance from the ships without being armed and under the direction of such officers as I could depend upon and who were well acquainted with the natives. During my former visits to this country I had not taken these precautions, nor were they, I believe, more necessary now than formerly; but after the tragic fate of the *Adventure*'s boat crew and of Captain Marion du Fresne and some of his people in the Bay of Islands, it was impossible totally to divest ourselves of all apprehensions of experiencing a similar calamity.

If the natives entertained any suspicion of our revenging these acts of barbarity, they soon laid it aside. During the course of the day a great number of families came from different parts of the coast and took up their residence close to us so that there was not a spot in the cove where a hut could be put up, except the place where we had fixed our little encampment. This, they left us in quiet possession of; but they came and took away the ruins of some old huts as materials for their new erections.

It is curious to observe with what facility they build these occasional places of abode. I have seen about twenty of them erected on a spot of ground that, not an hour before, was covered with shrubs and plants. They generally bring some part of the materials with them, the rest they find upon the premises. I was present when a number of people

landed and built one of these villages. The moment the canoes reached
shore the men leaped out and at once took possession of a piece of
ground by tearing up the plants and shrubs and then sticking up some
part of the framing of a hut. While the men were employed in raising
the huts, the women were stationed to take care of the canoes, others
secured the provisions and the few utensils, and the rest went to gather
dry sticks for a fire. As to the children: I kept them occupied in scram-
bling for beads till I had emptied my pockets.

The temporary habitations are abundantly sufficient to afford shelter from the wind and rain. Generally, if not always, the same tribe
or family, though large, associated and built together. Frequently we
saw a village, as well as their larger towns, divided into districts by
low palisades or similar mode of separation.

It was a great advantage to have the natives come to live with us.
Every day, when the weather would permit, some of them went out
to catch fish. We generally got, by exchange, a good share of the produce of their labors. This supply, and what our own nets and lines
afforded us, was so ample that we seldom were in want of fish. Nor
was there any deficiency in other refreshments. Celery, (*wild*) scurvy-
grass (*same family as water-cress*), and portable soup (*porridge*)
were boiled with peas and wheat for both ships' companies every day
during our stay; and they had spruce beer to drink. (*The needles and
small branches of the spruce tree were boiled with sugar and the decoction subsequently fermented. The beverage was greatly relished by
seamen even though at the same time their regular ration of grog was
often curtailed.*) If any of our people had contracted the seeds of
scurvy, such a regimen soon removed them. The truth is, when we
arrived here, there were only two invalids.

Besides the natives who took their abode close to us, we were visited
by others whose residence was not far off and by some who lived more
remote. Their articles of commerce were: curiosities, fish, and women.
The first two always come to a good market, but the women did not.
The seamen had taken a kind of dislike to these people and were
either unwilling or afraid to associate with them. I knew no instance
of a man quitting his station to go to their habitations. ॐ

John Ledyard, a marine corporal from Connecticut, who sailed with
Cook, wrote otherwise in his journal:

"Belonging to the *Discovery* was a youth with whom a young New
Zealander girl, about fourteen years of age, fell desperately in love, nor

was he indifferent to this engaging brunette. What time he could spare
he generally retired with her; and they spent the day, but oftener the
night, in a silent conversation. Though words were wanting, their
meaning was perfectly understood. The language of love among all
the languages in this sublunary world is the soonest comprehended.

"Though our sailor appeared amiable in her eyes in the habit of a
stranger, he was conscious that to ornament his person in the fashion
of New Zealand would recommend him more to his mistress. He
therefore submitted himself to be tattooed from head to foot. She, on
her part, had fine hair; and her chief pride was in the dressing of her
hair. The pains she took and the decorations she used would perhaps
have done honor to a European beauty. She was furnished with combs
and taught by her lover how to use them. He would by the hour amuse
himself with forming her hair into ringlets, rendering them fit for the
residence of little loves.

"On the twenty-fifth of February, the ships being ready for sea, the
precaution of mustering the ships' company was taken. It was found
that one was missing: This was our adventurer, who with his faithful
Gowannahee (that was her name), had completely made their escape.
A messenger was dispatched on board the *Resolution* to know how to
proceed. When the message was delivered, the captains and the officers
were joyous over their bottle. At first it only furnished a subject of
pleasantry; but it came at last to be seriously debated whether the
man should be sent for or not. Most were for leaving him to follow
his own humor; but Captain Cook, thinking it would be a bad prece-
dent and an encouragement for other inamoratos when they came to
happier climates to follow, was for sending an armed force and bringing the man back at all hazards.

"It was two in the morning before the guard found the spot where
the lovers were. They surprised them in a profound sleep locked in
each other's arms, dreaming no doubt of love, of kingdoms, of dia-
dems, of being the progenitors of a numerous family of princes to
govern the kingdoms of Ea-kei-nommauwee and T'avi-Poenammoo.

"Love like this is not to be found in those countries where the boasted
refinements of sentiment too often circumscribe the purity of affection and narrow it away to mere conjugal fidelity. God of love and
romance! This pair ought to have been better heeded by thee and
at least secluded from the pursuit of those who never did, and perhaps
never will be able to, offer to thy deityship one single sacrifice of pure,
sublimated romantic sentiment.

"The prisoner was carried on board to the Captain, where he underwent a long examination and made a full confession of all his views. Captain Cook, astonished at the young man's extravagant notions and pleased at his frankness, instantly forgave him and ordered him to duty, telling him he was convinced his present situation and feelings must be sufficient punishment."

Captain Cook's forbearance was impressive. On other ships, lashing nearly to death with a cat-o-nine tails was the usual punishment for desertion. The Captain gives us his views on relations with native women:

⋙ A connection with the women I allow because I cannot prevent it; but I never encourage it because I always dread the consequences. Many men are of the opinion that such intercourse is one of our greatest securities among savages; and perhaps they, who either from necessity or choice are to remain and settle with them, may find it so. With travelers and transient visitors, such as we, it is generally otherwise: A connection with their women betrays more men than it saves. What else can reasonably be expected, since all their views are selfish without the least regard or attachment? My own experience, at least, which has been pretty extensive, has not pointed out to me one instance to the contrary.

Among our occasional visitors was a Chief named Kahoora, who, I was informed, headed the party that cut off Captain Furneaux's people and himself killed Mr. Rowe, the officer who commanded. To judge the character of Kahoora, by what I heard from his countrymen, he seemed to be more feared than beloved among them. Not satisfied with telling me that he was a very bad man, some of them importuned me to kill him; and they were surprised that I did not listen to them. If I had followed the advice of all our friends, I might have extirpated the whole race; for the people of every hamlet or village, by turns, applied to me to destroy the other. One would almost have thought it impossible for these people to live in such a divided state. ⋙

Judging from these people of Polynesia, just now being discovered and understood by Western man, war and open aggression with intent to kill is the natural state of man. This was no idyllic paradise of the "noble savage." In their bountiful climate they had no fear of cold, starvation, or wild beasts; but their neighbors might at any time set upon them and kill them.

⋖§ From my own observations, and from the information of Chief Taweihorooa and others, it appears to me that the New Zealanders must live under perpetual apprehensions of being destroyed by each other. There are few tribes that have not, as they think, sustained wrongs from some other tribe, which they are continually upon the watch to revenge. And perhaps the desire of a good meal may be no small incitement.

Many years will sometimes elapse before a favorable opportunity happens; and the son never loses sight of an injury that has been done his father. They steal upon the adverse party in the night; and if they find them unguarded (which, I believe, is very seldom the case) they kill everyone indiscriminately, not even sparing the women and children. When the massacre is completed, they either feast and gorge themselves on the spot, or carry off as many of the dead bodies as they can and devour them at home. If they are discovered before they can execute their bloody purpose, they steal off again, and sometimes are pursued and attacked by the other party. To give quarter, or to take prisoners, makes no part of their military law. The vanquished can only save their life by flight. This perpetual state of war, and the destructive method of conducting it, produces habitual circumspection, so that one hardly ever finds a New Zealander off his guard either day or night.

On the sixteenth at daybreak, I set out with a party of men to collect food for our cattle. As we turned down the sound, we visited Grass Cove, the memorable scene of the massacre of Captain Furneaux's people. Here I met with my old friend Pedro (*a nickname the seamen had given this Polynesian on the previous voyage, by which he was thereafter called by both his countrymen and the English*). He and another received us on the beach armed with a patoo (*an elliptic club about 18 inches long with a handle of stone or bone*) and spear. If they had any apprehensions, a few presents soon removed them and brought down to the beach two or three more of the family; but the greatest part of them remained out of sight.

While we were at this place, our curiosity prompted us to inquire into the melancholy fate of our countrymen. We already knew that Pedro had not been concerned in the unhappy transaction.

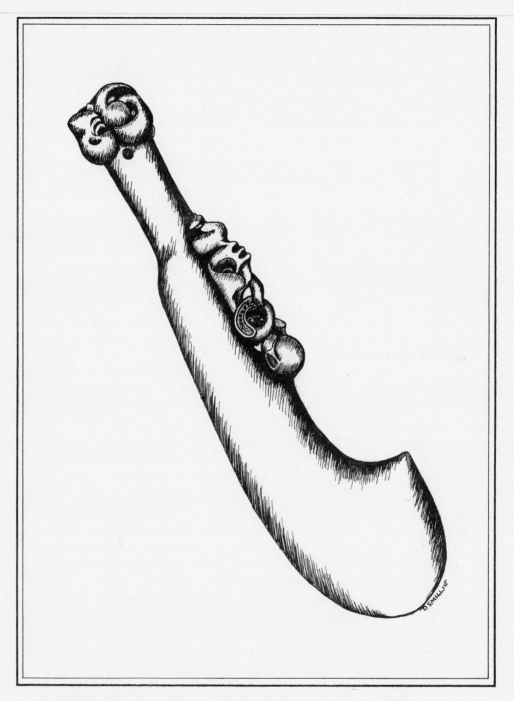

THE NEW ZEALANDER'S CLUB: A PATOO

Credit: Author's Private Collection

They told us that while our people were sitting at dinner, surrounded by several of the natives, some of the natives stole, or snatched from them, some bread and fish, for which they were beaten. This being resented, a quarrel ensued and two natives were shot dead. Before our people had time to load again, the natives rushed upon them, overpowered them with their numbers, and put them all to death. We were afterward told that a black servant of Captain Furneaux who was left on the boat to take care of her was a cause of the trouble. One of the natives was stealing something out of the boat and the Negro gave him a severe blow with a stick. The cries of the fellow being heard by his countrymen at a distance, they imagined he was killed and immediately began the attack on our people, who, before they had time to reach the boat, or arm themselves against the unexpected impending danger, fell a sacrifice to the fury of their savage assailants. This second manner of relating the transaction rests upon the authority of the young New Zealander who chose to abandon his country and go away with us, and who, consequently, could have no possible view in disguising the truth.

In attempting to get out of the bay we had not been long at anchor near Motuara before three or four canoes filled with natives came off to us from the southeast side of the sound. In one of these canoes was Kahoora, the leader of the party, who cut off the crew of the *Adventure*'s boat. This was the third time he had visited us without betraying the smallest appearance of fear. Omai pointed him out and solicited me to shoot him. Not satisfied with this he addressed himself to Kahoora, threatening to be his executioner if ever he presumed to visit us again.

The New Zealander paid so little regard to these threats that he returned the next morning with his whole family: men, women, and children, to the number of twenty and upward. Omai was the first to acquaint me with his being alongside the ship and desired to know if he should ask him to come on board. I told him he might; and accordingly he introduced the Chief into the cabin, saying, "Here is Kahoora, kill him!" But, as Omai had forgot his former threats, or was afraid that I should call upon him to perform them, he immediately retired.

In a short time, however, he returned, and seeing the Chief unhurt, he expostulated with me very earnestly saying, "Why do you not kill him? You tell me, if a man kills another in England, that he is hanged

for it. This man has killed ten, and yet you will not kill him, though
many of his countrymen desire it, and it would be very good!"

Omai's arguments, though specious enough, having no weight with
me, I asked the Chief, "Why have you killed Captain Furneaux's
people?" At this question, Kahoora folded his arms, hung his head,
and looked like one caught in a trap. I firmly believe he expected
instant death. No sooner was he assured of his safety than he became
cheerful. He did not, however, seem willing to give me an answer to
the question till I had, again and again, repeated my promise that
he should not be hurt. Then he ventured to tell us.

"One of my men brought a stone hatchet to barter. The Englishman
to whom it was offered took it and would neither return it nor give
anything for it. The owner of it snatched up the bread or an equivalent.
Then the quarrel began."

The remainder of Kahoora's account of this unhappy affair differed
little from what we had before learned. He mentioned a narrow escape
he had during the fray; a musket was leveled at him which he avoided
by skulking behind the boat, but another man, who stood close to him,
was shot dead. As soon as the musket was discharged, he instantly
seized the opportunity to attack Mr. Rowe, who defended himself with
his hanger (*a short, broad sword with an inward-cutting point carried
hung at the waist*), with which he wounded Kahoora in the arm.

All agree that there was no premeditated plan of bloodshed; and
that if these thefts had not been, unfortunately, too hastily resented,
no mischief would have happened. For Kahoora's greatest enemies—
those who solicited his destruction most earnestly—at the same time
confessed that he had no intention to quarrel, much less to kill, till
the fray had actually commenced. It also appears that the unhappy
victims were under no apprehension of their fate; otherwise they never
would have ventured to sit down to a repast at so considerable a distance from their boat, among people who were the next moment to be
their murderers.

When the *Adventure* arrived first in Queen Charlotte's Sound in
1773, Mr. Bayly fixed upon Hippah, a fortified village, for making his
astronomical observations. He, and the people with him, at their
leisure, planted several spots with English garden seeds. Not the least
vestige of these now remained. It is probable that they had been
all rooted out to make room for buildings when the village was re-
inhabited. At all the other gardens planted by Captain Furneaux,

although now wholly overrun with the weeds of the country, we found cabbages, onions, leeks, purslane, radishes, mustard, and a few potatoes. Though the New Zealanders are fond of the potato it was evident that they had not taken the trouble to plant a single one—much less any other of the articles which we had introduced.

While we were unmooring and getting under sail, Tomatongeauooranuc, Matahouah, and many more of the natives came to take leave of us, or rather to obtain, if they could, some additional presents from us before we left them. These two chiefs became suitors to me for some goats and hogs. Accordingly, I gave to Matahouah two goats— a male and female with kid—and to Tomatongeauooranuc, two pigs —a boar and sow. They made me a promise not to kill them; though I must own I put no great faith in this. The animals which Captain Furneaux sent on shore here and which soon after fell into the hands of the natives, I was told were all dead. I could get no intelligence about the fate of those I had left in West Bay and Cannibal Cove when I was there in the course of my last voyage. All the natives agreed that poultry are now to be met with wild in the woods behind Ship Cove. Tiratou, a popular chief among them, had a great many cocks and hens in his possession, and one of the sows.

On my present arrival at this place, I fully intended to have left not only goats and hogs, but sheep and a young bull with two heifers, if I could have found a chief powerful enough to protect and keep them. (*Samples of many of the domesticated animals of England were on board Cook's ships.*) I have, at different times, left in New Zealand no less than ten or a dozen hogs besides those put on shore by Captain Furneaux. It will be extraordinary if this race should not increase and be preserved here, either in a wild or in a domestic state.

For some time Omai had expressed a desire to take one of the natives with him to his own country. A youth about eighteen years of age named Taweiharooa offered to accompany him and took up his residence on board. Finding that he was fixed in his resolution to go with us, and having learned that he was the only son of a deceased chief, and that his mother, still living, was a woman much respected here, I was apprehensive that Omai had deceived him by giving him hopes and assurances of being sent back. I therefore caused it to be made known to them that if the young man went away with us, he would never return. This declaration seemed to make no sort of impression. The afternoon before we left the cove, Tiratoutou, his mother, came on board. She and Taweiharooa parted with all the marks of tender affection that might be expected between a parent and a child who will never meet again. She said she would cry no more; and sure enough, she kept her word. When she returned the next morning to take her last farewell, all the time she was on board she remained quite cheerful and went away wholly unconcerned.

That Taweiharooa might be sent away in a manner becoming his birth, another youth, a boy of about ten years of age named Kokoa, was presented to me by his own father, who, I believe, would have parted with his dog with far less indifference. The very little clothing the boy had, he stripped him of, and left him as naked as he was born. I endeavored to convince these people of the impossibility of these youths ever returning home. Not one, not even their nearest relations, seemed to trouble themselves about their future fate. I was well satisfied that the boys would be no losers by exchange of place and gave my consent to their going. ৪৯

The Captain and his surgeon made a number of notable observations during their stay in New Zealand.

৭৪ One day, on inquiring of Taweiharooa, how many ships such as ours had arrived in Queen Charlotte's Sound or its neighborhood, he began by giving an account of one absolutely unknown to us. This, he said, had put into a port on the northwest coast but a very few years before I arrived in the Sound in the *Endeavour.* At first I thought he might have been mistaken as to the time and place, and that the ship in question might be either that of Monsieur Surville (*a French navigator who went on to make the first detailed study of the Solomon Islands*), who is said to have touched upon the northeast coast the same year (*1769*) that I was there in the *Endeavour,* or else that of Monsieur Marion du Fresne, who was in the Bay of Islands on the same coast a few years later. He assured me that he was not mistaken either as to the time or place of this ship's arrival. He said that the Captain of her, during his stay, cohabited with a woman of the country, and that she had a son by him still living about the age of Kokoa. We were also informed by Taweiharooa that this ship first introduced venereal disease among the New Zealanders. I wish that subsequent visitors from Europe may not have their share of guilt in leaving so dreadful a remembrance of them among this unhappy race. The dis-

order now is but too common here. The only method they make use
of as a remedy is by giving the patient a hot bath which they produce
by the steam of certain green plants laid over hot stones. (*Producing
a fever by externally applied heat is an effective treatment of syphilis.
In Europe the same discovery was made in the early 1900's and used
until the discovery of penicillin for the brain-infected form of the
disease.*) I have not the least doubt that this testimony may be depended upon to believe that a ship really had been here prior to my
arrival in the *Endeavour.* ֍

The ship may have been Spanish. Vessels of this nation had sailed
back and forth across the Pacific for two hundred years before Cook
and kept their courses and discovery of lands secret, especially from
the British, who during the same period of years had been constantly
raiding the Spanish ships and settlements. K'ang-hsi dishes of china
have been recovered by divers off Florida's Cape Kennedy from a
Spanish ship that went down in 1715. The china came from the Orient
probably via Manila, east by ship to Acapulco, Mexico, headed for
Spain. These trading galleons had to swing north or south in the Pacific
to reach favorable winds, and some bound for Peru may have seen
these islands, but the British would be the last to know about it. Outside of the report of Taweiharooa, there is no other record of a European ship visiting New Zealand between Cook's first voyage and
Tasman's original discovery more than 100 years earlier in 1642.

֍ The land everywhere about Queen Charlotte's Sound is mountainous, rising immediately from the sea into large hills with blunted tops.
At considerable distances are valleys, each terminating toward the sea
in a small cove with a pebbly beach, behind which are small flats
where the natives build their huts and haul their canoes. The hills are
one continuous forest of lofty trees, flourishing with a vigor superior
to anything that imagination can conceive.

Though answering to our month of August, the weather was never
disagreeably warm, nor did it raise the thermometer higher than 66°.
The winter also seems equally mild; for in June 1773, which corresponds to our December, the mercury never fell lower than 48° and
the trees retained their verdure as if in the summer season. The northwest winds are the most prevailing and are almost constantly connected with fine weather. The only obstacle to this being one of the
finest countries upon earth is its great hilliness.

The large trees which cover the hills are chiefly of two sorts. One of them, the size of our largest firs, grows much after their manner, but the leaves and small berries on their points are much like the yew. It was this which supplied the place of spruce in making beer. This liquor when well prepared was acknowledged to be little inferior to the American spruce beer by those who had experienced both. The other sort of tree is like a maple and grows often to great size. The wood of this and the preceding was found to be too heavy for masts, yards, and similar repairs.

Among other plants that were useful to us may be reckoned wild celery and one that we used to call scurvy-grass though entirely different from the plant to which we give that name. This, however, is far preferable to ours, and may be known by its jagged leaves and small clusters of white flowers. Both sorts were boiled every morning with wheat ground in a mill (*hot cereal*) for the people's breakfast and also with their pea-soup for dinner; sometimes they were used as salad, or dressed as greens; in all ways they are good.

Insects are very rare. The only noxious one is the sandfly, very numerous here and almost as troublesome as the mosquito. We found no reptiles here except two or three sorts of small harmless lizards. Taweiharooa told us that there are snakes and lizards of enormous size. He described the lizards as being 8 feet in length and as big round as a man's body. He said they sometimes seize and devour men, that they burrow in the ground, and that they are killed by making fires at the mouths of the holes. We could not mistake him, for with his own hand he drew a very good representation of a lizard and also a snake to show what he meant.

It is remarkable that in their extensive land there should not even be the trace of any quadruped, only excepting a few rats and a sort of fox-dog, which is a domestic animal with the natives. ও

Mr. Anderson was correct about the absence of land mammals on New Zealand except for the dog and rat, which must have come with the Polynesian man when he first discovered and settled the land. The lizard must have been the Tuatara, a scientific curiosity—the sole survivor of a predinosaur and otherwise extinct order of reptiles, the *Rhynchocephalia*. The Tuatara lives in burrows but is not big enough to eat a man, being only about 2 feet long. There were no snakes on New Zealand. Taweiharooa's drawing that resembled a snake may have been a worm.

THE TUATARA

Credit: Author's Private Collection

*§ There is no mineral worth notice but a green jasper of which the New Zealanders make their tools and ornaments. It may be found, they say, in the channel of a large river far to the southward. It is deposited in the earth in thin layers. A piece was purchased about 18 inches long, a foot broad, and nearly 2 inches thick which yet seemed only the fragment of a larger piece. A trade for green talc is carried on throughout the whole northern island. They tell us that there is none of this stone to be found but at a place somewhere about the head of Queen Charlotte's Sound. I regretted much that I could not spare sufficient time for paying a visit to the place, as we were told a hundred fabulous stories about this stone, not one of which carried with it the least probability of truth, though some of their most sensible men would have us believe them. One of the stories is that this stone is originally a fish which they stick with a gig in the water, tie a rope to it, and drag it to the shore. They all agree that it is fished out of a large lake called by the natives Tavai Poenammoo, and the adjoining country is known to them by that name. (*The area is truly a "fabulous" one. Lake Taupo is in the center of a pumice-covered plateau, surrounded by active volcanoes with innumerable boiling pools, geysers, and fumaroles. Floating pumice can indeed by "fished out" of these pools with a stick and rope*).

Their boats are well built of planks raised upon each other and fastened with strong withes (*a tough, flexible small twig*). They also bind a long narrow piece on the outside of the seams to prevent their leaking. Some are 50 feet long and so broad as to be able to sail without an outrigger. The smaller boats commonly have one; and they often fasten two boats together by rafters which they call a double canoe (*a catamaran*). They carry from five to thirty men or more and often have at the bow a large head ingeniously carved and painted, which seems intended to represent a man with his features distorted by rage. Their paddles are about 4 or 5 feet long, narrow, and pointed. When they keep time, the boat is pushed along pretty swiftly. Their sail, which is seldom used, is made of a mat of a triangular shape having the broadest part above. There is not the least sign of cultivation of land; they depend principally for their subsistence on the sea, which, indeed, is very bountiful in its supply.

Their principal profession is war. Before they begin, they join in a war-song to which all keep exact time and soon raise their passion to a degree of frantic fury, attended with the most horrid distortion of their eyes, mouths, and tongues to strike terror into their enemies, which makes them appear more like demons than men, and would almost chill the boldest with fear. To this succeeds a circumstance, almost foretold in their fierce demeanor—horrid, cruel, and disgraceful to human nature—which is: cutting in pieces, even before being perfectly dead, the bodies of their enemies; and, after dressing them on a fire, devouring the flesh, not only without reluctance, but with peculiar satisfaction. (*In a land where there is no other red meat of mammals except man it may have tasted good.*) One might be apt to suppose that people capable of such excess of cruelty must be destitute of every humane feeling, even among their own party. And yet we find them lamenting the loss of their friends with a violence of expression which augurs the most tender remembrance of them. Both men and women, upon the death of those connected with them whether in battle or afterward, bewail them with the most doleful cries; at the same time cutting their foreheads and cheeks with shells or pieces of flint in large gashes until the blood flows plentifully and mixes with their tears. ❧

Ledyard says of the New Zealander:

"They wear a very coarse outer covering that affords good shelter from cold or wet weather. It is formed round and converging to the top, where there is an aperture just sufficient to admit the head to pass through and cover the body as low as the hip. If it storms they squat down upon their hams and the bottom of the garment, reaching the ground, forms a shelter to the whole body, the head excepted, which looks in that situation as if it had been fixed upon a haystack.

"After a labored inquiry on our part with regard to their ancestors and the original population of the country, the only information we have obtained is: Their forefathers at some very remote period, but how remote they knew not, came from a distant island called Hawyjee. I cannot think the information useless.

"Among all the savage sons of war I ever saw, they are the most formidable. When a New Zealander stands forth and brandishes his spear the subsequent idea is: There stands a man."

CHAPTER SEVEN

A NEW ISLAND

February 25, 1777———March 30, 1777

◄§ On the twenty-fifth of February, 1777, at ten o'clock in the morn-ing, a light breeze springing up at northwest by west, we weighed, stood out of the sound, and made sail through the strait. (*The ships were now proceeding through a passage that separates the North and South islands of New Zealand. This passage was discovered by Cook on his first voyage in the* Endeavour. *The Admiralty named it Cook Strait in recognition of his remarkable achievement of surveying, in the course of that voyage, the entire coast of both islands of New Zealand.*) We had hardly got the length of Cape Tierawhitte when the wind took us aback at southeast. It continued in this quarter till two the next morning, when we had a few hours calm. After which we had a breeze at north; but here it fixed not long before it veered to the east and after that to the south. At length on the twenty-seventh, at eight in the morning, we took our departure from Cape Palliser, when we had a fine gale, and I steered east by north. ξ»

The Captain, like many sailors, was beset by headwinds. His frus-tration is evident. It took him two days to make the 50 miles through Cook Strait. The Cape was named by Cook in remembrance of Admiral Hugh Palliser, who had been his friend and benefactor since his first days in the Navy and was a member of the Admiralty that sent him on this voyage.

◄§ We had no sooner lost sight of the land than our two New Zealand adventurers, the sea sickness they now experienced giving a turn to

71

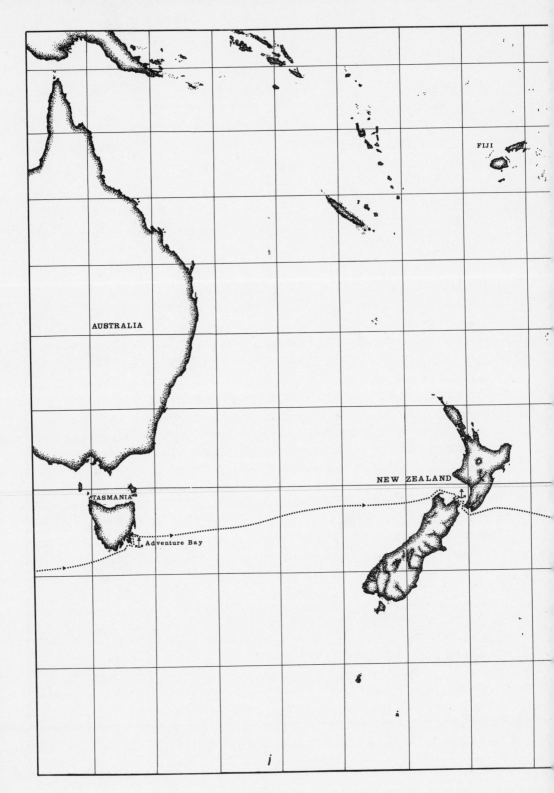

FIJI

AUSTRALIA

NEW ZEALAND

TASMANIA

⚓ Adventure Bay

ROUTE OF COOK'S SHIPS FROM

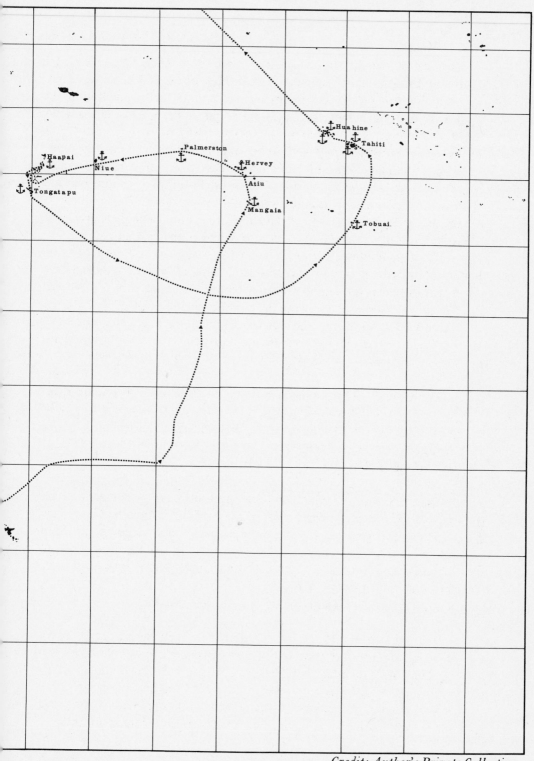

TASMANIA TO THE SOCIETY ISLANDS

their reflections, repented heartily of the steps they had taken. All the soothing encouragement we could think of availed but little. They wept, both in public and in private, and made their lamentations in a kind of song; which, as far as we could comprehend the meaning of the words, was expressive of their praises of their country and people, from which they were to be separated forever. Thus they continued for many days, till their seasickness wore off, and the tumult of their minds began to subside. Then these fits of lamentations became less and less frequent, and at length entirely ceased. Their native country and their friends were, by degrees, forgotten, and they appeared to be as firmly attached to us as if they had been born among us.

The wind continued invariably fixed at east-southeast, seldom shifting above two points on either side. It also blew very faint, so that it was the twenty-seventh of March before we crossed the Tropic (*of Capricorn*) and then we were only in the longitude of 201° 23′ east, which was 9 degrees to the westward of our intended port (*Tahiti*). We frequently made no better than a northerly course; nay, sometimes to the westward of north. ঌ

The Captain was having a trying time getting east against these prevailing easterly winds. He had all of the Pacific Ocean yet to cross from west to east. A month out of New Zealand, he had sailed only this small portion of the total distance. Summer in the Northern Hemisphere, the time to look for a "Northwest Passage," was fast arriving.

ঌ The hopes of the wind coming more southerly, or of meeting with it from the westward when a little south of the Tropic of Capricorn, as I had experienced in my former visits to this ocean, encouraged me to continue this course. Indeed it was necessary that I should run all risks, as my proceeding to the north this year in prosecution of the principal object of the voyage depended entirely on my making a quick passage to Tahiti or the Society Islands. ঌ

A NEW ISLAND ঌ On the twenty-ninth, at ten in the morning, as we were standing to the northeast, the *Discovery* made the signal of seeing land. We saw it from the masthead almost the same moment, bearing northeast by east by compass. We soon discovered it to be an island of no great extent and stood for it until sunset. The night was spent in standing off and on; and at daybreak the next morning, I

bore up for the lee or west side of the island. Neither anchorage nor
landing appeared practicable on the south side on account of a great
surf which broke everywhere with violence against the shore or against
the reef that surrounded it. (*The ships have come upon the first discovery of new land in this voyage.*)

We presently found that the island was inhabited and saw several
people on a point of land we had passed. They waded to the reef,
where, as they found the ship leaving them quickly, they remained;
others followed our course. They made a shouting noise nearly after
the manner of the inhabitants of New Zealand.

Between seven and eight o'clock we were at the west-northwest part
of the island. Being near the shore, we could perceive with our glasses
that several of the natives who appeared upon a sandy beach were all
armed with long spears and clubs, which they brandished in the air
with threatening signs, or as some on board interpreted their attitudes,
with invitations to land. Most of them appeared naked, except having
a girdle which, being brought up between the thighs, covered that part
of the body. Some of them had pieces of cloth of different colors, white-
striped, or checkered, which they wore thrown about their shoulders.
Almost all of them had a white wrapper about their heads, not much
unlike a turban or a high conical hat. The people were of tawny color,
of middling stature, but robust, and inclining to corpulence.

At this time, a small canoe was launched in a great hurry from the
beach and a man getting into it, put off, as with a view to reach the
ship. On perceiving this, I brought to that we might receive a visit.
But the man's resolution failing, he soon returned toward the beach,
where, after some time, another man joined him in the canoe and
they both paddled toward us. They stopped short, however, as if afraid
to approach, until Omai, who addressed them in the Tahitian language, in some measure quieted their apprehensions. They then came
near enough to take some beads and nails, which were tied to a piece
of wood and thrown into the canoe. They seemed afraid to touch
these things and put the piece of wood aside without untying them;
this attitude might have arisen from superstition. Omai told us that
when they saw us offering them presents they asked something for their
Eatooa, or god. He also, perhaps improperly, put the question to them:
Whether they eat human flesh. They answered in the negative with
a mixture of indignation and abhorrence. One of them, whose name
was Mourooa, being asked how he came by a scar on his forehead,

told us that it was the consequence of a wound he had gotten in fighting with the people of an island which lies to the northeastward, who
sometimes came to invade them. They afterward took hold of a rope;
still, however, they would not venture on board. They told Omai,
who understood them pretty well, that their countrymen on shore had
given them this caution, at the same time directing them to inquire
from whence our ship came and to learn the name of the Captain.
On our part, we inquired the name of the island, which they called
Mangeea. 𐫱

Whenever possible, Cook preferred to learn the name of geographical locations that the native inhabitants used, and record this name
on his charts. Today this island is called, with a slight change in spelling, the same name that Mourooa called it: Mangaia. A fragment of
the conversation between this Polynesian standing in his canoe and
Cook, high above in the English ship, is thus preserved forever. The
following passage is perhaps the finest description ever recorded of the
inhabitants of a South Sea atoll, heretofore untrampled by any previous European.

⤙ Mourooa was lusty and well made, but not very tall. His features
were agreeable, and his disposition no less so. He made several droll
gesticulations which indicated both good nature and a share of humor.
He also made others which seemed of a serious kind and repeated
some words with a devout air before he ventured to lay hold of the
rope of the ship's stern. His color was nearly the same cast as most
southern Europeans. The other man was not so handsome. Both of
them had strong, straight hair of a jet color, tied together on the crown
of the head with a bit of cloth. They wore girdles made from the
Morus papyrifera in the same manner as at the other islands of this
ocean. It was glazed like the sort used by the natives of the Friendly
(*Tonga*) Islands; but the cloth on their heads was white, like that
found at Tahiti. They had on sandals made of a grassy substance,
interwoven. These, we also observed, were worn by those who stood
upon the beach; and, as we supposed, were intended to defend their
feet against the rough coral rocks. Their beards were long. The inside
of their arms, from the shoulder to the elbow, and some other parts,
were punctured or tattooed after the manner of the inhabitants of
almost all the other islands in the South Sea. The lobes of their ears

A MAN OF MANGAIA

Credit: *Engraving, Author's Private Collection*

were pierced, or rather slit, and to such a length that one of them stuck there a knife and some beads which he had received from us. He had two polished pearl-shells and a bunch of human hair, loosely twisted, hanging about his neck. This was the only ornament we observed. The canoe they came in was not more than 10 feet long and very narrow, but both strong and neatly made. The forepart had a flat board fastened over it and projecting out to prevent the sea getting in on plunging, like the small canoes called Evaas at Tahiti. It had an upright stern, about 5 feet high, like some in New Zealand; and the upper end of this sternpost was forked. The lower part of the canoe was of white wood, but the upper was black. Their paddles were made of wood of the same color, not above 3 feet long, broad at one end and blunted. They paddled either end of the canoe forward indifferently, and only turned about their faces to paddle the contrary way. We now stood off and on. As soon as the ships were in a proper station, about ten o'clock, I ordered two boats, one of them from the *Discovery,* to sound the coast and to endeavor to find a landing place. With this view, I went in one of them myself, taking with me articles to give the natives that might gain their goodwill. I had no sooner put off from the ship than the canoe with the two men which had left us not long before, paddled toward our boat; and, having come alongside, Mourooa stepped into her without being asked, and without a moment's hesitation.

Omai, who was with me, was ordered to inquire of him where we could land. He directed us to two different places; but I saw with regret that the attempt could not be made at either place unless at the risk of having our boat filled with water or even staved to pieces. Nor were we more fortunate in our search for an anchorage; for we could find no bottom till within a cable's length (*720 feet*) of the breakers. There we met with from 20 to 40 fathoms depth over sharp coral rocks, so that anchoring would have been attended with much more danger than landing.

While we were thus employed in reconnoitering the shore, great numbers of the natives thronged down upon the reef, all armed as above-mentioned. Mourooa, who was now in my boat, probably thinking that their warlike appearance hindered us from landing, ordered them to retire. As many of them complied, I judged he must be a person of some consequence among them. Indeed, if we understood him right, he was the king's brother.

So great was the curiosity of several of them that they took to the water and, swimming off to the boats, came on board without reserve. Nay, we found it difficult to keep them out; and still more difficult to prevent their carrying off everything they could lay their hands upon. At length, when they perceived that we were returning to the ships, they all left us except our original visitor, Mourooa. He, though not without evident signs of fear, kept his place in my boat and accompanied me on board the ship.

Such parts of the coast of the island as fell under our observations are guarded by a reef of coral rock, outside of which the sea is of an unfathomable depth. It is a full 5 leagues in circuit. (*A league is 3 nautical miles or 3.45 U.S. statute [land] miles. The circumference of Mangaia is then about 17 "land" miles.*) The island is of moderate and equal height and in clear weather may be certainly seen at the distance of 10 leagues. The shore has several excavations made by the beating of the waves against a brownish sandstone. The descent is covered with trees of a deep green color, very thick, but not high, which seem all of one sort. Near the shore there are great numbers of that species of dracaena found in the woods of New Zealand and also scattered in some other places. (*These foliage plants are today often grown as house plants because of their strikingly patterned leaves.*) On the northwest part, the shore ends in a sandy beach beyond which the land is broken down into small chasms or gullies and has a broad border of trees resembling tall willows, which from its regularity might be supposed a work of art did not its extent forbid us to think so. The island has a pretty aspect and might be made a beautiful spot of cultivation.

The inhabitants seemed to be both numerous and well fed. It might be a matter of curiosity to know their method of subsistence; for our friend Mourooa told us they had no animals as hogs and dogs, both of which, however, they had heard of, but acknowledged they had plantains, breadfruit, and taro. The language of the inhabitants of Mangaia is a dialect of that spoken at Tahiti, though their pronunciation, as that of the New Zealander, was more guttural. ॐ

The common language, as well as the knowledge of hogs and dogs, of which there were none on this island, indicates that the inhabitants had some intercourse with other Pacific Islands, though we do not know if this was by planned voyages or by accidental drifting of their canoes.

◄§ The natives of Mangaia seem to resemble those of Tahiti and the Marquesas (*1,550 miles to the eastward*) in the beauty of their persons more than any other nation I have seen in these seas, having a smooth skin and not being muscular. They are not only cheerful but, as Mourooa showed us, are acquainted with all the lascivious gesticulations which the Tahitians practice in their dance (*the hula-hula*). We observed one house near the beach which much resembled in its mode of construction those of Tahiti. It was pleasantly situated in a grove of trees and appeared to be about 30 feet long and 7 or 8 feet high, with an open end which represented an ellipse divided transversely. Before it was spread something white on a few bushes which we conjectured to be a fishing net. They salute strangers much after the manner of the New Zealanders, by joining noses, adding, however, the additional ceremony of taking the hand of the person to whom they are paying civilities and rubbing it with a degree of force upon their nose and mouth.

On the ship, the cattle and other objects did not strike Mourooa with so much surprise as one might have expected. Perhaps his mind was too much taken up with his own safety to allow him to attend to other things. It is certain that he seemed very uneasy; and the ship, on our getting on board, happening to be standing off shore, this circumstance made him more so. I could get but little new information from him; and therefore after he had made a short stay, I ordered a boat to carry him in toward the land. As soon as he got out of the cabin, he happened to stumble over one of the goats. His curiosity now overcoming his fear, he stopped, looked at it, and asked Omai, "What bird was this?" And then he repeated the question to people upon the deck. The boat having conveyed him near the surf, he leaped into the sea and swam ashore. He had no sooner landed than the multitude of his countrymen gathered round him as if with an eager curiosity to learn what he had seen. In this situation they remained when we lost sight of them. As soon as the boat returned we hoisted her in and made sail from the land to the northward. Thus were we obliged to leave unvisited this fine island. §►

CHAPTER EIGHT

THE ISLAND OF ATIU

March 30, 1777——April 4, 1777

◄§ After leaving Mangaia on the afternoon of March 30, we continued our course northward all that night and till noon of the thirty-
first, when we again saw land. Next morning we had got abreast of its
north end and could now pronounce it to be an island near in appearance and extent to that we had so lately left. At the same time, another
island, but much smaller, was seen right ahead.

The largest one was most likely to furnish food for the cattle, of
which we began to be in great want. With this view, I determined to
work up to it; but as there was little wind, and that was unfavorable,
we were still 2 leagues to leeward the following morning. We observed
several single canoes coming from the shore. Three of these canoes
came alongside the *Resolution,* each conducted by one man. They
were long and narrow and supported by outriggers. The stern is
elevated about 3 or 4 feet, something like a ship's sternpost. The head
(*bow*) is flat above, but prowlike below.

With a little persuasion, one of the men made his canoe fast to the
ship and came on board. The other two, encouraged by his example,
soon followed him. Not long after, a double canoe in which were
twelve men, came toward us. As they drew near the ship, they recited
some words in concert by way of chorus. When they had finished their
solemn chant, they came alongside and asked for the Chief. As soon
as I showed myself, a pig and a few coconuts were conveyed up into
the ship. §►

The gift of a pig indicates that this island, unlike Mangaia only
150 miles away, supported a mammal other than man. As we shall

see, there were no other mammals on the island, not even dogs; but the inhabitants, nevertheless, knew of dogs, and valued them highly.

◄§ Our visitors were conducted into the cabin and other parts of the ship; they were afraid to come near the cows and horses, nor did they form the least conception of their nature. The sheep and goats did not surpass the limits of their ideas; for they gave us to understand that they knew these to be birds. It will appear rather incredible that human ignorance could ever make so strange a mistake, there not being the most distant similitude between a sheep or goat and any winged animal. (*Mourooa of Mangaia had also thought they were birds.*) These people seemed to know nothing of the existence of any other land animals besides hogs, dogs, and birds. Our sheep and goats they could see were very different creatures from hogs and dogs, and therefore they inferred that they must belong to the class of birds in which they knew there is a considerable variety of species. I made a present to my new friend (*note that the Captain calls him "friend"*); but on going away he seemed rather disappointed. I afterward understood that he was very desirous of obtaining a dog of which this island could not boast, though its inhabitants knew that the race existed in other islands of their ocean. §►

It was "their ocean" sure enough. Dogs and hogs, companions of men—cats did not exist here—must have accompanied mankind in his travels to these island. Some islands had all three—dogs, hogs, and men—some, like Mangaia, although populated, had neither hogs nor dogs, and others, like this island, had hogs but no dogs.

◄§ The people in these canoes were in general like those of Mangaia, though several were of a blacker cast. Some of their hair was of a frizzling disposition, yet for the most, that, as well as the straight sort, was long. §►

Kinky hair and dark skin color are characteristic traits of the inhabitants of lands west of here, such as Fiji and New Hebrides, and may indicate that contrary to the prevailing easterly winds there may have been, in prehistory, some movement of these races from the west to the east. This would imply the ability and knowledge to sail for long distances to windward. By the time of Cook's visit to this region the inhabitants did not have the knowledge, nor the sailing craft, to make such voyages.

Some of the men were rather handsome. They had girdles of glazed cloth, the inside of which, being brought betwixt their thighs, covered the adjoining parts. Ornaments, composed of broad grass, stained with red, and strung with berries of the night-shade were worn about their necks. Their ears were bored and they were punctured (*tattooed*) upon the legs from the knee to heel, which made them appear as if they wore a kind of boot. Their behavior was frank and cheerful, with a great deal of good nature.

(*Was it the warm tropical climate that made these people so much more peaceful than the New Zealander, or was it as Margaret Mead proposes—a difference in child-rearing and social habits?*) In general, the women were rather stout, with black hair flowing in ringlets down their neck and of an olive complexion. Their features were fuller than we allow to perfect beauties, and much alike. Their eyes were of a deep black and each countenance expressed a degree of complacency and modesty peculiar to the sex in every part of the world, but perhaps more conspicuous here where nature presented us with her productions in the fullest perfection, unbiased in sentiment by custom or unrestrained in manner by art. Their shape and limbs were elegantly formed. As their dress consisted only of a piece of glazed cloth fastened about the waist and scarcely reaching so low as the knees, we had an opportunity of observing every part.

At three o'clock in the afternoon, Mr. Gore returned with the boat and informed me that he had examined all of the west side of the island without finding a place where a boat could land or the ship could anchor, the shore being everywhere bounded by steep coral rock, against which the sea broke in a dreadful surf. Mr. Gore was of the opinion that by means of Omai, who could explain our request, the natives might be prevailed upon to bring off to the boats, beyond the surf, such articles as we most wanted, in particular the stems of plantain trees, which make good food for the cattle. Since we had little wind, the delay of a day or two was not of any moment; and therefore I determined to try the experiment. About ten the next morning, I dispatched Mr. Gore with three boats to try the experiment he had proposed. As I could confide in his diligence and ability, I left it entirely to him to act as he should judge to be most proper. The ships being a full league from the island when the boats put off, and having little wind, it was noon before we could work up to it. We then saw our three boats riding at their grapplings just without the surf, and a prodigious number of natives on the shore abreast of them. We concluded that Mr. Gore and others had landed. I kept as near the shore as was prudent. I was sensible, however, that the reef was as effective a barrier between us and our friends who had landed, and put them as much beyond the reach of our protection, as if half the circumference of the globe had intervened. At length, a little before sunset, we had the satisfaction of seeing the boats put off. Mr. Anderson's account I shall give a place here, nearly in his own words.

"We rowed toward a small sandy beach and came to anchor within a hundred yards of the reef, which extends about as far from the shore. Soon after, two canoes came off and to create a greater confidence in the islanders, we determined to go unarmed and run the hazard of being treated well or ill. Mr. Burney, the first Lieutenant of the *Discovery,* and I went in one canoe. Our conductors, watching attentively the motions of the surf, landed us safely upon the reef. An islander took hold of each of us with intentions to support us in walking over the rugged rocks to the beach, where several others met us, holding green boughs of a species of mimosa (*a shrub or small tree, often with yellow flowers*) in their hands, and saluted us by applying their noses to ours.

"We were conducted from the beach by our guides amidst a great crowd of people eager with curiosity to look at us. The number of people must have been at least two thousand. (*Even the small islands were heavily populated. The "great crowds" on these small islands are all gone now, killed off by European ways and diseases, especially measles.*) We were then led up an avenue of cocoa-palms; and soon came to a number of men, arranged in two rows, armed with clubs, which they held on their shoulders much in the manner we rest a musket. (*There was no disarmament program here. Even on this tiny island where there was no beast of prey and no one, except a close neighbor, to use a club on, everyone was armed.*) After walking a little way among them, we found a person who seemed a Chief, sitting cross-legged, cooling himself with a triangular fan made from a leaf of the cocoa-palm with a polished handle of black wood. In his ears were large bunches of beautiful red feathers which pointed forward. He had no other mark or ornament to distinguish him from the rest of the people, though they all obeyed him with greatest alacrity. He desired us to sit down, which we were very willing to do, being pretty well fatigued with walking up and the excessive heat we felt among the vast crowd that surrounded us.

"In a few minutes, these people were ordered to separate; and we saw about twenty young women with red feathers in their ears, engaged in a dance. They performed to a slow and serious song, sung by them all. We got up and went forward to see them. They seemed to be directed by a man who served as a prompter, and mentioned each motion they were to make. They never changed the spot as we do in dancing; though their feet were not at rest. This exercise consisted more in moving the fingers nimbly, at the same time holding their hands in a prone position near the face, and now and then clapping them together. Their motions and song were performed in such exact concert that it should seem they had been taught with great care. Few of those whom we saw in the crowd equaled them in beauty.

"After this, making use of Omai as his interpreter, Mr. Gore informed the Chief with what intention we had come on shore, but was given to understand that he must wait till the next day, and then he should have what was wanted. They now seemed to take some pains to separate us from each other; and everyone of us had his circle to surround and gaze at him. At the same time, I found the people began to steal several trifling things which I had in my pockets. (*Adolescents of today in their ardor to possess something of their current idol are apt to strip him clean of all removable objects, and maybe his shirt too.*) When I complained to the Chief of this treatment, he justified it. They did not seem to be of a disposition so savage as to make us anxious for the safety of our person, but it was vexing to be detained by their curiosity. In this situation I asked for something to eat, and they readily brought me some coconuts, breadfruit, and a sour pudding. Omai had observed that they had dug a hole in the ground for an oven, which they were now heating, and he could assign no other reason for this than that they meant to roast and eat us. He went so far as to ask them the question, at which they were greatly surprised, asking, in return, whether that was the custom with us?

"In this manner we were detained the greatest part of the day, being always in a crowd. Not satisfied with gazing at us, they frequently desired us to uncover parts of our skin, the sight of which commonly produced a great murmur of admiration."

The island, though never before visited by Europeans, actually happened to have other strangers residing in it. It was owing to Omai's being one of Mr. Gore's attendants that this curious circumstance came to our knowledge. He found among the crowd three of his own countrymen, natives of the Society Islands. At the distance of about 200 leagues (*about 700 miles*) from those islands, an immense unknown ocean intervening, with such wretched boats as they are known to make use of, and fit only for a passage where sight of land is scarcely ever lost, such a meeting, at such a place, may well be looked upon as one of those unexpected situations with which the writers of adventures love to surprise their readers, and which, when they really happen in common life, deserve to be recorded for their singularity.

Their story, as related by them, is an affecting one. About twenty persons of both sexes had embarked on board a canoe at Tahiti to cross over to the neighboring island of Raiatea. A violent contrary wind arising, they could reach neither Raiatea or go back to Tahiti. Their intended passage being a short one, their stock of provisions was scanty and soon exhausted. The hardships they suffered while driven along by the storm they knew not whither, are not to be conceived. They passed many days without having anything to eat or drink. Their numbers gradually diminished, worn out by famine and fatigue. Only four men survived. (*Similar occurrences happen today. In 1963 a young Tahitian started out with a companion in an outboard-motor boat to take a load of watermelons from the island of Maupiti on a short run to Bora Bora. Halfway across, the motor broke down and they drifted away. They ate the watermelons, fished, and drank rainwater. One died. One hundred and fifty-five days later, the survivor came ashore on the island of Samoa after drifting 1400 miles!*)

So well satisfied were the survivors that they refused the offer made to them of giving them passage on board our ship to restore them to their native islands. The similarity of manners and language more than naturalized them to this spot, and they had arrived upon this island at least twelve years ago.

This account brings to our knowledge a matter of fact not only very curious but very instructive. The applications of the above narrative is obvious. It will serve to explain, better than a thousand conjectures of speculative reasoners, how the detached parts of the earth, and in particular how the islands of the South Sea, may have originally been peopled; especially those that be remote from any other. It is indubitable that the natives of this island sprang originally from the same stock which has spread itself so wonderfully all over the immense extent of the South Seas.

This island is called Atiu by the natives. It lies in the latitude of 20° 1' south and in the longitude of 201° 45' east and is about 6 leagues in circumference. ঌ

Cook recorded his longitude, always east of Greenwich, past the 180° point, where today it would be shown on the map as west longitude, and measured in a westerly direction from Greenwich, 360° — 201° 45' = 158° 15' west of Greenwich longitude. Hereafter, the author will convert Cook's east longitude to the corresponding west longitude.

ঌ It is a beautiful spot with a surface composed of hills and plains, and covered with verdure of many hues. The language spoken at Atiu was equally well understood by Omai and our two New Zealanders. What its peculiarities may be, when compared with other dialects, I am not able to point out; for, though Mr. Anderson had taken care to note down a specimen of it, the natives, who made no distinction in the objects of their theft, stole the memorandum book. ঌ

CHAPTER NINE

DISCOVERY OF OTHER ISLANDS
IN THE COOK ARCHIPELAGO

April 4, 1777——April 27, 1777

OTHER ISLANDS IN THE COOK ARCHIPELAGO ᙩ Light airs and calms had prevailed all night, and the easterly swell had carried the ships some distance from Atiu before daybreak. As I had failed in my object of procuring at that place some effectual supply of fodder for the cattle, I saw no reason for staying there any longer. I therefore quitted it without regret, and steered for the neighboring island, which we had discovered three days before. ᙩ

TAKUTEA ᙩ We got up with it before ten o'clock in the morning. I immediately dispatched Mr. Gore with two boats to endeavor to land and get some food for our cattle. As there seemed to be no inhabitants here to obstruct our taking away whatever we might think proper, I was confident of his being able to make amends for our late disappointment, if the landing could be effected. There was a reef here surrounding the island, as at Atiu, and a considerable surf breaking against the rocks. Notwithstanding which, our boats no sooner reached the lee, or west side of the island, but they ventured in; and Mr. Gore and his party got safe on shore.

The supply here consisted of about a hundred coconuts for each ship; and besides this refreshment for ourselves, we got for our cattle some grass, and a quantity of leaves and branches.

This island lies in the latitude of 19° 51′ south and the longitude of 158° 23′ west, about three leagues from Atiu, the inhabitants of which called it Takutea. Mr. Anderson, who walked around it, guessed that it could not be much more than 3 miles in circuit. The beach within the reef is composed of white coral sand; above which, the land does not rise above 7 feet and is covered with a light reddish soil. One of our people caught a lizard of a most forbidding aspect, though small. Though there were at this time no inhabitants upon the island, indubitable marks remained of its being occasionally frequented. A few empty huts were found; and there were also several large stones, erected like monuments. &

HERVEY'S ISLAND & As soon as the boats were hoisted in, I made sail again to the northward with a light air of easterly wind, intending to try our fortune at Hervey's Island, which was discovered in 1773 during my last voyage. It was not more than 15 leagues distant, yet we did not get sight of it till daybreak on the morning of the sixth. As we kept on toward the island, six or seven canoes, all double ones, soon came near us with from three to six men in each of them. Their disorderly and clamorous behavior by no means indicated a disposition to trust us or treat us well. They even cut away, with a shell, a net with meat which hung over the ship's stern and absolutely refused to restore it, though we afterward purchased it from them. Those who were about our ship behaved in the same daring manner, for they made a hook of a long stick with which they endeavored openly to rob us.

These people seemed to differ as much in person, as in disposition, from the natives of Atiu, though the distance between the two islands is not very great. Their color was of a deeper cast and several had a fierce, rugged aspect resembling the natives of New Zealand. Not one of them had adopted the mode of ornament, so generally prevalent among the natives of this ocean, of tattooing their bodies. Though singular in this, their language approached still nearer to the dialect of Tahiti than that of Atiu or Mangaia. Like the inhabitants of these two islands, they inquired from whence our ships came, and whither bound, who was our chief, the number of men on board, and even the ship's name. &

This is seaman's talk and suggests that the inhabitants were familiar with sea voyage. There may have been some voyaging among these nearby islands at this time, though Cook never saw a native sailing canoe at sea. By means of the survivors at Atiu, and perhaps by other histories, the existence of the Tahiti Islands to the eastward was known to these people; but we have no information that in this period of their culture they made any voyages between the more distant groups of islands.

⋖§ They very readily answered such questions as we proposed to them. They told us they had seen two great ships like ours before, but they had sailed past. There can be no doubt that these were the *Resolution* and *Adventure* (*the previous voyage*). We further learned that they are subject to the King of Atiu. Their articles of food are coconuts, fish, and turtle; the island being destitute of hogs and dogs. Their canoes are pretty large and well built; in the construction of the stern, they bear resemblance to those at Atiu.

I sent Mr. King with two armed boats to sound and reconnoiter the coast. When he returned, Mr. King informed me that there was no anchorage for the ships, and the boats could only land on the outer edge of the reef, which lay about a quarter of a mile from dry land. Furthermore, a number of the natives came down upon this reef armed with long spikes and clubs as if they intended to oppose the landing.

Being thus disappointed at all the islands we had met with since our leaving New Zealand, and the unfavorable winds and other unforeseen circumstances having unavoidably retarded our progress so much, it was now impossible to think of doing anything this year in the high latitudes of the Northern Hemisphere, from which we were still at so great a distance, though the season for our operations there was already begun. In this situation it was absolutely necessary to pursue such measures as were most likely to preserve the cattle we had on board; and, which was still a more capital object, to save the stores and provisions of the ships that we might be better enabled to prosecute our northern discoveries, which could not now occur till a year later than was originally intended. It was my purpose to have stood back to the south till I met with a westerly wind. But the certain consequences of doing this without a supply of fodder would have been the loss of all the cattle. I therefore determined to bear away for the Friendly Islands, where I was sure of meeting with an abundance of everything I wanted. §⋗

At this point the Friendly Islands were about twice as far away as Tahiti, but the Captain had been frustrated in his attempt to get to windward against the prevailing east wind and must now turn and sail downwind before his supplies give out.

⋅⁵ It being necessary to run in the night as well as in the day, I ordered Captain Clerke to keep about a league ahead of the *Resolution*. I used this precaution, because his ship could best claw off the land, and it was very possible we might fall in with some in our passage. About noon the next day, those faint breezes that had attended and retarded us for so long again returned; and I found it necessary to haul more to the north to get into the latitude of Palmerston and Savage Islands, discovered in 1774 during my last voyage, so that if necessity required it, we might have recourse to them. This day, in order to save our water, I ordered the still (*distilling apparatus*) to be kept at work from five o'clock in the morning to four in the afternoon, during which time we procured 13 gallons of fresh water. There have been some improvements made, as they are pleased to call it, of this machine, which, in my opinion, is much for the worse.

These light breezes continued till the tenth of April, when we had the wind blowing fresh from the north and northwest, but in the afternoon we had some thunder squalls from the south attended with heavy rain, so that we collected enough water to fill five puncheons (*a puncheon is a cask containing about 70 imperial gallons or 84 U.S. gallons*). After these squalls had blown over, the wind came around to northeast and northwest and about noon the next day it fixed at northwest and blew a fresh breeze. We were persecuted with the wind in our teeth, whichever way we directed our course. We had the additional mortification to find here those very winds which we had reason to expect 8 to 10 degrees farther south. They came too late, for I dared not trust their continuance; and the event proved I judged right. ᣟ

PALMERSTON ISLAND ⋅⁵ At length, at daybreak, in the morning of the thirteenth, we saw Palmerston Island. However, we did not get up with it till eight o'clock the next morning. (*Palmerston is a low island and cannot be seen from a far distance, so this is very slow progress.*) Now we were under the absolute necessity of procuring from this island some food for the cattle, otherwise we would lose them.

What is comprehended under the name of Palmerston Island is a group of small islets of which there are, on the whole, nine or ten,

MAN-OF-WAR
BIRD

*Credit: Courtesy of
American Museum
of Natural History*

RED-TAILED TROPIC BIRD

Credit: Courtesy of American Museum of Natural History

lying in a circular direction and connected together by a reef of coral
rocks, and no bottom was to be found to anchor upon. The island
where we landed is scarcely a mile in circuit and not above 3 feet
higher than the level of the sea. It appeared to be composed entirely
of coral sand with a small mixture of blackish mold produced from
rotten vegetables. Notwithstanding this poor soil it is covered with
trees and bushes, among these are some cocoa-palms. We were the
only human beings on the island.

We found a great number of man-of-war birds, tropic birds, and
two sorts of boobies, which were so tame that they suffered us to take
them off with our hands. Their nests were only a few sticks loosely
put together; and the tropic birds laid their eggs on the ground under
the trees. These differ much from the common sort, being entirely of
a most splendid white, slightly tinged with red, and having two long
tail feathers of a deep crimson or blood color. Of each sort our people
killed a considerable number; and, though not the most delicate food,
they were acceptable enough to us, who had been long confined to
a salt diet. ॐ

Cook next describes the beauty of the underwater coral reef and
anticipates the colorful world beneath tropic seas that the modern
"scuba" diver has discovered.

ॐ At one part of the reef, which looks into or bounds the lake (salt-
water lagoon) that is within, there was a large bed of coral almost
even with the surface, which afforded one of the most enchanting pros-
pects that nature has anywhere produced. Its base was fixed to the
shore, but it seemed to be suspended in the water, which deepened
so suddenly that at a distance of a few yards there might be 7 or 8
fathoms. The sea was at this time quite unruffled, and the sun, shining
bright, exposed the coral in the most beautiful order—some parts
branching into the water with great luxuriance, others lying collected
in round balls, and in various other figures—all greatly heightened by
the spangles of the richest colors that glowed from a number of large
clams that were everywhere interspersed. But the appearance of these
was still inferior to that of the multitude of fishes that glided gently
along seemingly with the most perfect security. The colors were the
most beautiful that can be imagined—the yellow, blue, red, blacks,
etc., far exceeding anything that art can produce. Their various forms

A CORAL REEF

A GROUPER, SEA ANEMONE, SEVERAL VARIETIES OF CORAL, AND
THE ANTENNAE OF A SPINY LOBSTER.

Credit: Courtesy of American Museum of Natural History

contributed to increase the richness of their submarine grotto, which
could not be surveyed without a pleasing transport, mixed, however,
with regret that a work so stupendously elegant should be concealed
in a place where mankind could seldom have an opportunity of rendering the praises justly due to so enchanting a scene.

We found a great number of fish upon the reefs. Among these
were some large eels, beautifully spotted, which when followed would
raise themselves out of the water and endeavor with an open mouth
to bite their pursuers. (*This was probably the dangerous moray eel
that inhabits coral reefs.*) The other sorts were chiefly parrot fish,
snappers, and a brown-spotted rock-fish, about the size of a haddock,
so tame that instead of swimming away it would remain fixed and
gaze at us. (*This must be the grouper, which today's scuba diver
always finds hanging around inspecting his operations and looking for
handouts.*) Thousands of clams stuck upon the reef, some of which
weighed 2 or 3 pounds. Several sharks came in over the reef, some
of which our people killed, but they rendered it rather dangerous to
walk in the water at that time.

There were no traces of inhabitants having ever been here, if we
except a small piece of a canoe that was found upon the beach, which
may have drifted from some other island. On the next islet two pieces
of board, one of which was rudely carved, and an elliptical paddle,
were found on the beach. These had probably belonged to the same
canoe. But what is pretty extraordinary, we saw several small brown
rats on this spot; a circumstance perhaps difficult to account for unless
we allow that they were imported in the canoe of which we saw the
remains.

The nine or ten low islets, comprehended under the name of
Palmerston Island, may be reckoned the heads or summits of the reef
of coral rock that connects them together, covered only with a thin
coat of sand, yet clothed with trees and plants, most of which are of
the same sorts that are found on the low ground of the high islands
of this ocean.

There are different opinions among ingenious theorists concerning
the formation of such low islands as Palmerston. Some will have it
that, in remote times, these little separate heads or islets were joined
and formed one continued and more elevated tract of land, which the
sea (over the ages) has washed away, leaving only the higher ground,
which in time also will—according to this theory—share the same

fate. Another conjecture is that they have been thrown up by earth-
quakes and are the effect of internal convulsions of the globe. A third
opinion, and the one which appears to me as the most probable, main-
tains that they are formed from coral banks and, of consequence, are
increasing. In support of this argument, I shall describe such parts of
Palmerston Island as fell under my observation.

The foundation is everywhere a coral rock. The soil is coral sand
with which the decayed vegetables have intermixed so as to form a
soil. From this a very strong presumption may be drawn that these
little spots of land are not of very ancient date, nor the remains of
larger islands, for upon either of these suppositions some part of the
original soil must have remained. Another circumstance confirmed
this doctrine of the increase of the islets. We found upon them, far
beyond the reach of the sea, elevated coral rocks, perforated in the
same manner as the rocks that now compose the outer edge of the
reef. This evidently shows that the sea had formerly washed these
rocks, now almost in the center of the land. But the strongest proof
of the increase was the gentle gradation observable in the plants round
the skirts of the islands—from within a few inches of the high-water
mark to the edge of the wood. In many places, the division of plants
of different growth was very distinguishable, especially on the lee, or
west side. The regular and gentle operation of high tides, as well as
gales from the westward, heaped up the sand beyond the reach of
common tides enough to form a barrier so as to prevent the next tide
reaching as far and destroying the plants that have begun to vegetate.
We found many coconuts and some other things just sprouting up
only a few inches beyond where the sea reaches at present. The increase of vegetation will add to the height of this newly created land,
as the fallen leaves and broken branches are, in such a climate, soon
converted into a true black mold, or soil.

Perhaps there is another cause which will accelerate the increase
of these islands as much as any other. This is the spreading of the coral
bank into the sea, which in my opinion is continuously, though im-
perceptibly effected. The waves receding as the reef grows in breadth
and height leave a dry rock behind ready for the reception of broken
coral, sand, and other deposits necessary for the formation of land
and the vegetation of plants. There is little doubt that in time the whole
reef will become an island, and, I think, will extend gradually inward
upon the beds of coral within the enclosed lake. ❧

Subsequent studies of coral atolls down to the present time concur
with Cook that the small animals that are responsible for coral, like
other living things, grow. Thus the reef of coral slowly enlarges until
the sea and waves pulverize and heave up enough material for plants
to get a start. The coral animals are unlike many other animals in
that they live their lives in a stationary spot, building around their
bodies the deposits of calcium, which become the coral rock. These
organisms, unlike plants, are unable to derive food stuffs by photo-
synthesis, but instead eat the microscopic plankton and bits of other
material washed to them by the sea. They live in organized clusters
to give rise to various shapes, according to their kind, such as brain
coral, staghorn coral, and structures that visibly resemble plants, like
the sea-fans (Gorgonians).

⋖§ Upon the whole, we did not spend our time unprofitably at this
islet, for we got there about 1200 coconuts, which were equally
divided among the whole crew and were of great use to them both
on account of the juice and the kernel. There was no water on either
of the islets where we landed. For the cattle we collected palm-
cabbage, young coconut trees, and the tender branches of the wharra
tree.

After leaving Palmerston Island, I steered west with a view to make
the best of my way to Nomuka (*lying in the central Tonga [Friendly
Islands] group*). We still continued to have variable winds, with
squalls, some thunder, and much rain. During these showers, which
were generally very copious, we saved a considerable quantity of
water. Finding that we could get a greater supply by the rain in one
hour than we could get by distillation in a month, I laid aside the
still as a thing attended with more trouble than profit.

The heat, which had been great for about a month, now became
much more disagreeable in the close rainy weather; and, from the
moisture attending it, threatened soon to be noxious. The ships could
not be kept dry, nor the skuttles (*hatchways for the men*) open, for
the sea would come in. It is remarkable that though the only refreshment we had received since leaving the Cape of Good Hope was that
at New Zealand, there was not a single person on board sick from
the constant use of salt food or the vicissitude of climate. ॐ

CHAPTER TEN

THE FRIENDLY ISLANDS

April 28, 1777——June 9, 1777

During this visit to the Friendly (Tonga) Islands, where, as he has indicated, he had been before, Cook provides us with a fine documentation of Polynesian life before the advent of the European. The islands, at that time, were heavily populated with thousands of people who were healthy and well-fed. They were employed in agriculture and fishing, and had a centralized government, with peace among all the member islands. There are many indications that at the time of Cook's voyage, the Tonga group was the most highly developed and enjoyed the most advanced culture in all of Polynesia. Their sailing canoes were regularly making voyages to all the islands of this archipelago spread over 170 miles of Pacific Ocean in the north-south directions, and there was commerce with the Fiji Islands, 400 miles to the west, and probably with Samoa, 550 miles to the north.

Cook records many details of their customs, but more than that, he actually participated in their daily life. He knew the language and was able to walk the island paths at will.

On the twenty-eighth of April, at ten o'clock in the morning, we sighted the islands which lie to the eastward of Nomuka. The weather being squally with rain, I anchored at the approach of night in 15 fathoms over a bottom of coral sand. Soon after we anchored, two canoes, one with four and the other with three men, paddled toward us and came alongside without the least hesitation. They brought coconuts, breadfruit, plantains, and sugarcane, which they bartered

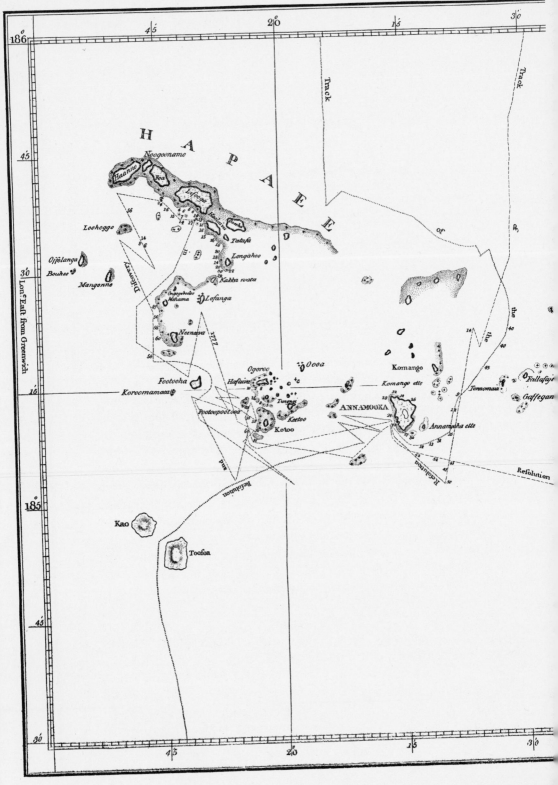

CHART OF THE FRIENDLY

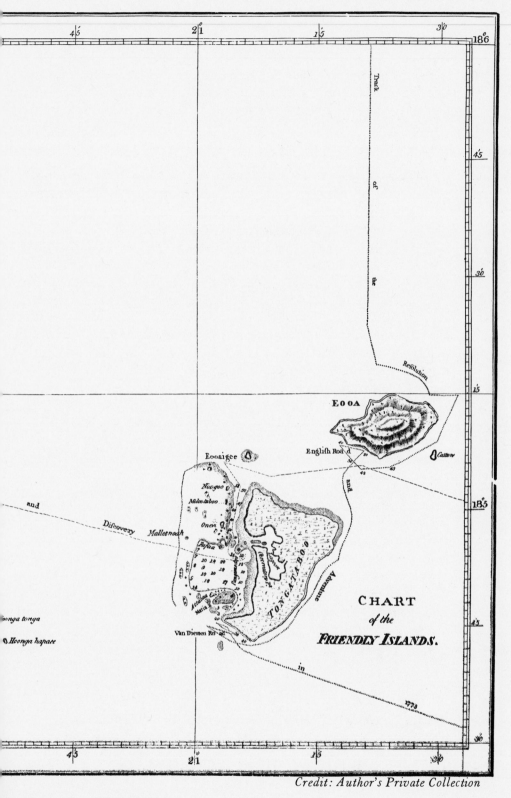

CHART
of the
FRIENDLY ISLANDS.

TONGA) ISLANDS

with us for nails. (*The plantain is what we call a banana.*) Mango, the island nearest us, was at least 5 miles off; which shows the hazards these people would run in order to possess a few of our most trifling articles.

I ordered a boat to be hoisted out and sent the master to sound the southwest side of Nomuka, where there appeared to be a harbor. In the meantime the ships were got under sail and wrought up to the island. When the master returned, he reported that he had sounded between Great and Little Nomuka, where he found 10 and 12 fathoms depth of water, the bottom coral sand. The place was very well sheltered from all winds; but there was no fresh water to be found. For this reason only, and it was a very sufficient one, I determined to anchor on the north side of the island, where, during my last voyage, I had found a place fit both for watering and landing. It was not above a league distant, and yet we did not reach it till five o'clock in the afternoon, being considerably retarded by the great number of canoes that continually crowded round the ships bringing to us abundant supplies of the produce of their island. Among these canoes there were some double ones with a large sail that carried between forty and fifty men each. These sailed round us, apparently with the same ease as if we had been at anchor. (*These catamarans were large, fast, and compared with the English ships had superb sailing characteristics. They were large enough and fast enough to transport men and material over large distances.*) ✌

NOMUKA ✌ I came to an anchor about three-quarters of a mile distant in a cove on the north shore. Thus I resumed the very same stations which I had occupied when I visited Nomuka three years before; and anchored probably almost in the same place where Tasman, the first discoverer of the islands, anchored in 1643.

The following day, I went ashore to fix a place where the observatory could be set up, the natives having already given us leave. ✌

When time permitted the moving of the telescopes and equipment from the ship to the shore, a shore-based astronomical observatory was established to more carefully determine their position, and to check on the accuracy of their chronometer.

✌ The natives accommodated us with a boathouse to serve as a tent, and showed us every other mark of civility. Toobou, the Chief of the island, conducted me and Omai to his house, which we found situated on a pleasant spot in the center of his plantation. A fine grass plot surrounded it, which he gave us to understand was for the purpose of cleaning their feet before they went indoors. I had not before observed such an instance of attention to cleanliness at any of the places I had visited in this ocean; but afterward found it was very common at the Friendly Islands. The floor of Toobou's house was covered with mats, and no carpet in the most elegant English drawing room could be neater. When we got on board again, the ship was crowded with natives. Few of them came empty-handed; every necessary refreshment was now in the greatest plenty. In the afternoon the horses and cattle, in a weakly state, were sent on shore.

Next day our various operations on shore began. Some were employed in making hay for the cattle; others in filling water casks at the neighboring pool; and a third party in cutting wood. But the trees here, which our people erroneously supposed to be manchineel but were a species of pepper called faitanoo by the natives, yielded a juice of a milky color and of so corrosive a nature that it raised blisters on the skin and injured the eyes of our workmen. They were therefore obliged to desist. Other wood more suitable to our purpose was furnished to us by the natives. Messrs. King and Bayly began this day to observe equal altitudes of the sun in order to get the rate of the timekeepers. &

The speed with which the sun appears to move across the sky is constant, it being determined by the revolution of the earth. By comparing this known and constant speed of the sun with the rate of movement of their timekeeper, a check on the accuracy of the timekeeper could be obtained. Such a check is possible only with precise observations using shore-based sighting equipment. Small errors which would become significant over the long period of this voyage would not necessarily be revealed.

&° On the sixth of May we were visited by a great Chief from Tongatapu whose name was Feenou and whom Taipa was pleased to introduce to us as King of all the Friendly Islands. I was told that on my arrival a canoe had been dispatched to Tongatapu with the news, in consequence of which the Chief immediately passed over to Nomuka. &

It is about 67 miles from Tongatapu to Nomuka. Cook arrived at Nomuka during the afternoon of May 1. The Chief from Tongatapu was there on May 6. In the four-day interval between May 1 and May 6, the native canoe covered the round-trip distance of 134 miles. Not even the great Chief hesitated a moment to put to sea for this distance.

◄§ When the King arrived all the natives were ordered out to meet him and paid their obeisance by bowing their heads as low as his feet, the soles of which they also touched with each hand, first with the palm and then with the back part. There could be little room to suspect that a person received with so much respect could be anything less than the King. In the afternoon I went to pay this great man a visit, having first received a present of two fish from him brought on board by one of his servants. As soon as I landed, he came up to me. He appeared to be about thirty years of age, tall and thin, and his features were more European than anyone else's I had yet seen here.

Feenou became so fond of associating with us that he dined on board every day, though sometimes he did not partake of our fare. Some of his servants brought a mess which had been dressed for him on shore. It consisted of fish, soup, and yams. Instead of common water to make the soup, a coconut liquor had been used in which the fish was boiled or stewed, probably in a wooden vessel with hot stones. It was carried on board in a plantain leaf. I tasted of the mess and found it so good that I afterward had some fish dressed in the same way. Though my cook succeeded tolerably well, he could produce nothing equal to the dish he imitated.

It was remarkable that none but Taipa was allowed to sit at the table with him, or to eat in his presence. I own that I considered Feenou a very convenient guest on account of this etiquette. Before his arrival I generally had a larger company than I could find room for, and my table overflowed with crowds of both sexes. It is not the custom at the Friendly Islands, as it is in Tahiti, to deny to their females the privilege of eating with the men.

The first day of our arrival, one of the natives had stolen a large axe. I now applied to Feenou to exert his authority to get it restored to me, and so implicitly was he obeyed that it was brought on board while we were at dinner. These people gave us very frequent opportunities of remarking what expert thieves they were. Even some of their chiefs did not think this profession beneath them. One of them was detected carrying out of the ship, concealed under his clothes, the bolt belonging to the spun-yarn winch. I sentenced him to receive a dozen lashes and kept him confined till he paid a hog for his liberty. After this we were not troubled with thieves of rank. Their servants, or slaves, however, were still employed in this dirty work and upon them a flogging seemed to make no greater impression than it would have done upon the main-mast. When one of them happened to be caught in the act, their masters, far from interceding for them, would often advise us to kill them. As this was a punishment we did not choose to inflict, they generally escaped without any punishment at all. They appeared to be equally insensible to the shame and pain of corporal chastisement. Captain Clerke at last hit upon a mode of treatment which we thought had some effect. He put them under the hands of the barber and completely shaved their heads, thus pointing them out as objects of ridicule to their countrymen and enabling our people to deprive them of future opportunities for a repetition of their rogueries by keeping them at a distance. The only defect sullying the characters of these people that we know of is this propensity to thieving, to which we found those of all age and both sexes addicted, and in an uncommon degree. (*Magellan, the first to discover a Polynesian isle, called the island he landed upon: the* "Islas de los Ladrones," *Spanish for: "Island of Thieves."*)

It should, however, be considered that this exceptionable part of their conduct seemed to exist merely with respect to us; for, in their general intercourse with one another, I have reason to be of the opinion that thefts do not happen more frequently (perhaps less so) than in other countries. Great allowances should be made for the foibles of these poor natives of the Pacific Ocean whose minds we overpowered with the glare of objects, equally new to them as they were captivating. The thefts of what we had brought along with us may be traced to less culpable motives than ordinary stealing. They seemed to arise from an intense curiosity or desire to possess something which they had not been accustomed to, and belonging to a people so different from themselves. They steal everything indiscriminately before they can have the least conception of converting their prize to any useful object. And perhaps if it were possible that a set of beings seemingly as superior in our judgment, as we are in theirs, should appear among us, it might be doubted whether or not our natural regard to justice would be able to restrain many from falling into the same error.

Finding that we had quite exhausted the island of almost every article of food that it afforded, I employed the eleventh of May in moving off the things we had landed, intending to sail as soon as the *Discovery* recovered her best bower anchor, which had been cut away by the coral rocks. Feenou, understanding that I meant to proceed directly to Tongatapu, importuned me strongly to alter this plan, to which he expressed as much aversion as if he had some particular interest to promote by diverting me from it. In preference, he warmly recommended a group of islands called Ha'apai lying to the northeast. There, he assured us, we could be supplied plentifully with every refreshment in the easiest manner. To add weight to his advice, he engaged to attend us thither in person. He carried his point with me and Ha'apai was chosen for our next station. As it had never been visited by a European ship, the examination of it became an object with me.

The twelfth and thirteenth were spent in attempting the recovery of Captain Clerke's anchor, which, after much trouble, was happily accomplished. On the fourteenth, we got under sail and left Nomuka. To the north and northeast in the direct tract to Ha'apai the sea is sprinkled with a great number of small isles. Amidst the shoals and rocks adjoining this group, I could not be assured that there was a free or safe passage for such large ships as ours, though the natives sailed through the intervals in their canoes. For this substantial reason, I thought it necessary to go to the westward of the above islands and steered north-northwest toward Kao and Tofua, the two most westerly islands in sight and remarkable for their great height.

Feenou and his attendants remained on board the *Resolution* till near noon, when he went into the large sailing canoe which had brought him from Tongatapu and stood in among the cluster of islands. Most of the islands are entirely clothed with trees, among which are many cocoa-palms, and each forms a prospect like a beautiful garden placed in the sea. The serene weather we now had contributed to heighten this, and the whole might supply the imagination with an idea of some fairy land.

We had in the afternoon been within 2 leagues of Tofua, the smoke of which we saw several times a day. The Friendly Islanders have some superstitious notions about the volcano upon it and say it is an

Otooa, or divinity. They say it sometimes throws up large stones and they compare the crater to the size of a small islet. We sometimes saw the smoke while we were at Nomuka, though at the distance of at least 10 leagues.

It was our intention to have anchored for the night, but it came upon us before we could find a place in less than 55 fathoms, and rather than come to in this depth, I chose to spend the night under sail. In the course of the night we could plainly see flames issuing from the volcano.

About ten o'clock the next day, Feenou came on board and remained with us all day. After passing Fotuha'a we met with a reef of rocks, and as there was but little wind it cost us some trouble to keep clear of them. Being past this reef of rocks, we hauled for Niniva in hopes of finding anchorage but were again disappointed and obliged to spend the night making short boards (*tacking back and forth*). Although we had land in every direction, the sea was unfathomable.

At daybreak, on the morning of the sixteenth, with a gentle breeze at southeast, we steered for Ha'apai, which was now in sight. The wind scanting upon us, we could not fetch the land, so we were forced to ply to windward. In doing this, we once passed over some coral rocks on which we had only 6 fathoms. We got up with the northernmost of these isles by sunset and there found ourselves in the very same distress for want of anchorage that we had experienced the two preceding evenings, so that we had another night to spend under sail with land and breakers in every direction. Toward the evening, Feenou and Omai went in the canoe to Ha'apai. They did not forget our disagreeable situation and kept up a good fire all night by way of a landmark. As soon as daylight returned, being then close in with Foa, I dispatched a boat to look for anchorage. A proper place was soon found and we came to, abreast of a reef which joins Lifuka to Foa. We were not above three-quarters of a mile from the shore. (*Negotiating this cluster of unsurveyed islands, rocks, reefs, and coral beds, always under sail, in vessels that went to windward with difficulty, was a remarkable feat of seamanship.*) &

HA'APAI ⋅§ By the time we had anchored, the ships were filled with natives and surrounded by a multitude of canoes also filled with them. They brought from the shore hogs, fowls, fruit, and roots, which were exchanged for hatchets, knives, nails, beads, and cloth. On shore, the

Chief conducted me to a house, or rather a hut, situated close to the beach, which I had seen brought thither but a few minutes before our reception. In this, Feenou, Omai, and myself were seated. The other Chiefs and multitude composed a circle on the outside. I was asked how long I intended to stay. Upon my saying "Five days," Taipa was ordered to come and proclaim this to the people. He then harangued them in a speech mostly dictated by Feenou. The purport of it, as I learnt from Omai, was that they were all to look upon me as a friend who intended to remain with them a few days; that during my stay they must not steal anything nor molest me in any other way, and that it was expected they should bring hogs, fowls, fruit, etc., to the ships, where they would receive in exchange for them such things as he enumerated.

Next morning, early, Feenou came to ask my presence upon the island. Upon landing I saw a large concourse of people already assembled. I guessed that something more than ordinary was in agitation. I had not been long seated before a hundred natives appeared in sight and advanced laden with jams, breadfruit, plantains, coconuts, and sugarcane. They deposited their burdens in two heaps upon our left. Soon after arrived a number of others from the right bearing the same kind of articles which were collected into two piles upon that side.

Presently a number of men entered the circle before us armed with clubs made of the green branches of the coconut tree. These paraded about for a few minutes and seated themselves before the spectators, and then they successively entered the area and entertained us with single combat which continued till their weapons were broken. At intervals there were both wrestling and boxing matches, the latter differed very little from the method practiced in England.

What struck us with most surprise was to see a couple of lusty wenches step forth and begin boxing without the least ceremony, and with as much art as the men. The conquering heroine received the same applause from the spectators as they bestowed upon the successful combatants of the other sex. Two other females then entered; they seemed to be girls of spirit and certainly would have given each other a good drubbing if two old women had not interposed to part them. These combats were exhibited in the midst of at least three thousand people and were conducted with the greatest of good humor on all sides, though some of the champions, women as well as men, received blows which doubtless they must have felt for some time after.

Feenou had expressed a desire to see the marines go through their military exercise. As I was desirous to gratify his curiosity, I ordered them all ashore, from both ships, on the morning of the twentieth. After they had performed various evolutions and fired several vollies, with which the numerous body of spectators seemed well pleased, the Chief entertained us, in his turn, with an exhibition which, as was acknowledged by us all, was performed with a dexterity and exactness far surpassing the specimen we had given of our military maneuvers. It was a kind of dance, so entirely different from anything I had ever seen that I fear I can give no description that will convey any tolerable idea of it. It was performed by men; one hundred and five persons bore their parts in it. Each of them had in his hand an instrument neatly made, shaped somewhat like a paddle of 2½ feet in length with a small handle and a thin blade so that it was very light. With these instruments they made many and various flourishes, each of which was accompanied with a different attitude of the body. The musical instruments consisted of two drums, or rather hollow logs, from which some varied notes were produced by beating on them with two sticks. They sang a chorus of music in which all performers joined at the same time. Their song was not destitute of pleasing melody, and all their corresponding motions were executed with so much skill that the numerous body of dancers seemed to act as if they were one great machine. It was the opinion of every one of us that such a performance would have met with universal applause in a European theater.

We then had a succession of dances which Feenou had got ready for our entertainment. As a prelude, a chorus of eighteen men seated themselves before us in the center of the circle composed by the numerous spectators. Four of this band had pieces of large bamboo from 3 to 5 feet long, each man held it in a vertical position, the upper end open, but the other end closed by one of the joints. With this closed end, the performers kept constantly striking the ground, though slowly, thus producing different notes according to the lengths of the instrument—all the notes were of a hollow or bass sort. Another person kept striking quickly with two sticks a piece of bamboo, split and laid along the ground, and by that means furnished a tone as acute as those produced by the others were grave. The rest of the band, as well as those who performed upon the bamboos, sang a low and soft air which so tempered the harsher notes of the instruments that no bystander,

A NIGHT DANCE BY

Credit: Engraving, Author's Private Collection

HE WOMEN OF HA'APAI

however accustomed to hearing the most perfect and varied modulations of sweet sounds, could avoid confessing the vast power and pleasing effect of this simple harmony.

The concert having continued about a quarter of an hour, twenty women entered the circle. Most of them had upon their heads garlands of crimson flowers of the china rose. Many of them had ornamented their persons with leaves of trees cut with a great of deal of nicety about the edges. They made a circle around the chorus of men, turning their faces toward them and began by singing a soft air to which responses were made by the chorus in the same tone. All the while the women accompanied their song with very graceful motions of their hands toward their faces, making constantly a step forward, and then back again, with one foot, while the other was fixed. They then turned their faces to the assembly, sang awhile, and retreated slowly in a body to where the principal spectators sat.

Their manner of dancing was now changed to a quicker measure. They made a half turn by leaping, clapped their hands, and snapped their fingers, repeating some words in conjunction with the chorus. As the music increased, their gestures and attitudes were varied with wonderful vigor and dexterity. Some of their motions perhaps would, with us, be reckoned rather indecent, though this part of the performance, most probably, was not meant to convey any wanton ideas but merely to display the astonishing variety of their movements. ॐ

Here, then, is a description of what the "hula-hula" was like when first seen by a European in the Tonga Islands. Most of the dancing and singing, however, was done by the men.

ॐ This female ballet was followed by a performance by fifteen men. Some of them were old but their age seemed to have little abated their agility or ardor for the dance. After this, at a considerable interval, another act, as we may call it, began. Twelve men placed themselves in double rows, fronting each other on opposite sides of the circle, and they sang slowly and afterward danced and sang more quickly. (*After this there was one other performance by the women.*)

Nine women exhibited themselves and sat down fronting the hut where the Chief was. A man then rose and struck the first of these women on the back with both fists joined. He proceeded, in the same manner, to the second and third, but when he came to the fourth, instead of the back, he struck her on the breast. Upon this, a person rose instantly from the crowd and brought him to the ground with a blow on the head and he was carried off. This did not save the other five women from so odd a discipline, or perhaps necessary ceremony, for a person succeeded him who treated them in the same manner. Their disgrace did not end here, for when they danced they had the mortification to find their performance twice disapproved of and were obliged to repeat it. At the end, they repeated, with great agility, the brisk movements in which the former group of female dancers had shown themselves so expert.

The place where the dances were performed was an open space among the trees, just by the sea, with lights, at short intervals, placed round the inside of the circle. The concourse of people was large— some of our gentlemen guessed there might be present about five thousand persons.

The next day I began to have time to look about me. I took a walk into the Island of Lifuka. (*Cook apparently felt free to walk about the islands unguarded and often alone.*) The plantations were both numerous and extensive, enclosed in such a manner that the fences running parallel to each other, from fine, spacious public roads, would appear ornamental in countries where rural conveniences have been carried to the greatest perfection.

I happened to step into a house where I found a woman shaving a child's head with a shark's tooth stuck into the end of a piece of stick. The operation seemed to give no pain to the child, although the hair was taken off as if one of our razors had been employed. I soon after tried one of these singular instruments upon myself and found it to be an excellent succedaneum (*substitute*). However, the men of these islands have recourse to another contrivance when they shave their beards. The operation is performed with two shells; one of which they place under a small part of the beard, and with the other, applied above, they scrape that part off. In this manner they are able to shave very close. It was common to see our sailors go ashore to have their beards scraped off after the fashion of Ha'apai.

On the morning of the twenty-third, as we were going to unmoor in order to leave the island, Feenou and others came alongside in a canoe and informed me that they were setting out for Vavaoo, an island which, they said, lies about two days' sail to the northward of Ha'apai. (*Feenou's information was correct. There is such an island, about 70 miles north, now spelled* Vava'u.) I thought this a good opportunity to get some knowledge of Vava'u and proposed to him to go thither with my ships. But he seemed not to approve of the plan, and by way of diverting me from it told me that there was neither harbor nor anchorage about it (*which is untrue*). I resolved to change our station and to await Feenou's return in some other convenient anchoring place. Accordingly, we got under sail and stood to the southward along the reef off the islands, having 13 and 14 fathoms of water with a sandy bottom. Having passed several shoals, and seeing more of them before us, I hauled into a bay that lies at the south end of Lifuka.

Near the south end of the island and on the western side, we met with an artificial mount. From the size of some trees growing upon it, and from other appearances, I guessed that it had been raised in remote times. I judged it to be about 40 feet high, and the diameter of the summit measured 50 feet. At the bottom of this mount stood a stone which must have been hewn out of coral rock. It was 4 feet broad, 2½ feet thick, and 14 feet high. We were told by the natives present that not more than half its length appeared above ground. They called it "Tangata Arekee." *Tangata,* in their language, is man; *Arekee,* king. They said that it had been set up, and the mount raised, by some of their forefathers in memory of one of their kings. How long since, they could not tell.

Here in western Polynesia is an archaeological discovery that indicates ancient culture on these islands and which brings to mind the upright, half-buried stone statues on Easter Island at the eastern limit of the Polynesian Islands. Also on Uoleva, the next island south, connected to Lifuka by a reef passable on foot at low tide, and uninhabited, Cook found that another artificial mount had been raised upon it as high as some of the surrounding trees.

At daybreak I weighed with a fine breeze at east-northeast and stood to the westward with a view to return to Nomuka by the track we had already experienced. We were followed by several sailing canoes, in one of which was the King. As soon as he got on board the *Resolution* he inquired for his brother and others who had remained with us all night. We also had the company of a chief, just then arrived from Tongatapu. The moment he arrived he sent his canoe away and declared that he and five more who came with him would sleep on board. Now my cabin was filled with visitors. This, indeed, was some inconvenience; but I bore with it willingly.

We made no progress to windward, and being apprehensive of losing the islands with so many of the natives on board, I tacked and stood back, intending to wait for some more favorable opportunity. We did but just fetch in with two small islands, where we spent the night under reefed topsails and foresail. The wind blew fresh and with squalls and rain, and we were not without apprehensions of danger. I kept the deck till midnight, when I left it to the master with such directions as, I thought, would keep the ships clear of the shoals and rocks that lay round us. But after standing back again to the south, our ship, by a small shift of the wind, fetched farther to the windward than was expected. By this means she was very near running full upon a low sandy isle surrounded with breakers. It happened, very fortunately, that the people had just been ordered upon the deck to put the ship about and most of them were at their stations. The necessary movements were not only executed with judgment but also with alertness. This alone saved us from destruction. Such hazardous situations are the unavoidable companions of the man who goes upon a voyage of discovery.

This circumstance frightened our passengers so much that they expressed a strong desire to get ashore. As soon as daylight returned, I hoisted out a boat and ordered the officer who commanded her, after landing them at Kotu, to sound along the reef for anchorage. I was full as much tired as they could be, with beating about among the surrounding isles and shoals, and determined to get to an anchor, somewhere or other, if possible. We were obliged to anchor in 50 fathoms, with the sandy isle one mile distant, and we lay there three days.

On the fourth (*June 1777*), at seven in the morning, we weighed; and with a fresh gale at east-southeast, stood away for Nomuka, where we anchored next morning nearly in the same station which we had so lately occupied.

I went on shore soon after and found the inhabitants very busy on their plantations, digging up yams to bring to market. About two hundred assembled on the beach and traded with as much eagerness as during our late visit. Before I returned on board, I visited the several places where I had sown melon seeds and had the mortification to find that most of them were destroyed by a small ant; but some pineapple plants, which I had also left, were in a thriving state. ৯

Cook does not say where he obtained the pineapple plants, which he planted at Nomuka, but the species came originally from the Caribbean. When it was planted in Hawaii it took hold so well that Hawaii became the center of pineapple culture. But Cook does not tell us if he ever planted any pineapples in Hawaii as he did in Nomuka.

৯ At eight o'clock on the morning of June 8, we weighed and steered for Tongatapu, having a gentle breeze at northeast. (*Tongatapu is the largest of the Friendly Islands and is the center of government for all the other islands of the group.*) About fourteen sailing vessels belonging to the natives set out with us, but every one of them outran the ships considerably. Feenou was to have taken his passage in the *Resolution* but preferred his own canoe, and put two men on board to conduct us to the best anchorage.

We continued till two o'clock the next morning, when, seeing some lights ahead and not knowing whether they were on shore or on board the canoes, we hauled the wind and made a short trip each way till daybreak. We then resumed our course to the south by west and presently saw several small islands before us, and Eua and Tongatapu beyond them. We had at this time 25 fathoms water over a bottom of broken coral and sand. The depth gradually decreased as we drew near the isles. By the direction of our pilots we steered for the middle and for the widest space between the small isles, having our boats ahead employed in sounding. We were insensibly drawn upon a large flat, upon which lay innumerable coral rocks of different depths below the surface of the water. Notwithstanding all our care and attention to keep the ship clear of them, we could not prevent her from striking on one of these rocks. Nor did the *Discovery,* though behind us, fare any better. Fortunately, neither of the ships stuck fast, nor received any damage. We could not get back without increasing the danger, as we had come in almost before the wind. Nor could we cast anchor but with the certainty of having our cables instantly cut in two by the rocks. We had no other recourse but to proceed. To this, indeed, we were encouraged, not only by being told but by seeing that there was deeper water between us and the shore. That we might be better informed the moment we found a spot where we could drop the anchor clear of rocks, we came to and sent the masters, with the boat, to sound. While we were plying up to the harbor, to which the natives directed us, the King kept sailing round us in his canoe; and there were, at the same time, a great many small canoes about the ships. Two of these, which could not get out of the way of his royal vessel, he ran over with as little concern as if they had been bits of wood. At length we arrived at our intended stations. It was a very snug place, formed by the shore of Tongatapu on the southeast, and two small islands on the east and northeast. Here we anchored in 10 fathoms, over a bottom of oozy sand, one-third of a mile distant from the shore. ॐ

CHAPTER ELEVEN

TONGATAPU

June 10, 1777——July 16, 1777

TONGATAPU ✍ Soon after we anchored, but having first dined, I landed, accompanied by Omai and some of the officers. We found the King waiting for us upon the beach. He immediately conducted us to a small, neat house, situated a little within the skirts of the woods, with a fine large area before it. This house, he told me, was at my service during our stay on the island; and a better situation we could not wish for.

A root of the kava plant being brought and laid down before the King, he ordered it to be split into pieces and distributed to several people of both sexes, who began the operation of chewing it, and a bowl of their favorite liquor was soon prepared. (*After the kava root is thoroughly chewed, it is spit out into a large bowl. The masticated root combined with the digestive juices of the saliva constitute the beverage.*) The first cup was brought to the King, which he ordered to be given to one who sat near him. The second was also brought to him, and this he kept. The third was given to me, but their manner of brewing having quenched my thirst, it became Omai's property. ✍

A SUPPLY BASE ESTABLISHED ✍ As I intended to make some stay at Tongatapu, we pitched a tent by the house that Poulaho had assigned for our use. The horses, cattle, and sheep were afterward landed. The observatory was then set up and Mr. King sent on shore to attend the observations and to superintend the several operations necessary to be conducted here; and the sails were carried thither to be repaired.

The gunners were ordered to remain upon the spot to conduct the traffic with the natives, who thronged from every part of the island with hogs, yams, coconuts, and other articles of their produce. In a short time, our landpost was like a fair, and the ships were so crowded with visitors that we had hardly room to stir upon the decks. &

During one of Mr. Anderson's explorations inland, he came upon another ancient stonework. He describes it thus: "This work begins on one side as a narrow causeway which, becoming gradually broader, rises with a gentle ascent to the height of 10 feet, where it is five paces (*25 feet*) broad and the whole length seventy-four paces (*370 feet*). Joined to this is a ring whose diameter is thirty paces (*150 feet*), and not more than a foot or two higher than the causeway that joins it, with some trees planted in the middle. On the opposite side, another causeway of the same sort descends, but this is not more than forty paces long and is partly in ruin. The whole is built with large coral stones, with earth on the surface, which is quite overgrown with low trees and shrubs. From its decaying in several places, it seems to be of no modern date. Whatever may have been its use formerly, it seems to be of none now. All that we could learn of it from the natives was that it is called *Etchee*."

& In the course of a walk, Mr. Gore and I had the opportunity of seeing the whole process of making cloth. The manufacturers, who are females, take the slender stalks or trunks of the paper-mulberry, which they cultivate for the purpose, and which seldom grows more than 7 feet in height, and about four fingers' thickness. From these they strip the bark and scrape off the outer rind with a mussel shell. The bark is then rolled up to take off the convexity which it had round the stalk and macerated in water for a night. After this it is laid across the trunk of a small tree, squared, and then beaten with a square wooden instrument, about a foot long, full of coarse grooves. According to the size of the bark a piece of cloth is soon produced. It is spread out to dry, the pieces being from 4 to 6 feet in length and half as broad. They are given to another person, who joins the pieces by smearing part of them over with the viscous juice of a berry called *taoo*, which serves as a glue. Having been thus lengthened, they are laid over a large piece of wood, with a kind of stamp made of a fibrous substance closely interwoven placed beneath. They then take a bit of cloth and dip it in a juice expressed from the bark of a tree called "kokka," which they rub briskly upon the piece that is being made. This leaves a dull brown color, and a dry gloss upon its surface. In this manner they proceed, joining and staining by degrees, till they produce a piece of cloth of such length and breadth as they want. Throughout the whole, if any parts of the original pieces are too thin, or have holes, which is often the case, they glue spare bits upon them till they become of equal thickness. ❧

Cook notes that the island was heavily populated. At a particular gathering for dances and sporting events he remarks:

❧ Vast numbers of their own people attended as spectators. Their numbers could not be computed exactly, but by reckoning the inner circle and the number in depth which was between twenty and thirty in many places, we supposed that there must be near four thousand. At the same time there were round the trading place at the tent and straggling about at least as many more. Some of us computed that there were not less than ten or twelve thousand people in our neighborhood; that is, within the compass of a quarter of a mile. ❧

The Tonga islanders were inveterate souvenir-hunters, or thieves, depending upon how you look at it.

❧ All our care and attention did not prevent their plundering us in every quarter, and that in the most daring and insolent manner. There was hardly anything they did not attempt to steal. They once, at noonday, ventured to aim at taking an anchor from off the *Discovery*'s bow. They would certainly have succeeded, if the stock had not hooked one of the chain plates in lowering down the ship's side from which they could not disengage it; fortunately tackles were things they were unacquainted with. A man got out of a canoe into the quarter galley of the *Resolution* and stole from thence a pewter basin. He was discovered, pursued, and brought back alongside the ship. (*The quarter galley is the officer's toilet, which is simply an enclosed opening in the overhanging portion at the stern of the ship. Apparently our Tonga "souvenir-hunter" climbed in the opening.*) One morning one of our kids (*goat*) and two turkey-cocks were missing. I could not be so simple as to suppose that this was merely an accidental loss; and I was determined to have them again. The first step I took was to seize on those canoes that happened to be alongside the ships. I then went ashore, and having found the King and other chiefs in the house that we occupied, I immediately put a guard over them and gave them to understand that they must remain under restraint till not only the kid and turkeys, but the other things that had been stolen from us, were restored. It was not long before an axe and an iron wedge were brought to me. In the meantime, some armed natives began to gather behind the house; but when our guard marched against them, they dispersed. On asking the King and Chiefs to go aboard with me to dinner, they readily consented. (*Cook treated his prisoners like guests.*) Some objected to the King's going, but he rose up and declared he would be the first man, and accordingly we came on board. I kept them there until four o'clock, and soon thereafter the kid and turkey-cock were brought back.

After the Chiefs had left us, I walked out with Omai to observe how the people fared. (*Even though he had only a few moments earlier released the Chiefs from hostage, Cook apparently felt he could safely walk about the island with only Omai for company.*) In this walk we met about half a dozen women at supper. Two of the company, I observed, were fed by the others. On our asking the reason, they said, *"Taboo mattee."* (*The word these women spoke,* taboo, *eventually found its way into common English usage.*) On further inquiry, we found that they had washed the dead corpse of a chief, and that, on this account, were not to handle any food for five months.

Early the next morning, the King came on board to invite me to an entertainment, which he proposed to give the same day. He had already been under the barber's hands, his head being all besmeared with red pigment in order to redden his hair, which was naturally of a dark brown color.

After breakfast, I attended him to the shore. There we found his people busy in the front of our area, fixing, in an upright position, four very long poles, near 2 feet from each other, in a square position. The space between the poles was afterward filled with yams. As they went on filling it they fastened pieces of sticks across from post to post, at a distance of about every 4 feet to prevent the posts from separating by the weight of the inclosed yams, and also to get up by. When the yams reached the top of the first post, they fastened others to them, and so continued till each pile was the height of 30 feet, or

upward! It was a matter of curiosity to observe with what facility and
dispatch these two piles were raised. Had our seamen been ordered to
execute such a work, they would have sworn that it could not be
performed without carpenters; and the carpenters would have called
to their aid a dozen different tools and expended a hundred weight
of nails; and it would have employed them as many days as it did
these people hours. But seamen, like most other amphibious animals,
are always the most helpless on land.

Some of the officers who had made an excursion into the interior
parts of the island, without my leave, and indeed without my knowledge, returned this evening after an absence of two days. They had
taken with them their muskets with the necessary ammunition, and
several personal articles; all of which, the natives had the dexterity
to steal from them in the course of their expedition. Our plundered
travelers, upon their return, without consulting me, employed Omai
to complain to the King. He, not knowing what step I should take,
and fearing lest I might lay him again under restraint, went off early
the next morning, followed by Feenou, so that we had not a chief of
any authority remaining in our neighborhood.

I reprimanded Omai for having presumed to meddle. This repri-
mand put him upon his mettle to bring his friend Feenou back; and
he succeeded in the negotiation. The Chiefs very justly observed that,
if any of my people wanted to go into the country, they ought to be
acquainted with it; in which case they would send proper people along
with them, and then they would be answerable for their safety. And
I am convinced, from experience, that, by taking this very reasonable
precaution, a man and his property may be as safe among these
islanders as in the civilized world.

On the twenty-fifth, two boats, which I had sent to look for a channel by which we might commodiously get to sea, returned. The masters
who commanded them reported that the channel to the north, by
which we came in, was highly dangerous and full of coral rocks from
one side to the other. To the eastward there was a very good channel,
which, however, was very much contracted in one place by small
islands, so that a leading (fair) wind would be requisite to get through;
but a westerly wind did not often blow here. We had now recruited
the ships with wood and water; we had finished the repair of our sails;
and had little more to expect from the inhabitants of the produce of
their island. However, as an eclipse of the sun was to happen upon

the fifth of next month, I resolved to defer sailing in order to have a chance of observing it.

Having therefore some days of leisure before me, a party of us set out in a boat for Mu'a, the village where Poulaho and other great men usually reside. As we rowed up the inlet we met with fourteen canoes fishing in company. Poulaho's son was in one. I desired to see their method of fishing, which they readily complied with. A school of fish upon one of the banks was instantly enclosed in a long net like a seine. One fisher got into the water out of each boat with a triangular net extended between two poles in his hands and scooped the fish out of the seine, or caught them as they attempted to leap over it. The whole process of this operation seemed to be a sure one.

As soon as we got on shore, the King desired Omai to tell me that I need be under no apprehension about the boat or anything in her, for not a single article would be touched by anyone; and we afterward found this to be the case.

Some of us, accompanied by a few of the King's attendants, walked up to take a view of a *fiatooka,* or burying place, which we were told belonged to the King. It consisted of three large houses situated upon rising ground, all ranged longitudinally. The middle house of the three, much the largest, was placed in a square about twenty-four paces by twenty-eight (*120–140 feet*) and raised about 3 feet. The floor of these houses, as also the tops of the mounts around them were covered with loose, fine pebbles, and the whole enclosed by large, flat stones of hard coral rock, all properly hewn. One stone measured 12 feet in length, two in breadth, and more than one in thickness. (*Therefore the Tonga islanders, or their ancestors, knew the art of cutting, hewing, and setting stone.*) One of the houses, contrary to what we had seen before, was open on one side and within it were two rude, wooden busts of men, one near the entrance, the other farther in. The natives told us that they were memorials of some Chiefs who had been buried there and not the representations of any deity. Such monuments, it should seem, are seldom raised, for these had probably been erected several ages ago. In one of them was the carved head of a Tahiti canoe which had been driven ashore on their coast and deposited here. (*We are not told if it was Cook, the Chiefs, or both, who recognized the carving on the canoe as originating from Tahiti, 1800 miles to the east. Nor are we told if anyone recalled whether there were any people in that canoe. But here, as at the Island of Atiu,*) *is an instance of a canoe coming downwind from the east and from Tahiti.*)

There were many public and well-beaten roads, and an abundance of footpaths leading to every part of the island. The roads being good, and the country level, travel was easy. It is remarkable that when we were on the most elevated parts, at least a hundred feet above the level of the sea, we often met with the same coral rock which is found at the shore. It was cut into those inequalities which are usually seen in rocks that lie within the wash of the tide. (*The supposition is that the sea-washed coral rocks that compose all of this island, including the high elevations, were lifted out of the ocean by geologic action in prehistoric times.*)

When we returned from our walk, which was not till the dusk of evening, our supper was ready. It consisted of a baked hog, some fish, and yams, all excellently well cooked. As there was nothing to amuse us after supper, we followed the custom of the country and lay down to sleep, our beds being mats spread upon the floor, and cloth to cover us. The King, who had made himself very happy with some wine and brandy which we had brought, slept in the same house, as well as several other natives. Our sleep was disturbed by a singular luxury in which the principal men indulge themselves: that of being beaten while they are asleep. Two women sat by Futtafaike and performed this operation, which is called *tooge tooge*, by beating briskly on his body and legs with both fists, as on a drum, till he fell asleep. They continued the whole night, abating a little in the strength and quickness of the beating when once the person was asleep; but resumed if they observed any appearance of his awakening. Futtafaike's women relieved each other, and slept by turns. It would be supposed that such a practice would put an end to all rest, but here it certainly acts as an opiate. Long before daybreak, he and they all rose and sat conversing by moonlight. Before it was light, they made a hearty meal of fish and yams, which were brought to them by a person who seemed to know very well the appointed time for this nocturnal refreshment.

As soon as it was day, they dispersed, some one way and some another. But it was not long before they returned, bringing with them several more of their countrymen. Now they began to prepare a bowl of kava. We had seen the drinking of kava sometimes at other islands, but by no means so frequently as here, where it seems to be the only forenoon employment of the principal people. The kava is a species

of pepper which they cultivate about their houses, taking great care
to defend young plants from injury. It seldom grows to more than
a man's height, and branches considerably with large heart-shaped
leaves and jointed stalks. The root is the only part that is used. After
the root is dug up it is given to servants, who break it to pieces, scrape
the dirt off with a shell, and then chew a portion and spit it into a
plantain leaf. A person collects all these mouthfuls and puts them into
a large wooden bowl, adding as much water as will make the proper
strength. ॐ

Saliva contains a digestive enzyme, ptyalin, that acts upon starch
to convert it into sugar. The chewing, then, is a perfectly effective
method of converting the starches of the kava root into sugar. If all
it needed was to be pulverized, this could have been done in a mortar.
In a small island of constant population, every individual nurtures
similar bacterial flora in his mouth and saliva, so it was immaterial
if one chewed the root for oneself or let the servant do it. No infection
would result, as everyone had the same germs.

ॐ It is thus well mixed with the hands, and some loose stuff, the
same as mats are made of, is thrown upon the surface to intercept the
fibrous part, and is wrung hard to get as much liquid out from it as
possible. The quantity which is put into each cup is about a quarter
of a pint. Some of our people, who ventured to try it, though so un-
tidily prepared, found it had the same intoxicating power as spirits;
or rather, it produced that kind of stupefaction which is the consequence of using opium. Though these islanders have this liquor always
freshly prepared and may drink it seven times before noon, it is nevertheless so disagreeable that the greatest part of them cannot swallow
it without making wry faces and afterward shuddering. The intoxicating effect is not perceptible in these people, who use it so frequently.

When we got on board after this expedition, I found that everything had been quiet during my absence, not a theft had been committed. The good conduct of the natives was, however, of short duration; for the next day six or eight of them assaulted some of our people
who were sawing planks. They were fired upon by the sentry; one was
wounded and three taken prisoner. These I kept confined till night,
and did not dismiss them without punishment. After this they behaved
with a little more circumspection and gave us less trouble. The re-

peated insolence of the natives had induced me to order the muskets loaded with small shot, and to authorize men to fire on particular occasions. I took it for granted, therefore, that this man had only been wounded with small shot; but Mr. King and Mr. Anderson, in an excursion into the country, met with him and found indubitable marks of his having been wounded, but not dangerously, with a musket ball. I never could find out how this musket happened to be charged with a ball; and there were people enough ready to swear that its contents were only small shot.

On the morning of the fifth, the day of the eclipse, the weather was dark and cloudy, with showers of rain, so that we had little hopes of an observation. It was totally obscured, till within a minute or two of the beginning of the eclipse. We were all at our telescopes, viz., Mr. Bayly, Mr. King, Captain Clerke, Mr. Bligh, and myself. I lost the observation by not having a suitable dark glass at hand; Mr. Bligh did not get the sun into the field of his telescope, so the commencement of the eclipse was only observed by the other three gentlemen, and by them with an uncertainty of several seconds. The disappointment was of little consequence, since the longitude was more than sufficiently determined, independently of this eclipse, by lunar observations.

We were now ready to sail, but the wind being easterly, we had not sufficient daylight to turn through the narrow, either with the morning or with the evening flood, the one falling out too early, and the other too late. Without a leading wind, we were under the necessity of waiting two or three days. ॐ

When in a tight spot, the careful navigator takes the time to wait for the right conditions rather than rush on into what might be trouble. Each day the tide would be about an hour later, and in several days that morning flood would come about noon to give him time enough between sunup and the end of the ebb to move out through the narrows.

ॐ I took the opportunity of this delay to be present at a public solemnity; but we were informed that in about three months there would be performed on the same account (the initiation of Poulaho's son and heir into certain privileges) a far more important and grander solemnity. On this occasion, not only the tribute of Tongatapu, but that of Ha'apai, Vava'u, and all the other islands would be brought to the Chief, and confirmed more awfully by sacrificing ten human victims from among the inferior sort of people. A horrid solemnity indeed! This is a most significant instance of the influence of gloomy and ignorant superstitions over the minds of one of the most benevolent and humane nations upon earth.

On the tenth, at eight o'clock in the morning, we weighed anchor, and with a steady gale at southeast turned through the channel between the small isles called Makaha'a and Fafa. The flood set strong in our favor till we were the length of the channel leading up to the lagoon, where the flood from the eastward meets that from the west; this, together with the indraught of the lagoon, caused strong ripplings and whirlpools. To add to these dangers, the depth of water in the channel exceeds the length of a cable, so that there is no anchorage except close to the rocks; but here a ship would be exposed to the whirlpools. We continued to ply to windward, between the two tides, without either gaining or losing an inch, till near high water, when, by a favorable slant, we got into the eastern tide's influence. About five in the afternoon, finding that we could not get to sea before dark, I came to an anchor under the shore of Tongatapu in 55 fathoms, about two cables' length from the reef. The *Discovery* dropped anchor under our stern; but before the anchor took hold, she drove off the bank and did not recover it till after midnight. We remained at this station until eleven o'clock the next day, when we weighed and plyed to the eastward. It was ten at night before we weathered the east end of the island and were enabled to stretch away for Eua. ᢟ

EUA ᢞ That evening we anchored at Eua, being nearly in the same place where I had my station in 1773. We had no sooner anchored than Taoofa, the Chief, and several other natives visited us on board. Taoofa had been my friend when I was here during my last voyage; consequently, we were not strangers to each other.

On the thirteenth, in the afternoon, a party of us made an excursion to the highest part of the island. Halfway up about 200 or 300 feet above the level of the sea, the valley was composed of hardly anything but coral rock. The coral was perforated into all the holes and inequalities of this substance when in the reach of the tide. Indeed, we found the same coral rock till we began to approach the summits of the highest hills. Remarkably, the summits were chiefly composed of yellow, soft, sandy stone, and the soil a reddish clay, in many places very deep. ৯

Eua rises to an elevation of 1,078 feet. The coral rock indubitably was elevated to the height Cook found it by the geologic forces that raised this mountain out of the sea. At the highest points, sedimentary material, chiefly sandstone and clay make their appearance. All the Tonga Islands, indeed all the scattered islands of the Pacific, are the tops of mountains rising from the floor of the sea. The "low islands," like Tongatapu and Ha'apai, are barely above sea-level and are formed from the growing coral extending itself upon sea-mount summits that lie just beneath the surface of the ocean. The "high islands" are mountaintops that project above sea-level. Tiny Kao, in this group, juts sharply to 3,380 feet. Tofua, when Cook saw it, was, and still is, an active volcano, spewing steam and smoke. The Friendly Islands ascend from a valley 30,000 feet beneath the ocean. What we can see above the ocean actually are the tops of a chain of mountains rising higher from the floor of the sea than does Mount Everest above sea-level.

৩ On the most elevated part of the island we found a round platform supported by a wall of coral stones, which to bring to such height must have cost much labor. They called it *Etchee*. ৯

This is the third instance in which Cook has observed architectural stonework in the Tonga Islands. Craftsmanship in stone is not found west of here, at least not in the New Hebrides, New Caledonia, Solomon Islands, and New Guinea. East of here it reaches its apogee in the stone statues of Easter Island. Much further east, as Thor Heyerdahl so forcibly brings to our attention in *Kon-Tiki,* superb stone constructions are found in Peru, especially walls and platforms on mountaintops, such as Cook has here come upon.

৩ From the elevation to which we had ascended, we had a full view of the whole island. The plains and meadows, of which there are some of great extent, are adorned with tufts of trees, intermixed with plantations. They form a very beautiful landscape from every point of view. While I was surveying this delightful prospect, I could not help flattering myself with the pleasing idea that some future navigator may behold these meadows stocked with cattle brought to these islands by the ships of England. This, independent of all other considerations, would mark to posterity that our voyages had been useful to the interests of humanity. I had some encouragement that my endeavors of this kind would not be fruitless; for, this day, there was served up at my dinner a dish of turnips, the produce of seeds I had left here during my last voyage.

Omai, who was a great favorite with Feenou and these people in general, was tempted with the offer of being made Chief of this island if he would stay among them. He would have been glad to stay, if the scheme had met my approbation. I own, I did disapprove of it. &

Curiously, we are not told anything of the reception and activities of the other two young Polynesians who boarded the ships in New Zealand.

Although neither Omai nor the New Zealand boys were left on the Tonga Islands, and although not mentioned here, tradition has it that Captain Cook left behind Chief Tuimalila. Chief Tuimalila still lives and only about eleven years ago was elevated to the status of Chief by Queen Salote of the Tongas—Chief Tuimalila is a tortoise. Legend has it that the royal tortoise was given to a Tonga noble by Captain Cook before he left. For centuries this old turtle roamed the streets of Nukualofa, but Queen Salote, before she died, saw to it that he had a permanent home on the palace grounds, and a constant valet.

&§ According to the information that we received, the Tonga archipelago is very extensive. The natives used bits of leaves to ascertain their number, and up to 150 islands were reckoned. Some of them are high, such as Tofua and Eua; and thirty-five of them are large, of these only three were seen this voyage: Ha'apai, Tongatapu, and Eua. (*Cook was misled here; besides these three, there is only one other large island of this group, and that is Vava'u, which he had heard about but not seen. However, thirty-two of the islands sustain regular inhabitants.*)

Upon my inquiring one day of Poulaho from what quarter they had procured a small iron tool which I had seen when I first visited their island during my former voyage, he informed me that they had received this iron from a nearby island. I found him perfectly acquainted with its history. He said that one of those islanders sold a club for it to a ship which had touched there. He added that this was the first iron known among them. So what Tasman left of that metal must have worn out and been forgotten long ago. He said there was but one ship and she did not come to an anchor. From many circumstances which he mentioned, it could not be many years since this had happened. This ship, so pointedly referred to in their conversation, could be no other than the *Dolphin,* the only ship from Europe as far as we have ever learned that had touched, of late years, at any island in this part of the Pacific Ocean prior to my former visit. (*The* Dolphin *was in command of Captain Wallis, who sailed in 1767 and was the first English explorer in the area. During this voyage he discovered Tahiti and did indeed sight islands of the Friendly group before sailing on around the world.*)

The most considerable islands in the neighborhood that we heard of (and we heard a great deal about them) are Hamoa, Vava'u, and Feejee. No European that we know of has, as yet, seen any of them. Tasman lays down in his chart an island nearly in the situation where I suppose Vava'u to be; that is, about the latitude of 19°. (*This is the correct latitude for Vava'u, and it must be that Tasman had sighted it.*) Vava'u, according to the united testimony of all our island friends at Tongatapu, exceeds the size of their own island and has high mountains. (*Not precisely true. The highest elevation is 670 feet and the land area is slightly smaller than Tongatapu.*) I should certainly have visited it if Feenou had not discouraged me by representing it to be very inconsiderable and without any harbor. But Poulaho, the king, assured me that it was a large island that produced everything in common with Tongatapu and with as good a harbor as that at Tongatapu. I had not the least doubt of the truth of his intelligence, and was satisfied that Feenou, from some interested view, attempted to deceive me. ࠫ

What treacherous Feenou had on his mind came to light some years later. According to William Mariner, who as a boy of thirteen served as a captain's clerk aboard the privateer *Port au Prince* and was the only eventual survivor after Feenou's son, in company with his subjects, attacked his ship, Feenou and the other chiefs had hatched a plan to seize Cook's ships and murder everyone aboard. They consequently wished to detain him until the time was ripe. Lack of agreement among the chiefs as to the best way to go about it prevented them from initiating their bloody design. The plot was to have been hatched at the time of all the dancing and celebration that Feenou had staged for Captain Cook back on the island of Ha'apai. Will Mariner reported in his journal:

Finow [Feenou] (at that time tributory Chief of the Ha'apai Islands, Toogoo Ahoo being King), was not the designer of this conspiracy, but he gave counsel and advice respecting it. The other Chiefs proposed to invite the captain and his officers to a grand *bo-mée* (a night dance by torchlight), and at a signal to massacre him, his officers, and all the marines; but Finow objected to this, as the darkness of the night would be unfavorable to their operations in taking the two vessels, and proposed rather that it should be done by day, and that they should seize the opportunity of making the attack on the occasion of a grand entertainment which was shortly to be given to him in honor of his arrival, and after they were all destroyed, the men, who would naturally come in search of him, were to be conducted to the further part of the island under pretense that he was there, and they were then to be destroyed in like manner and thus the two ships, their crews being so weakened, might be taken (as they supposed) with ease. The entertainment was prepared, and Captain Cook and several officers being invited were present; it happened, however, a little before the appointed time when the signal was to be given, that most of the chiefs still expressed their opinion that the nighttime would have been better than the day, and Finow, finding that the majority were of this opinion, was much vexed, and immediately forbade it to be done at all. Thus, no signal being given, the amusements went on without interruption, and Captain Cook and his officers were much pleased with their entertainment, acknowledging it to be far better than any other that they had received at the Friendly islands.

Old Feenou's son carried out his father's bloody design when Will Mariner's ship, the *Port au Prince,* anchored off their coast at nearly the same spot where Cook had put in.

◄§ Hamoa, which is also under the dominion of Tongatapu, lies two days' sail northwest from Vava'u. (*"Hamoa" must be* Samoa, *which in truth lies north north*east *from Vava'u about 350 miles distant.*) It was described to me as the largest of all their islands, as affording harbors and good water (*all true of Samoa*). Poulaho himself frequently resides there. (*Poulaho, Chief of Tongatapu, would have had to travel 550 miles to reach Samoa.*) It would seem that the people of Hamoa are in high estimation at Tongatapu. We were told that some of the songs and dances with which we were entertained had been copied from theirs; and we saw some houses said to be built after their fashion. (*Samoan dances, music, and house construction are all distinctive and especially refined.*) Fiji, we are told, lies three days' sail from Tongatapu in the direction northwest by west (*the direction is correct*). It was described to us as a high, very fruitful island, abounding with hogs, dogs, fowl, and all kinds of fruit and roots. It is much larger than Tongatapu and not subject to them; on the contrary, Fiji and Tongatapu frequently make war on each other. The men of Fiji are formidable on account of the dexterity with which they use their bows and arrows, but much more so on account of the savage practice, like that of New Zealand, of eating their enemies whom they kill in battle.

We met with several Fiji people at Tongatapu. They were of a color that was a full shade darker than the inhabitants of the Tonga Islands. The Fiji men, whom we saw, were much respected for their ingenuity. They excel the inhabitants of Tongatapu in respect to their skill of workmanship, such as clubs and spears, which were carved in a very masterly manner, cloth beautifully checkered, and earthen pots. (*Pottery had not developed in Polynesia, probably because there was no source of clay.*)

I have mentioned that Fiji lies three days' sail from Tongatapu. These people have no other method of measuring distance but by expressing the time required to make the voyage in one of their canoes. In order to ascertain, with some precision, how far these canoes can sail in a moderate gale, I went on board one. When under sail, by several trials with the log, I found she went 7 knots an hour, close-hauled in a gentle gale. (*This is swift windward sailing. An America's Cup 12-meter racing yacht makes about the same speed.*) The length of each day is not to be reckoned at twenty-four hours. Two days' sail, with them, signifies from the morning of the first day to the evening of the second, and so on, for any number of days. (*Three days of sailing, then, comes to sixty hours. At 7 knots a distance of 420 nautical miles would be covered, which is very close to the actual distance from Tongatapu to Fiji.*)

In their navigations the sun is their guide by day, and the stars by night. When these are obscured, they have recourse to points from whence the winds and waves come upon their vessel. If, during an obscuration, both the wind and waves should shift (which, within the limits of the trade wind, seldom happens), they are then bewildered and frequently miss their intended port and are never more heard of. The history of Omai's countrymen, who were driven to Atiu, leads us to infer that those not heard of are not always lost. ✌

By the time of Cook's arrival, the art of long sea voyages had been lost by all the Polynesians except the Tonga islanders. These people had regular commerce over a large section of their ocean, extending 500 miles to Samoa, and nearly the same distance to Fiji. Furthermore, the voyage from Fiji to Tongatapu would be against the wind; consequently, closehauled sailing and tacking would be required. They had to find their way even though constantly changing course when beating to windward. The Fiji men Cook saw at Tongatapu testify that voyages from Fiji were not uncommon. One wonders why Cook did not sail over to Fiji to have a look for himself. The Fiji Islands were first sighted by Bligh, who sailed past them after being put adrift in a small boat by the mutineers of the *Bounty*.

✌ The natives of the Friendly Islands are very strong and well made. They are generally broad about the shoulders, and some are really handsome. A fullness at the point of the nose is very common, but we met with hundreds of truly European faces and many genuine Roman noses. The bodies and limbs of most of the females are well proportioned; and some are absolutely perfect models of a beautiful figure. The most remarkable distinction in the women is the uncommon smallness and delicacy of their fingers. The general color is a cast deeper than copper brown, but several have a true olive complexion. These people walk with a graceful air and firm step. They consider this a thing so natural that nothing used to excite their laughter sooner than to see us stumbling upon the roots of trees or other inequalities of the ground. Their countenance expresses the abundant mildness and good nature which they possess. They are entirely free from that savage keenness which marks the nations in a barbarous state. They are, at the same time, frank, cheerful, and good humored. They never appeared in the smallest degree hostile; but, on the contrary, like most civilized people, they have courted an intercourse with their visitors by bartering, which is the only medium that unites all nations in friendship.

They are uncommonly healthy. Not a single person was seen during our stay to be confined to the house by sickness of any kind. Some are afflicted with blindness by a disease of the cornea. Ringworm seems to affect almost half of them and leaves whitish, serpentine marks behind it. Another disease, which is very frequent, appears on every part of the body in large broad ulcers with thick white edges, discharging a thin, clear matter. Those on the face are shocking to look at. Yet we met with some who seemed to be cured of it, but this was not without the loss of the nose or the best part of it. (*This latter disease was undoubtedly leprosy.*) We know for a certainty that the people of these islands were subject to this loathsome disease before the English first visited them.

There are two other diseases frequent among them. One of these is an indolent firm swelling which affects the legs and arms and increases them to an extraordinary size in their whole length. The other is a tumor in the testicles, which sometimes *exceed* the size of two fists. (*The "two diseases" are actually one: elephantiasis. This disease is due to infection of the body by a small worm called filaria.*)

The men are all circumcised, or rather, supercised, as the operation consists in cutting off only a small piece of the foreskin at the upper part, so that it is rendered incapable, ever after, of covering the glans. They say the operation is practiced from a notion of cleanliness.

The men have their beards cut short and both men and women strip the hair from their armpits. The men are tattooed from about the middle of the belly to about halfway down the thighs with a deep blue color. They trace lines and figures, some of which are very elegant. The women have only a small line or spots on the inside of their hands. The Kings, as a mark of distinction, are exempted from this custom.

The dress of both men and women is the same, and consists of a piece of cloth about two yards wide that goes around the waist and hangs down like a petticoat as low as the middle of the leg. So are the ornaments worn by both sexes the same. The most common are necklaces made of sweet-smelling flowers, others composed of small shells, the wing and leg bones of birds, and sharks' teeth; all which hang loose upon the breast. They often wear a ring of mother-of-pearl shell, neatly polished on the upper part of the arm, or rings of tortoise shell on the fingers. The lobes of the ears (frequently only one) are perforated with two holes in which they wear cylindrical bits of ivory, about 3 inches long. The women rub themselves all over with a fine powder of tumeric in the same manner as our ladies use dry rouge upon the cheeks.

Nothing appears to give them greater pleasure than personal cleanliness. They frequently bathe in ponds; they prefer them to the sea. They are so sensitive that salt water hurts their skin, and when necessity obliges them to bathe in the sea they commonly have some coconut shells filled with water poured over them. They are immoderately fond of coconut oil, a great quantity of which they not only pour upon their heads and shoulders but rub their bodies all over with it. None but those who have seen this practice can conceive how the appearance of the skin is improved by it.

They are very fond of associating together, so that it is common to find several houses empty and the owners of them convened in some other one, or rather, upon a convenient spot in the neighborhood where they recreate themselves by conversing and other amusements. Their private diversions are chiefly singing, dancing, and music performed by the women.

As female chastity, at first sight, seemed to be held in no great estimation, we expected to find frequent breaches of their conjugal fidelity, but we did them great injustice. I do not know that a single instance happened during our whole stay. Neither are those of the better sort, that are unmarried, more free with their favors. It is true that there is no want of those of a different character, but it appeared to me that most of them were of the lowest class. Such of them as permitted familiarities with our people were prostitutes by profession.

We took leave of the Friendly Islands and their inhabitants after a stay of two and one-half months, during which time, we lived together in the most cordial friendship. We weighed with a slight breeze at southeast and stood out to sea, and Taoofa and a few other natives who were in the ship left us. Other canoes came off to us with a few coconuts and haddocks to exchange them for what they could get. The eagerness of these people induced them to follow us out to sea and to continue their intercourse with us to the last moment. At the approach of night, these men, finding that we would not return, left us. &

CHAPTER TWELVE

TAHITI REVISITED

July 17, 1777——September 29, 1777

⋙ In the evening of the seventeenth of July, the body of Eua bore northeast by north, distant 3 or 4 leagues. The wind was now at east and blew a fresh gale. With it I stood to the south, until the next morning, when a sudden squall took our ship aback. ⋙

A square-rigged ship is taken "aback" when the wind is blowing upon the sails from over the bow and consequently presses the square sails and yards backward against the masts and rigging instead of billowing them out ahead of the masts as in normal sailing. A ship is apt to be taken aback when tacking, for the ship in this maneuver must be steered into the eye of the wind in order to get over on the other tack. For this reason, in light airs or when the ship does not have enough way on to carry her over to the other tack, the commander may "wear" ship by turning her all the way around, bringing the wind over the stern to arrive at the same course that he might have, if he had tacked. In a squall, a sudden, major shift in the direction of the wind often occurs, so that a ship might easily be caught aback by this shift in wind, which can come on too strong and too fast for the yards to be trimmed, or the course altered.

⋙ Before the ships could be trimmed on the other tack, the mainsail and the top-gallant-sails were much torn. I continued to stretch to the east-southeast till the evening of the twenty-ninth, when we

137

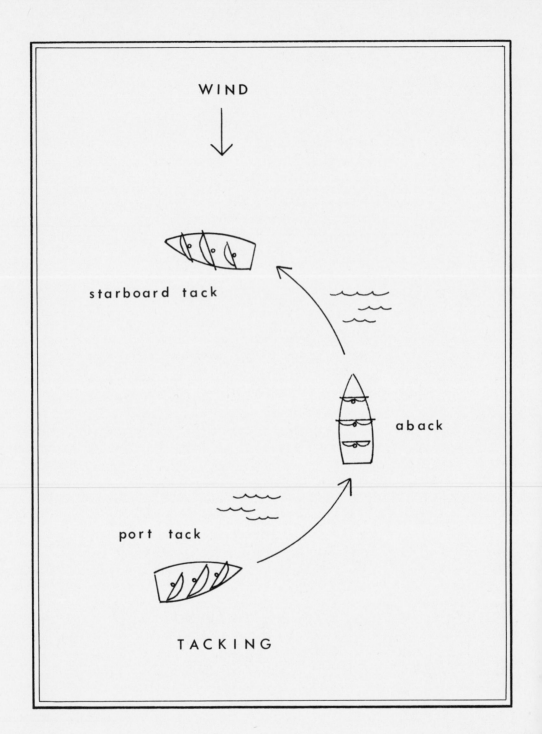

WIND

starboard tack

aback

port tack

TACKING

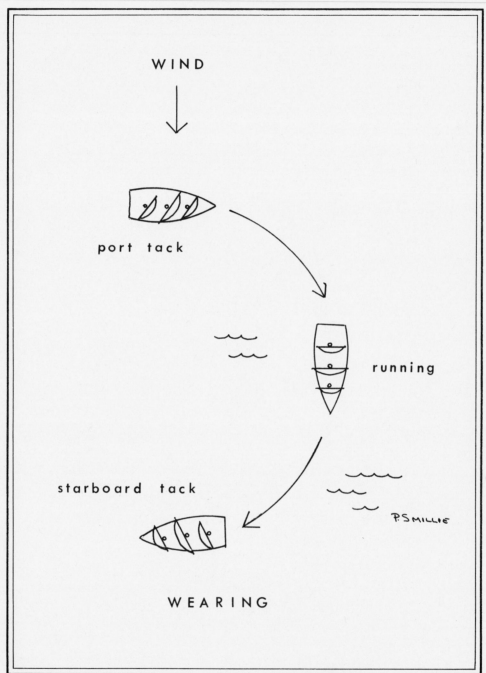

WIND

port tack

running

starboard tack

P. SMILLIE

WEARING

WEARING SHIP

had a sudden and very heavy squall of wind from the north. We were under single-reefed top-sails, courses (*the lower square-rigged sails*), and stay-sails. Two of the latter were blown to pieces and it was with difficulty that we saved the others. We observed lights moving about on board the *Discovery* and concluded something had given way. The next morning we saw that her main-top-mast had been lost.

On the thirty-first, Captain Clerke made a signal to speak to me. He informed me that the head of his main-mast had been discovered to be sprung in such a manner as to render the rigging of another top-mast very dangerous. Therefore he must rig something lighter in its place. He also informed me that he had lost his main-top-gallant yard and that he neither had another, nor a spar to make one, on board. The *Resolution*'s sprit-sail–top-sail yard which I sent him, supplied his want. The next day he got up a jury-top-mast, on which he set a mizzen-top-sail and this enabled him to keep way with the *Resolution*. We were now in the latitude of 28° 6' south. ॐ

The ships were headed for Tahiti, which lies north of Tonga at 17° south latitude, but Cook turned *south* from Tonga, expecting more favorable winds there to help him get east against the prevailing trade winds, eventually to turn north again to Tahiti.

ANOTHER ISLAND DISCOVERED ॐ I steered east and northeast until the eighth of August, when land was seen. I steered directly for it but did not reach it before dark, so the night was spent standing off and on. At daybreak I steered for the northwest, or lee side. We saw it everywhere guarded by a reef of coral rock, extending in some places a full mile from the land and a high surf breaking upon it.

We saw men launch two canoes, and they paddled toward us. I shortened sail to give these canoes time to come up with us, and they advanced to about the distance of a pistol shot from the ship, and there stopped. Their canoes appeared to be about 30 feet long and 2 feet above the water. The sides were incrusted with flat white shells in concentric semicircles; each carried seven or eight men, and they were managed with small paddles whose blades were nearly round. During their vicinity of our ship we got from them the name of their island, which they called Tubuai. (*A good map of the Pacific will show that this little spot of land is directly on the Tropic of Capricorn.*)

Omai was employed to use all his eloquence to prevail upon the men to come nearer. But no entreaties could induce them to trust themselves within our reach. They kept eagerly pointing to shore, which we considered an invitation to land. We could have done this, as the reef had a break or opening in it which was more than sufficient for the boats; but I did not think to risk losing the advantage of a fair wind for the sake of examining an island that appeared to be of little consequence. For this reason, after making several unsuccessful attempts to induce these people to come alongside, I made sail to the north and left them.

After leaving this island, I steered to the north with a fresh gale at east by south, and at daybreak on the morning of the twelfth we saw the Island of Mehetia, and soon after, Tahiti made its appearance. About a league from the bay, the wind suddenly died away and was succeeded by baffling light airs from every direction, consequently we were obliged to stand off and spend the night at sea. ᥱ

TAHITI ᥱ§ Next day, when we first drew near the island, several canoes came off to the ship, each conducted by two or three men. As they were common fellows, Omai took no particular notice of them, nor they of him. They did not even seem to perceive that he was one of their countrymen. At length, Omai's brother-in-law came on board; yet there was nothing either tender or striking in their meeting. There seemed to be a perfect indifference on both sides until Omai took him down to the cabin, opened the drawer where he kept his red feathers, and gave him a few; then the face of affairs entirely turned, and Ootee, who would hardly speak to Omai before, now begged that they might be *tayos* (friends) and exchange names. Had he not shown them his treasure of red feathers, I question much whether they would have bestowed even a coconut upon him.

From the natives we learned that two ships had twice been to Tahiti since my last visit to this land in 1774. They told us that these ships had come from a place called "Reema." We guessed that Lima, the capital of Peru, was meant, and that these visitors were Spaniards. The first time they came they built a house and left four men behind, viz., two priests, a servant, and a person called Mateema. When they sailed they carried away with them four natives. In about ten months the same two ships returned, bringing back two of the islanders, the other two having died in Lima. After a short stay they took away their own people, but the house was left standing.

A VIEW OF TAHITI

Credit: Peabody Museum, Harvard University

The Spaniard called Mateema seems to have studied their language, or at least spoke it so as to be understood. He took uncommon pains to impress the minds of the islanders with the most exalted ideas of the greatness of the Spanish nation, and to make them think meanly of the English. He even went so far as to assure them that we no longer existed as a nation, "Pretane" (*Britain*) was only a small island which they, the Spaniards, had entirely destroyed. As for me, they had met with me at sea and with a few shots had sent my ship and every soul in her to the bottom. If Spain had no other views in this expedition but to depreciate the English, they had better have kept their ships at home. My revisiting Tahiti was, of course, very unexpected and a complete confutation of all that Mateema had said. (*Spain and England were not on very good terms in those days.*) I was informed that they, the Spaniards, meant to return with men and women and settle, live, and die on the island. This shows with what facility a settlement might be made at Tahiti, which I hope will never happen. A permanent establishment among them, conducted as have been most European establishments among Indian nations, would, I fear, give them just cause to lament that our ships had ever found them out. It is unlikely that any measure of this kind should ever be seriously thought of, as it can neither serve the purpose of public ambition nor of private avarice. Without such inducement, I may pronounce, it will never be undertaken. ?

Both "public ambition" and "private avarice" did ensue with the sad consequences that Cook predicted. The culture and government of the Polynesian nation were destroyed and its people were decimated by European diseases. (Measles was the great killer.) Only remnants of the race and culture remain.

On the basis of early discoveries, Tahiti was claimed in turn by three European powers. Wallis was first to come upon the island in June 1767. Shortly thereafter, Bougainville, on his voyage around the world, also chanced to find Tahiti in April 1768 and claimed the island for France. Spain undoubtedly knew of the discoveries of Wallis and Bougainville but wanted to assert her authority in the Pacific, where she had held sway for the preceding two hundred years. A Spanish expedition under Captain Don Bonechea sailed from Peru and landed on Tahiti in November 1772.

The two additional Spanish expeditions to Tahiti, reported here by

Captain Cook, were incipient efforts to follow up on the voyage of
Don Bonechea and colonize the island. However, no nation consoli-
dated its position in Tahiti until France formally annexed the island
in 1843 without much protest from either Spain, England, or the
Tahitians. Since that time, the islands have remained French territory.

⋅⋅⋅ As I knew that Tahiti and the neighboring islands could furnish
us with a plentiful supply of coconut liquor which is an excellent
succedaneum for any artificial (*alcoholic*) beverage, I was desirous
of prevailing upon my people to abridge their stated allowance of
spirits to mix with water. As the stoppage of a favorite article, without assigning some reason, might have occasioned a general murmur,
I thought it most prudent to assemble the ship's company and to make
known the intent of the voyage and the extent of our future operations. (*The Captain has elected to take his men into his confidence,
which was unheard of in his day*.) I took notice of the rewards offered
by Parliament to such of His Majesty's subjects as shall first discover
a communication between the Atlantic and Pacific in the Northern
Hemisphere, and also to such as shall first penetrate beyond the 89th
degree of northern latitude. I told them that to give us the best chance
of succeeding it would be necessary to observe the utmost economy
in the expenditure of our stores and provisions. I reminded them that
our voyage must last a year longer than had been originally supposed
by our having already lost the opportunity of getting north this summer. I begged them to consider the difficulties we might still meet with,
and the aggravated hardships they would labor under if it should be
necessary to put them on short allowance in a cold climate. I submitted to them that rather than run the risk of having no spirits left
when such a cordial would be most wanted, to content themselves
to be without their grog now, when we had so excellent a liquor as
that of coconuts to substitute in its place. I left the determination
entirely to their own choice. (*Even more unheard of, the Captain does
not make a ruling but instead asks for a vote*.) I had the satisfaction
to find that this proposal was unanimously approved of without any
objection. Accordingly, we stopped serving grog, except on Saturday
nights, when the ships' companies had full allowances of it, that they
might drink the healths of their female friends in England, lest they,
among the pretty girls of Tahiti, should be wholly forgotten.

The next day we began to inspect the provisions that were in the main and forehold to get the casks of beef, port, and coal out of the ground tier (*lowest level*), and to put some ballast in their place. The caulkers were set to work to caulk the ship, which they stood in great need of, having made much water on our passage from the Friendly Islands. The *Discovery*'s main-mast was carried ashore and made as good as ever, our sails and water casks were repaired, and the rigging was all overhauled. We also inspected the bread that we had in casks and had the satisfaction to find little of it damaged.

I intended to leave all my European animals at this island. I thought Omai would be able to give some instruction about the management of them and about their use; but unfortunately, poor Omai conducted himself in so imprudent a manner that he soon lost the friendship of Otoo (*Tu, the reigning King of Tahiti*) and of every other person of note in Tahiti. We found here a Spanish bull which they kept tied to a tree near Otoo's house. Without a cow he could be of no use; so I sent the three cows that I had on board to this bull. The bull I had on board, the horse and mare, and the sheep, I put ashore at Matavai. Having thus disposed of these passengers, I found myself lightened of a very heavy burden. The trouble and vexation that attended the bringing of this living cargo thus far is hardly to be conceived.

I must do Otoo the justice to say that he took every method prudent I could suggest to prevent thefts and robberies. His own people constantly kept watch; thus stationed, they not only guarded us in the night from thieves but could observe everything that passed in the day and were ready to collect contributions from such girls as had private connections with our people, which was generally done every morning. The measures adopted by him to secure our safety at the same time served the more essential purpose of enlarging his own profits.

One morning a messenger arrived desiring Otoo's attendance the next day at the *marae* (*burying ground*) to give thanks to the gods for the peace he had concluded with the neighboring Island of Moorea. I was asked to go, but being much out of order was obliged to decline it. I sent Mr. King and Omaifi and returned on board ship attended by Otoo's mother, his three sisters, and eight more women. At first I thought that this numerous train of females came into my boat with no other view than to get a passage to Matavai. But when we arrived at the ship they told me they intended passing the night on board for the express purpose of undertaking the cure of the dis-

order I complained of, which was a pain of the rheumatic kind, extending from the hip to the foot. (*The Captain, from his description, must
have what we commonly term "sciatica," which is a painful disorder
of the sciatic nerve due to inflammation or pressure, usually at the
nerve roots, where it leaves the spine and causes pain and muscle
spasms in the back and legs.*) I accepted the friendly offer, had a bed
spread for them upon the cabin floor, and submitted myself to their
directions. I was desired to lay myself down among them (*There were
altogether twelve women with Captain Cook on that cabin-floor bed.*)
Then, as many of them as could get round me began to squeeze me
with both hands, from head to foot, but more particularly on the parts
where the pain lodged, till they made my bones crack and my flesh
became a perfect mummy. In short, after undergoing this discipline
about a quarter of an hour, I was glad to get away from them. However, the operation gave me immediate relief, which encouraged me
to submit to another rubdown before I went to bed. It was so effectual
that I found myself pretty easy all the night after. My female physicians repeated their prescription the next morning, and again in the
evening, after which I found the pains entirely removed, and the cure
being perfected they took their leave of me. (*The "physiotherapy"
method of these primitive women was perfectly sensible and effective
for the disorder that Cook suffered.*) ঞ

HUMAN SACRIFICE ঞ That the offering of human sacrifices is part
of the religious institutions of this island had been mentioned by
Monsieur Bougainville. I have satisfied myself that such a practice,
however inconsistent with the general humanity of the people, is here
adopted, for I was present myself at such a solemnity.

When we landed, Otoo expressed his desire that the seamen be
ordered to remain in the boat, and that we take off our hats as soon
as we came to the marae, to which we proceeded, attended by a great
many men, but not one woman. We found four priests and their
attendants waiting for us. The dead body, or sacrifice, was in a small
canoe that lay on the beach.

The unhappy victim offered to the object of their worship upon
this occasion seemed to be a middle-aged man and, as we were told,
was one of the lowest class of people. He had not been pitched upon
on account of any particular crime committed by him meriting death.
They make a choice of common, low fellows who stroll about from

place to place, and from island to island, without any fixed abode or any visible way of getting an honest livelihood, of which description of men enough are to be met with on these islands. I could observe that he was bloody about the head and face, and a good deal bruised upon the right temple, which marked the manner of his being killed. We were told that he had been privately knocked on the head with a stone. Those who are chosen to suffer in order to perform this bloody act of worship are never apprised of their fate till the blow is given that puts an end to their existence. Whenever a Chief thinks a human sacrifice necessary, he pitches upon the victim.

The dead body was now uncovered. Then one of the priests, standing at the feet of it, pronounced a long prayer in which he was joined by the others, each holding in his hand a tuft of red feathers. In the course of this prayer some hair was pulled off the head of the sacrifice and the left eye taken out; both were presented to Otoo. The priests, having again seated themselves round the body, renewed their prayers while some of the attendants dug a hole into which they threw the unhappy victim and covered it with earth and stones. While they were putting him into the grave a boy squealed aloud, and Omai said to me, "That was the Eatooa" (*God*).

The marae where the sacrifice was offered is where the supreme Chief of the whole island is always buried. At one place, more particular than the rest, is a heap of stones before which the sacrifice was offered with a platform at one side. On this are laid the skulls of all the human sacrifices, which are taken up after they have been several months under ground. I counted no less than forty-four skulls of former victims. As none of these skulls had as yet suffered any considerable change from the weather, it may be inferred that no great length of time had elapsed since, at least, this considerable number of unhappy wretches had been offered upon this altar of blood.

Among other artifacts I saw at this marae was a long piece of native cloth, the maro, ornamented with red and yellow feathers, ranged in square compartments and rows, so disposed as to produce a pleasing effect. The whole was then sewed to the upper end of the pendant, which Captain Wallis had displayed and left flying ashore the first time he landed in Matavai. We could easily trace the remains of the English pendant.

Early on the morning of the twenty-second of September, Otoo and his father came on board to know when I proposed sailing. For, having been informed that there was a good harbor at Mooréa, I had told them that I should visit that island on my way to Huahiné. They were desirous of taking a passage with me, and of their fleet sailing at the same time. ॐ

The Island of Mooréa is separated from Tahiti by only 12 miles. In those days there were frequent internecine wars between the people of Tahiti and Mooréa. The fighting was done largely on the water in their war canoes. Some of the double canoes had platforms erected upon them as stages for armed men to stand upon and attack the enemy.

ॐ As I was ready to take my departure, I left it to them to name the day. Wednesday following was fixed upon, but we were detained some days longer than I expected by light breezes and calms, so that we could not get out of the bay. During this time the ships were crowded with our friends and surrounded by a multitude of canoes. Not one would leave the place till we were gone. At length, on the afternoon of the twenty-ninth, the wind came at east and we weighed anchor. As soon as the ships were under sail, at the request of Otoo, I fired seven guns, after which all our friends, except him and a few others, left us with such marks of affection and grief as sufficiently showed how much they regretted our departure. Otoo, being desirous of seeing the ships sail, I made a stretch out to sea, and then in again; then he also bid us farewell and went ashore in his canoe. ॐ

CHAPTER THIRTEEN

THE FIRST VISIT TO MOOREA

September 30, 1777——October 10, 1777

On the morning of the thirtieth, after leaving Tahiti, I stood for the north end of Mooréa, the harbor which I wished to examine being at that part. Omai, in his canoe, had arrived there long before us and took measures to show us the place. However, we were not without pilots, having several men of Tahiti on board and not a few women. Not caring to trust entirely to these guides, I sent two boats to examine the harbor. Upon their making the signal for safe anchorage, we stood in with the ships and anchored close to the head of the inlet, in 10 fathoms, over a bottom of soft mud, and moored with a hawser fast to the shore. The harbor runs south, between the hills, above 2 miles. For security and goodness of its bottom it is superior to any harbor that I have met with in any of the islands of this ocean. It has the advantage over most of them in that a ship can sail in and out, with the reigning trade wind. There are several rivulets that fall into it, and the one at the head is so considerable as to admit boats to a quarter of a mile up, where we found the water perfectly fresh.

MOOREA We had no sooner anchored than the ships were crowded with the inhabitants, whom curiosity alone brought on board; but the next morning several canoes arrived from more distant parts with an abundance of breadfruit, coconuts, and a few hogs. These they exchanged for hatchets, nails, and beads.

The ship being pestered with rats, I hauled her within 30 yards of the shore, as near as the depth of water would allow, and made a path

*THE SHIPS AND NATIVE CANOES IN
COOK'S BAY ON THE ISLAND OF MOOREA*

Credit: Peabody Museum, Harvard University

for them to get to land, by fastening hawsers to the trees. It is said that this experiment has sometimes succeeded, but, I believe, we got clear of very few, if any, of the numerous tribe that haunted us.

We employed two or three days in getting up all our spirit casks, to tar their heads, which we found necessary to save them from the efforts of a small insect to destroy them. In the evenings, Omai and I mounted on horseback and rode along the shore. On the sixth, we hauled the ship off into the stream, intending to put to sea the next day, but an accident happened that prevented it, and gave me a good deal of trouble.

We had sent our goats ashore in the daytime to graze, with two men to look after them. Notwithstanding this precaution, the natives had contrived to steal one of them. The loss of this goat would have been of little consequence if it had not interfered with my views of stocking other islands with these animals. This being the case, it became necessary to recover it, if possible. We got intelligence that it had been carried to Maheine, the Chief, who was at a neighboring harbor. Two old men offered to conduct any of my people whom I might send to bring back the goat. Accordingly, I dispatched them in a boat, charged with a threatening message to Maheine.

Not thinking that anyone would dare steal a second at the very time I was taking measures to recover the first, the goats were put ashore again; and in the evening a boat was sent to bring them on board. As our people were getting them onto the boat, one was carried off undiscovered. I had no doubt of recovering it without much trouble, as there had not been time to carry it any considerable distance. Ten or twelve natives set out in different directions to bring it back. Not one of them would own that it was stolen, but all tried to persuade us that it had strayed into the woods; and, indeed, I thought so myself. I was convinced to the contrary, however, when I found that none of those who went in pursuit of it returned. Their only view was to amuse me until their prize was beyond my reach, and night coming on, put a stop to all further search. About this time the boat returned with the other goat, bringing also one of the men who had stolen it.

The next morning I found that most of the inhabitants had moved off, and that Maheine himself had retired to the most distant part of the island. It seemed now that a plan had been laid to steal what I had refused to give, and that, though they had restored one, they were resolved to keep the other. I was equally fixed in my resolution that they should not keep it. I therefore applied to the two old men who had been instrumental in getting back the first. They told me that the second had been carried to a district on the south side of the island by Hamoa, the Chief of that place, but that, if I would send anybody for it, it would be delivered up. They offered to conduct some of my people across the island, but on my learning from them that a boat might go and return the same day, I sent one with two petty officers.

Late in the evening, the boat returned; and the officers informed me that after proceeding as far in the boat as rocks and shoals would permit, Mr. Shuttleworth, with two marines and one of the guides, landed and traveled to the house of Hamoa, where the people of the place amused them for some time by telling them that the goat would soon be brought, and pretended they had sent for it. However, it never came, and the approach of night obliged them to return without it.

I was now sorry that I had proceeded so far, as I could not retreat with any tolerable credit and without giving encouragement to the people of the other islands here to rob us with impunity. I asked Omai and the two old men what methods I should next take. They, without hesitation, advised me to go with a party of men into the country and shoot every soul I should meet with. This bloody counsel I could not follow, but I resolved to march a party of men across the island. At daybreak the next morning, I set out with thirty-five of my people, accompanied by one of the old men and Omai. At the same time I ordered three armed boats around the western part of the island to meet us.

I had no sooner landed, than the few natives who still remained in the neighborhood, fled before us. The first man that we met with upon our march ran some risk of his life, for Omai, the moment he saw him, asked me if he should shoot him, so fully was he persuaded that I was going to carry his advice into execution. I immediately made it known that I did not intend to hurt, much less kill, a single native. These glad tidings flew before us like lightning, and stopped the flight of the inhabitants, so that no one quitted his house or employment afterward.

As we began to ascend the ridge of hills over which lay our road, we got intelligence that the goat had been carried that way before us. But when we had reached the uppermost plantation on the ridge, the people told us that what we were in search of had, indeed, been kept there the first night, but had been carried the next morning to Wateo by Hamoa. We then crossed the ridge and came within sight of Wateo, where they showed us Hamoa's house and told us that the goat was there. I had no doubt of getting it immediately upon my arrival; but when I reached the house, to my very great surprise, the few people we met with denied that they had ever seen it or knew anything about it. Even Hamoa himself came and made the same declaration.

I observed several men running to and fro in the woods with clubs and bundles of darts, and Omai had stones thrown at him, so that it seemed they had intended to oppose any step I should take. After getting a few of the people together, I desired Omai to expostulate with them on the absurdity of the conduct they were pursuing, and to tell them that I was well assured that the goat was in their possession and that I insisted upon its being delivered up, otherwise, I would burn their houses and canoes. Notwithstanding all that I or Omai could say, they continued to deny having any knowledge of it. The consequence was that I set fire to six or eight houses, which were presently consumed, and two or three war canoes. This done, I marched off to join the boats, which were about 8 miles from us and, on our way, burned six more war canoes. In one place information came back that a great many men were getting ready to attack us. We made ready to receive them, but instead of enemies we found petitioners with plantain trees in their hands who begged that I would spare a canoe that lay close by. This I readily complied with.

At length, about four in the afternoon, we got to the boats. All the principal people of the place fled to the hills, though I touched not a single thing of their property. After resting about an hour, we set out for the ships, where we arrived about eight o'clock in the evening. No account of the goat had been received, so that the operations of this day had not produced the desired effect.

Early the next morning I dispatched one of Omai's men to Maheine with this peremptory message: If he persisted in his refusal, I would not leave a single canoe upon the island, and that he might expect a continuation of hostilities as long as the stolen animal remained in his possession. That the messenger might see that I was in earnest, I sent the carpenter to break up three or four canoes that lay ashore at the head of the harbor. The planks were carried on board as materials for building of a house for Omai at the place he intended to settle. I afterward went to the next harbor, where we broke up and burnt six to eight canoes. On my return, about seven in the evening, I received word that the goat had been brought back about half an hour before.

In consequence of the message I sent to the Chief in the morning, it was judged prudent to trifle with me no longer. Thus ended this troublesome and unfortunate business. It grieved me to reflect that after refusing the pressing solicitations of my friends at Tahiti to favor their invasion of this island, I should so soon find myself reduced to the necessity of engaging in hostilities against its inhabitants, which, perhaps, did them more mischief than they suffered from Towha's expedition. The next morning our intercourse with the natives was renewed, and they brought breadfruit and coconuts to barter. It was natural for me to conclude that they were conscious it was their own fault that I had treated them with severity. The cause of my displeasure being removed, they had full confidence that no further mischief would ensue. ॐ

The Captain's patience was tried to the limit. He unwillingly found himself in need of asserting a principle that he valued more highly than the goat. This principle, which he maintained throughout his voyage among all the people he visited, could be stated in many ways. The central theme was that he expected, and insisted upon, fair treatment from the natives and was careful to treat them in the same manner. To have insisted upon bloody retribution for the theft of a goat or even to have incautiously or unwittingly excited the natives to combativeness would, of course, have defeated the whole principle he meant to maintain.

The Captain believed that men here, and elsewhere, would understand fair and equal treatment once this principle for useful intercourse among men had been shown them.

This narrative indicates that the men of the crew, such as Mr. Shuttleworth as well as Captain Cook, were able to converse with the natives in their language. In addition to the advantages gained by being able to communicate with these people, Cook had considerable Polynesian assistance. In this encounter, he received the help of "two old men," Omai, and "one of Omai's men," who must have been a New Zealand boy. These men in Cook's company, familiar as they were with Polynesian ways, served as a bridge of understanding between Cook and these islanders to the effect that the principle of fair treatment could be maintained, even insisted upon, without bloodshed.

CHAPTER FOURTEEN

OMAI RETURNS HOME

October 11, 1777——November 3, 1777

HUAHINE ⁀§ The next morning, October 11, 1777, at about nine o'clock, we weighed with a breeze down the harbor, but it proved so faint that it was noon before we got to sea. I steered for Huahiné, attended by Omai and a pilot in his canoe. They shaped as direct a course for the island as I could (*Huahiné is about 100 miles from Mooréa*). At daybreak the next morning, we saw Huahiné, and at noon we anchored at the entrance of the harbor on the west side of the island. The afternoon was spent in warping the ships into a proper berth and mooring.

Omai entered the harbor just before us in his canoe, but did not land; nor did he take much notice of his countrymen, though many crowded to see him. So many came off to the ship that we could hardly work on account of their number. Our passengers acquainted them with what we had done at Mooréa, and multiplied the number of houses and canoes that we had destroyed by ten, at least. I was not sorry for this exaggerated account, as I saw that it made a great impression on all who heard it; and I had hopes it would induce the inhabitants of this island to behave better to us than they had during my former visits.

Our arrival brought all the principal people of the island to our ships. This was just what I wished, as it was high time to think of settling Omai. The presence of these Chiefs, I guessed, would enable me to do it in the most satisfactory manner. Omai now seemed to have an inclination to establish himself at Ráiatéa (*another of the Society*

155

A VIEW OF

HUAHINE

Islands, 40 miles west of Huahiné), where his father had been dis-
possessed by the men of Bora Bora when they conquered Raiatéa.
I had no doubt of being able to get it restored to Omai in an amicable
manner; but for that purpose it was necessary that he should be upon
good terms with those who were now masters of Raiatéa; and he was
too great a patriot to listen to any such thing, and was vain enough to
suppose that I would reinstate him in his forfeited lands by force. This
made it impossible to fix him at Raiatéa and pointed out to me Huahiné
as the proper place. I therefore resolved to avail myself of the presence
of the chief men of the island to make this proposal to them.

After the hurry of the morning was over, we got ready to pay a
formal visit to Taireetareea, meaning then to introduce this business.
Omai dressed himself very properly for the occasion, and prepared a
handsome present for the Chief. After Omai had got clear of the gang
that surrounded him at Tahiti, he behaved with such prudence as to
gain respect. Our landing drew most of our visitors from the ships, and
the concourse of people assembled was very great. There appeared
to be a greater proportion of personable men and women than we
had ever seen in one assembly at any of these new islands. The bulk
of the people seemed much stouter and fairer than those of Tahiti.

We waited some time for Taireetareea, as I would do nothing until
he came; but when he appeared I found that his presence might have
been dispensed with, as he was not above ten years of age. Omai began
with making his offering to the gods, consisting of red feathers, cloth,
etc. The priest took each article in the same order in which it had been
laid before him and after repeating a prayer, sent it to the marae,
which was not at a great distance. These religious ceremonies having
been performed, Omai sat down by me and we entered upon our business by giving the young Chief my present and receiving his in return.
Some arrangements were next agreed upon as to the manner of carrying on the intercourse betwixt us, and I pointed out the consequences
that would attend their robbing us as they had done during my former
visits. Omai's establishment was then proposed to the assembled Chiefs.

Omai began: He said that he had been carried by us into our country, where he was well received by the great King and treated with
every mark of regard and affection; that he had been brought back,
enriched by our liberality with a variety of articles useful to his countrymen, and that, besides, two horses were to remain with him. He
then signified that it was my request, in return for all my friendly

offices, that they would give him a piece of land to build a house upon, and to raise provisions for himself and servants. He added that if this could not be obtained for him in Hauhiné either by gift or by purchase, I was determined to carry him to Raiatéa and fix him there.

I observed that what he had concluded with, about carrying him to Raiatéa, seemed to meet with the approbation of all the Chiefs. I instantly saw the reason. Omai vainly flattered himself that I meant to use force in restoring him to his father's lands in Raiatéa. The present assembly dreamed of nothing less than a hostile invasion of Raiatéa, and of being assisted by me in driving the Bora Bora men out of that island. It was of consequence therefore that I should undeceive them. I signified, in the most peremptory manner, that I neither would assist them in such an enterprise, nor would suffer it to be put into execution while I was in their seas. If Omai fixed himself in Raiatéa, he must be introduced as a friend and not forced upon the Bora Bora men as their conqueror. ॐ

Cook not only refused to take sides or participate in any of the internecine wars among the Polynesians, but also attempted to teach them the ways of purchase and friendly agreements. The dreams of invasion and the actual sending of expeditionary forces of conquest to a neighboring island seemed to be a constant occupation of the men of the Society Islands. In a land that figured in the minds of Europeans as being close to Paradise, war and the preparations for war were a constant occupation of the inhabitants. The name "Society" did not come from their being sociable with one another, rather Cook gave them their name in honor of the Royal Society when he discovered this group of islands lying west of Tahiti in his first voyage.

ॐ My declaration gave a new turn to the sentiments of the council. One of the Chiefs expressed himself to this effect: "The whole island of Huahiné, and everything in it, was mine, and that I might give what portion I pleased to my friend." Omai, who like most of his countrymen seldom sees things beyond the present moment, was greatly pleased to hear this, thinking I would be very liberal. But to offer what it would have been improper to accept, I considered as offering nothing at all. Therefore I now desired that they would not only assign the particular spot but also the exact quantity of land. Upon this, some Chiefs were sent for, and after a short consultation among themselves, my request was granted by general consent. The ground pitched upon adjoined the house where our meeting was held. The extent along the shore of the harbor was about 200 yards, and its depth to the foot of the hill, somewhat more.

This business being settled to the satisfaction of all parties, I set up a tent ashore, established a post, and erected the observatories. The carpenters of both ships were set to work to build a small house for Omai in which he might secure the European commodities that were his property. Omai began seriously to attend to his affairs and repented heartily his ill-judged prodigality while at Tahiti. He found at Huahiné a brother, a sister, and a brother-in-law. These did not plunder him, as he had lately been by his other relations. I was sorry, however, to discover that, though they were too honest to do him any injury, they were of too little consequence on the island to do him any good. They had neither authority nor influence to protect his person or his property. In that helpless situation, I had reason to apprehend that he ran great risk of being stripped of everything he had gotten from us as soon as he should cease to have us within his reach to enforce the good behavior of his countrymen by an appeal to our irresistible power. A man who is richer than his neighbors is sure to be envied by numbers who wish to see him brought down to their own level. In countries where civilization, law, and religion impose their restraints, the rich have reasonable grounds of security—there being, in all such communities, a diffusion of property so that no single individual need fear that the efforts of all the poorer sort can ever be united to injure him. It was very different with Omai. He was to live among those who were strangers to any other principle of action besides the immediate impulse of their natural feelings. His principal danger was to be placed in the singular situation of being the only rich man in the community. Having, by a fortunate connection with us, got into his possession an accumulated quantity of treasure which none of his countrymen could create by any art or industry, while all coveted a share of this envied wealth, it was natural to fear that all would be ready to join in attempting to strip its sole proprietor. To prevent this, if possible, I desired Omai to make a proper distribution of some of his movables to two or three of the principal Chiefs, who, being thus gratified themselves, might be induced to take him under their patronage and protect him from the injuries of others. Not trusting, however, to the operation of gratitude, I had recourse to the more forcible motive of intimidation. I took every opportunity of notifying the inhabitants that it was my intention to return to their island again, after being absent the usual time, and that if I did not find Omai in the same state of security in which I left him, all those whom I should then discover to have been his enemies might expect to feel the weight of my resentment. This threatening consideration will probably have considerable effect. Our successive visits of late years have taught these people to believe that our ships are to return at certain periods.

Omai's house being nearly finished, many of his movables were carried ashore on the twenty-sixth. Among a variety of other useless articles was a box of toys, which seemed greatly to please the gazing multitude. As to his pots, kettles, dishes, plates, drinking mugs, and glasses, hardly one of his countrymen would so much as look at them. Omai himself now began to think that they were of no manner of use to him—that a hog was a more savory food baked than boiled, that a plantain leaf made as good a dish as pewter, that a coconut shell was as convenient as a goblet.

The following particulars are added to complete the view of Omai's domestic establishment. He had picked up at Tahiti four or five servants; the two New Zealand youths remained with him, and his brother and some others joined him at Huahiné. His family consisted of eight or ten persons, if that can be called a family to which not a single female as yet belonged. At present Omai did not seem at all disposed to take unto himself a wife. The house which we erected for him was 24 feet by 18 feet and 10 feet high. It was composed of boards—the spoils of our military operations at Mooréa. In building it, as few nails as possible were used that there might be no inducement, from the love of iron, to pull it down. His European weapons consisted of a musket, a bayonet, a cartridge box, a fowling piece, two pairs of pistols, and two or three swords, or cutlasses. The possession of these made him quite happy, but I was of the opinion that he would have been happiest without firearms and other European weapons, as such implements of war, in the hands of one whose prudent use of them I had some grounds of mistrusting, would increase his danger rather than establish his superiority.

As soon as Omai was settled in his new habitation, I began to think of leaving this island; but first we carried ashore the bread remaining in the bread room, to clear it of vermin. The number of cockroaches that infested the ship at this time was incredible. The damage they

did us was very considerable, and every method devised by us to
destroy them proved ineffectual. These insects had now become a real
pest and so destructive that few things were free from their ravages.
If food of any kind was exposed, only for a few minutes, it was
covered with them and they soon pierced it full of holes resembling
a honeycomb. They were particularly destructive to the stuffed birds
preserved as specimens, and, what was worse, were uncommonly fond
of ink, so that the writing on the labels fastened to different articles
was quite eaten out. According to Mr. Anderson, they were of two
sorts: the *germanica* and the *blatta orientales*. The first of these had
been carried home in the ship on her former voyage, where they
withstood the severity of the hard winter of 1776, though she was in
dock all the time. The others made their appearance since leaving
New Zealand. They had increased so fast that they even got among
the rigging so that when a sail was loosened, thousands of them fell
upon the decks. The *orientales* came out in the night, when, from
their noise in crawling about, they made everything in the cabin seem
as if in motion. They did great mischief to our bread, which was so
bespattered with their excrement that it would have been badly relished
by delicate feeders.

On the second of November, at four in the afternoon, I took advantage of a breeze which then sprung up at east and sailed out of the
harbor. Most of our friends remained on board until the ships were
under sail; then all took their leave, except Omai, who remained till
we were at sea.

We had come to sail by a hawser fastened to the shore. In casting
the ship, it parted, being cut by the rocks. It became necessary to send
a boat to bring it on board; and in this boat Omai went ashore. Taking
a very affectionate farewell of all the officers, he sustained himself
with manly resolution until he came to me; then his utmost efforts to
conceal his tears failed. Mr. King, who went in the boat, told me that
he wept all the time in going ashore.

It was no small satisfaction to reflect that we had brought him safe
back to the very spot from which he was taken, but such is the
strange nature of human affairs that it is probable we left him in a less
desirable situation than he was before his connection with us. I do not
mean that because he has tasted the sweets of civilized life, he must
become more miserable from being obliged to abandon all thoughts
of continuing them. The disagreeable circumstance is that the advan-

tages he received from us have placed him in a more hazardous situation. Omai, from being much caressed in England, lost sight of his original condition. He seemed to have forgotten their customs, otherwise he must have known the extreme difficulty there would be in getting himself admitted as a person of rank where there is, perhaps, no instance of a man's being raised from an inferior station by the greatest merit. Rank seems to be the very foundation of all distinction and power here, and so pertinaciously or blindly adhered to, that unless a person has some degree of it, he will certainly be despised and hated if he assumes the appearance of exercising any authority. Revenge, rather than a desire of becoming great, appeared to motivate Omai from the beginning. This, however, may be excused if we consider that it is common to his countrymen. Whether he imagined that his own personal courage and superiority of knowledge would be sufficient to dispossess the conquerors of Raiatéa is uncertain, but from the beginning of the voyage this was his constant theme. The objection to admitting him to some rank would have been lessened if he had fixed at Tahiti, as a native will always find it more difficult to accomplish such a change of state among his countrymen than will a stranger. But Omai remained determined to the last and would not, I believe, have adopted my plan of settlement at Huahiné if I had not so explicitly refused to employ force in restoring him to his father's possessions. I can only conjecture that his greatest danger will arise from the very impolitic declarations of his antipathy to the inhabitants of Bora Bora. To the very last, he continued determined to take the first opportunity that offered of satisfying his revenge in battle.

Omai's return encouraged many to offer themselves as volunteers to attend me to "Pretane." I took every opportunity of expressing my determination to reject all such applications. If there had been the most distant probability of any ship being again sent to New Zealand, I would have brought the two youths of that country with me. Both of them were very desirous of continuing with us. Tiarooa, the eldest, was an exceedingly well-disposed young man and capable of receiving any instructions. The other was so strongly attached to us that he was taken out of the ship and carried ashore by force. He was a witty, smart boy, and on that account much noticed on board. ॐ

Perhaps Cook misjudged the time it would take for ships of other European nations, and those of England, to follow him into the

Pacific. Eleven years later, Bligh, now a commissioned officer and Captain of the *Bounty,* returned to Tahiti on the twenty-sixth of October, 1788. He, of course, immediately inquired after Omai, his former shipmate. From Otoo, still a powerful Chief of Tahiti, Bligh learned that Cook's misgivings were borne out. Soon after they left these islands, hostilities resumed between the inhabitants of Huahiné and those of Raiatéa and Bora Bora, with Omai a leader of the campaign. He used his muskets and firearms to gain a victory for Huahiné, but Cook's fears for his safety were justified. Only two and one-half years later, Omai, together with the two New Zealand boys, were killed— whether by men of Bora Bora or jealous countrymen of Huahiné— Otoo did not say.

If Cook had known that he was yet to discover another, much larger group of Polynesian Islands, he might have yielded to the pleas of the New Zealand youths to continue with him; and thereby, perhaps, saved both of them and himself from the all too common murderous belligerence of the Polynesian.

&s The boat which carried Omai ashore having returned to the ship with the remainder of the hawser, we hoisted her in, and immediately stood over for Raiatéa, where I intended to touch next. &

CHAPTER FIFTEEN

RAIATEA AND BORA BORA

November 3, 1777——December 7, 1777

RAIATEA ◄ We sailed around the south end of Raiatéa, where we met with calms and light airs, so that at noon we were still a league from the harbor; while we were thus detailed, my old friend Oreo, Chief of the island, came to visit. Being resolved to push for the harbor, I ordered all the boats to be hoisted out and sent them ahead to tow. We were obliged to come to an anchor at the harbor entrance and to warp in, which employed us till night set in. ►

To "warp in" a ship means to row out an anchor in a small boat, set it, haul the ship up to the anchor by the capstan winch, place another anchor farther in, and so repeat the assiduous process until the ship is pulled into the harbor.

◄ As soon as we were within the harbor, the ships were surrounded with canoes, filled with people who brought hogs and fruit to barter with us for our commodities.

On the night of the thirteenth, John Harrison, a marine, deserted, carrying with him his musket and accoutrements. A party was sent for him, but they returned in the evening after an ineffectual inquiry and search. The next day I applied to the Chief to interest himself in this matter. He promised to send a party of men after him, and gave me hopes that Harrison would be brought back the same day; but this did not happen, and I had reason to suspect that no steps had been taken, and then the Chief and his whole family fled. Having got intelligence that Harrison was at a place called Hamoa on the other side of the island, I went thither with two armed boats accompanied by one of the natives. On our way, we found the Chief, who also embarked with me. I landed about a mile from the place and marched quickly, lest the sight of the boats should give alarm and allow the man time to escape to the mountains. The natives had gotten information of my coming and were prepared to deliver him up.

I found Harrison with the musket lying before him, sitting down, between two women who, the moment I entered the house, rose up to plead in his behalf. I frowned upon them and bid them be gone. Upon this they burst into tears and walked off. The fellow had nothing to say in his defense but that the natives had enticed him away. This might in part be true; the two women had been at the ship the day before he deserted. As it appeared that he had remained upon his post until within a few minutes of the time he was to have been relieved, the punishment I inflicted upon him was not very severe.

While we lay moored to the shore, we heeled and scrubbed both sides of the bottoms of the ships. At the same time, we fixed some tin plates under the binds, first taking off the old sheathing. These plates I had from the ingenious Mr. Pelham, Secretary to the Commissioners for Victualling his Majesty's Navy, with a view of trying to learn whether this would answer the same end as copper on the bottoms of ships.

On the twenty-fourth, I was informed that a midshipman and a seaman belonging to the *Discovery* were missing. As the midshipman was known to have expressed a desire to remain on these islands, it seemed certain that he and his companion had gone off with this intention. As these two were not the only persons on the ships who wished to end their days at these favorite islands, it was necessary to get them back at all events in order to put a stop to further desertion. We were told that they had quit this island and had gone over to Bora Bora. I did not think it proper to follow them thither, but determined to have recourse to a measure which I guessed would oblige the natives to bring them back.

Soon after daybreak, the Chief, his son, daughter, and son-in-law came on board the *Resolution*. The three last I resolved to detain until the two deserters should be brought back. With this in view, Captain Clerke confined them in his cabin. The Chief was with me when the news reached him. He began to have apprehensions as to his own situation and his looks expressed the utmost perturbation of mind. I soon made him easy by telling him that he was at liberty to leave the ship whenever he pleased and to take such measures as he should judge best calculated to get our two men back. If he succeeded, his friends would be delivered up; if not, I was determined to carry them away with me.

Although relieved from apprehensions about their own safety, the people continued under the deepest concern for those who were prisoners. Many of them went under the stern in canoes to bewail their captivity, which they did with long and loud exclamations. The Chief's daughter resounded from every quarter, and the women seemed to vie with each other in mourning her fate.

Oreo himself did not give way to unavailing lamentations, but instantly began his exertions to recover our deserters by dispatching a canoe to Bora Bora.

The natives did not think it proper to trust to the return of our people for the prisoners' release. Their impatience was so great that it hurried them to make an attempt which might have involved them in still greater distress had it not been fortunately prevented. Their first, and great plan of operations, was to have laid hold of me. It was my custom every evening to bathe in fresh water. Very often I went alone, and always without arms. Expecting me to go as usual this evening, they had determined to seize me, and Captain Clerke too, if he accompanied me. In the course of the afternoon the Chief asked me several times if I would not go to the bathing place. When he found I could not be prevailed upon, he went off with the rest of his people. I had no suspicion at this time of their design.

Finding themselves disappointed as to me, they fixed on those who were more in their power. Between five and six in the evening, I observed all their canoes in the harbor begin to move off as if some sudden panic had seized them. I inquired in vain to find out the cause, till our people called to us from the *Discovery* and told us that a party of the natives had seized Captain Clerke and Mr. Gore. Struck with the boldness of this plan of retaliation which counteracted me so effectually in my own way, there was no time to deliberate. I instantly ordered the people to arm and in less than five minutes a strong party was sent to rescue our gentlemen. Mr. Williamson went after the flying canoes to cut off their retreat. Not a musket was fired except two or three to stop the canoes. To that firing Messrs. Clerke and Gore owed their safety, for at that very instant a party of natives, armed with clubs, was advancing toward them. On hearing the report of the muskets, they disappeared. It was fortunate for all parties that they did not succeed and that no mischief was done on this occasion.

This conspiracy, as it may be called, was first discovered by a girl whom one of the officers had brought from Mooréa. She, overhearing some of the Raiatéans say that they would seize Captain Clerke and Mr. Gore, ran to inform our people. Those who were in the conspiracy threatened to kill her as soon as we should leave the island. Being aware of this, we contrived that her friends should convey her to a place of safety where she might be concealed till they could have an opportunity to send her back to Mooréa. ❧

No doubt this Mooréan girl shared the cabin of the officer, and such arrangements were very likely frowned upon by Captain Cook, but her love for the ship's men saved Clerke and Gore. In the affair of the goat at Mooréa, and the first deserter here at Raiatéa, as well as in the Captain's efforts to get the second two deserters back in this present tense situation, close friendships with certain natives provided Cook with much-needed information and served him well, so that open hostilities were prevented.

❧ Oreo, the Chief, as well as I, being uneasy that no account had been received from Bora Bora regarding the deserters, set out for that island and desired me to follow down the next day with the ships. This was my intention, but the wind, which kept us in the harbor, brought Oreo back from Bora Bora with the two deserters. As soon as they were on board, our three prisoners were released. I would not have exerted myself so resolutely but for the reason before mentioned and to save the son of a brother officer from being lost to his country. Thus ended an affair which gave me much trouble and vexation. ❧

The lovely Polynesian Islands were as appealing and attractive to Cook's crew as they are for most people of the Western world. The crew's desire to remain among these green spots in the ocean, and among these happy, healthy, inhabitants, created an incessant desertion problem. Desertion began at New Zealand, and now three more of his crew had run away at Raiatéa.

Captain Bligh's greatest problem when he returned to Tahiti eleven years later was the desertion of his crew. He succeeded in getting them all back on board before he left for home, but the lure of the islands was too great, and this enticement as much as Bligh's reputed harshness, incited the crew to mutiny, and to turning the *Bounty* back to Tahiti.

Captain Clerke of the *Discovery,* who was ill with tuberculosis, also would have liked to remain here. If he could have done so, he might have recovered and lived, rather than dying later on in this voyage while cruising the cold arctic seas.

BORA BORA ⋙ As soon as we had gotten clear of the harbor, we took leave of Raiatéa and steered for Bora Bora. The sole object I had in view by visiting that island was to procure from its monarch one of the anchors Monsieur de Bougainville had lost at Tahiti. Having been taken up by the natives at Tahiti, it had, as they informed me, been sent as a present to the Chief. My desire to get possession of it did not arise from our being in want of anchors, but, having expended all the hatchets and other iron tools which we had brought from England, we were now reduced to the necessity of creating a fresh assortment of trading articles by fabricating them out of the spare iron we had on board, and a great part of that had been already expended. I thought that Monsieur de Bougainville's anchor would supply our want of this useful material. I had no doubt that I should be able to tempt Opoony (*the Chief*) to part with it.

Oreo and six or eight men from Raiatéa, took passage with us to Bora Bora. Indeed, most of the natives in general, except the Chief himself, would have gladly taken a passage with us to England. At sunset, being the length of the south point of Bora Bora, we shortened sail and spent the night making short boards. At daybreak we made sail for the harbor, which is on the west side of the island. The wind was scant, so we had to ply up, and it was nine o'clock before we got near enough to send away a boat to sound the entrance. I had thoughts of running the ships in and anchoring for a day or two.

When the boat returned, the master reported that though the entrance of the harbor was rocky, there was good ground within, and the depth of water was 27 to 35 fathoms, and there was room to turn the ships in, the channel being one-third of a mile broad. We attempted to work the ships in; but the tide, as well as the wind, being against us, I found, after making two or three trips, that it could not be done until the tide should turn in our favor. I gave up the design of carrying the ships into the harbor and ordered the boats to be gotten ready. I embarked in one of them, accompanied by Oreo, and was rowed in to the island.

Soon after we landed I was introduced to Opoony in the midst of a great concourse of people. Having no time to lose, as soon as the necessary formality of compliments was over, I asked the Chief to give me the anchor, and produced the present I had prepared for him consisting of: a linen nightshirt, a shirt, some gauze handkerchiefs, a looking-glass, some beads, other toys, and six axes. At the sight of these last, there was a general outcry. Opoony absolutely refused to receive my present till I should get the anchor. He ordered three men to go and deliver it to me, and I was to send by them what I thought proper in return. With these messengers, we set out in our boats for an island lying at the north side of the entrance of the harbor, where the anchor had been deposited. I found it to be neither so large nor so perfect as I expected. It had originally weighed 700 pounds according to the mark upon it, but the ring, with part of the shank and two points, were now wanting. I was no longer at a loss to guess the reason for Opoony's refusing my present. He doubtless thought that it so much exceeded the value of the anchor in its present state that I would be displeased when I saw it. Be this as it may, I took the anchor as I found it, and sent him every article of the present that I first intended. Having completed my negotiations, I returned on board, hoisted in the boats, and made sail from the island to the North. ❧

Cook, and his surgeon-naturalist Mr. Anderson, recorded some of their observations of the culture they found in the Society Islands, and the changes that culture had undergone since the islands were discovered by Wallis and Bougainville.

Mr. Anderson writes: ❧ Perhaps there is scarcely a spot in the universe that affords a more luxuriant prospect than the southeast part of Tahiti. The hills are high and steep, and in many places craggy. They are covered to the very summits with trees and shrubs in such a manner that the spectator can scarcely help thinking that the very rocks possess the property of producing and supporting their verdant clothing. The valleys also teem with productions that grow with the most exuberant vigor and fill the mind of the beholder with the idea that no place on earth can outdo this in strength and beauty of vegetation. On viewing these charming scenes, I have often regretted my inability to transmit to those who have had no opportunity of seeing them, such a description as might convey and impression of what must be felt by everyone who has been fortunate enough to be upon the spot.

It is doubtless the natural fertility of the country, combined with the mildness and serenity of the climate, that renders the natives so careless in their cultivation. The cloth plant, which is raised from seed brought from the mountain, and the intoxicating pepper *kava,* which they defend from the sun, are almost the only things they seem to pay any attention to. I have inquired into their manner of cultivating the breadfruit tree, but was answered that they never plant it. It will be observed that the tree springs from the roots of the old ones, which run along the surface of the ground. The inhabitants of Tahiti, instead of being obliged to plant their bread, will rather be under a necessity of preventing its progress. The plantain requires a little more care. After it is planted, it shoots up, and in about three months begins to bear fruit, then it gives off young shoots which supply a succession of fruit. The old stocks are cut down as the fruit is taken off.

A delicacy and whiteness distinguishes the inhabitants of Tahiti. Their women struck us as superior in every respect and as possessing all those delicate characteristics which distinguish them from the other sex in many countries.

I never saw the Tahitian in any misfortune labor under the appearance of anxiety after the critical moment has past. Neither does care ever seem to wrinkle their brow. Such a disposition leads them to direct all their aims to what can give them pleasure and ease. Their amusements all tend to excite and continue their amorous passions, and their songs, which they are immoderately fond of, answer the same purpose.

Their behavior on all occasions seems to indicate a great openness and generosity of disposition. But Omai often said that they are sometimes cruel in punishing their enemies. According to him, they torment them very deliberately: at one time tearing out small pieces of flesh from different parts; at another, taking out the eyes; then cutting off the nose; and lastly killing them by opening the belly.

On walking one day about Matavai Point, I saw a man paddling in a small canoe so quickly and looking about him with such eagerness as to command my attention. At first I imagined he had stolen something from one of the ships. He went out from the shore till he was near the place where the swell begins to take its rise. Watching the swell's motion very attentively, he paddled before it with great quickness till he found that it overlooked him and had acquired sufficient force to carry his canoe before it without passing underneath. He sat motionless and was carried along at the same swift rate as the wave till he landed on the beach. Then he emptied his canoe and went in search of another swell. I could not help concluding that this man felt the most supreme pleasure while he was driven on—so fast and so smoothly—by the sea. Two or three natives came up who shared his felicity and always called out when there was an appearance of a favorable swell. By them I understood that this exercise, which is called *choroee,* was frequent among them. (*This is the first recorded description of surfing. Twentieth-century American surfers show in their bodies and countenance the same ecstatic emotions experienced in surfing that Mr. Anderson observed in this Tahitian the first time he saw the sport. Today the cry still goes out when a "favorable swell" is running.*)

In customs respecting the females, there seems to be no obscurity, especially as to their connections with men. If a young man and woman, from mutual choice, cohabit, the man gives the father of the girl such things as hogs, cloth, or canoes in proportion to the time they are together. If the father thinks that he has not been sufficiently paid for his daughter he makes no scruple of forcing her to leave her friend and cohabit with another person who may be more liberal. The man, on his part, is always at liberty to make a new choice; but should his consort become pregnant, he may kill the child and after that either continue his connection with the mother or leave her. If he should suffer the child to live, the parties are then considered as in the married state and they commonly live together ever after. It is thought no crime for the man to join a more youthful partner to his first wife and to live with both. The custom of changing their connection is so common that they speak of it with great indifference. The Erreoes are those of the better sort, who from their fickleness and their possessing the means of purchasing a succession of fresh connections, are constantly roaming about. So agreeable is this licentious plan of life that the most beautiful of both sexes commonly spend their youthful days habituated to the practice of enormities which would disgrace the most savage tribes, and are peculiarly shocking among a people whose character, in other respects, has evident traces of the prevalence of humane and tender feelings. When an Erreoe woman is delivered of a child, a piece of cloth, dipped in water, is applied to the mouth and nose, which suffocates it.

The women have the mortification of being obliged to eat by themselves and in a different part of the house from the men, and by a strange policy, are excluded from a share of the better sorts of food. It is seldom that even those of the first ranks are suffered to eat pork. The women serve up their own victuals; and they would certainly starve before any grown man would do them such office. As in such a life, their women must contribute a very large share of its happiness, it is surprising to find them treated with a degree of harshness or even brutality which one would scarcely suppose a man would bestow on an object for whom he had the least affection. Nothing is more common than to see a man beat a woman without mercy. They seem scarcely susceptible of those delicate sentiments that are the result of mutual affection. I believe that there is less platonic love in Tahiti than in any other country.

Cutting or incising the foreskin is a practice adopted among them from a notion of cleanliness. They have a reproachful epithet in their language for those who do not observe that custom. When there are five or six lads pretty well grown up in a neighborhood, the father of one of them goes to a Tahoua, or a man of knowledge. He goes with the lads to the top of the hills. Seating one of them properly, he introduces a piece of wood underneath the foreskin, desires the boy to look aside at something he pretends is coming, and cuts through the skin upon the wood with a shark's tooth, generally at one stroke. After ten days, a thickness of prepuce remaining where it was cut, they go again to the mountain with the Tahoua. Some heated stones are prepared and the Tahoua puts the prepuce between two of them and squeezes gently, which removes the thickness. The lads then return home with their heads and bodies adorned with flowers.

The productions, the people, the customs, and the manners of all the islands in the neighborhood may, in general, be reckoned the same as at Tahiti. Besides the chain of high islands from Mehetia to Maupiti, the people of Tahiti are acquainted with a low uninhabited island which they name Mopélia and seems to be Howe's Island laid down to the westward of Maupiti in our charts. There are also several low islands to the northeastward of Tahiti which they have sometimes visited and are said to be at the distance of two days' sail with a fair wind. Forty men of Bora Bora, incited by curiosity, roamed as far as one of them called Mataeeva in a canoe. These low islands are doubtless the farthest navigation which those of the Society Islands perform at present. ६⤳

The low islands to the northeastward must be the Tuamotu archipelago. These islands lie 300 miles in that direction from Tahiti. The prevailing east wind might bring a canoe from the nearer islands of the Tuamotu group to Tahiti in two days, but it must have taken more days than that to sail back again. The island of "Mataeeva" visited by the men of Bora Bora must be Matahiva, which is among the islands of the Tuamotu group nearest to Bora Bora.

Captain Cook adds: ⤳ I own, I cannot avoid expressing it as my real opinion, that it would have been far better for these poor people never to have known our superiority in the arts that make life comfortable, than, after once knowing it, to be again left and abandoned to their original incapacity for improvement. Indeed, they cannot be restored to that happy mediocrity in which they lived before we discovered them. It seems to me that it has become, in a manner, incumbent on the Europeans to visit them once in three or four years in order to supply them with those conveniences which we have introduced among them. It may be too late to go back to their old less perfect contrivances, which they now despise and have discontinued since the introduction of ours. By the time the iron tools which they now possess are worn out, they will have almost lost the knowledge of their own. A stone hatchet is, at present, as rare a thing among them as an iron one was eight years ago. A chisel of bone or stone is not to be seen. At Tahiti they expect the return of the Spaniards every day, and they will look for the English two or three years hence. It is to no purpose to tell them that you will not return. They think you must, though not one of them knows, or will give himself the trouble to inquire, the reason of your coming. ६⤳

In the brief span of eight years since his first visit to Tahiti, the Captain has seen the stone age come to an end. He has observed that the inhabitants have been irrevocably altered by their contact with the eighteenth-century Europeans and will never be the same. He laments the passing of the primitive period of these people and is aware that he has been instrumental in bringing it about. Seeing that this alteration in the economy of the islands has occurred, and that there can be no return, Europe, in his opinion, is obligated to assume the responsibility of continuing to provide what have now become economic necessities. The islanders did not ask to be "discovered."

The Captain has discovered more than islands, more than geographical points, more even than a heretofore unknown culture—he has discovered the forces that one culture works upon another; that exploration leads to new responsibilities; that in human affairs, there is no going back, no matter how much men might wish it, whether they be the discovered or the discoverer. He senses the future and thinks "it would have been far better for these poor people never to have known" superior comforts. How right! In a hundred years the inroads of western ways and western diseases caused the "great crowds" to disappear. Few of the original race remained. Tahitian culture was obliterated. Cook was one of a few persons who saw the need for, and cared to take, *responsibility*.

CHAPTER SIXTEEN

DISCOVERY OF HAWAII

December 8, 1777———February 2, 1778

AT SEA ⋖§ After leaving Bora Bora, I steered to the northward, close-hauled with the wind between northeast and east, hardly ever having it to the southward of east, till after we had crossed the line and had gotten into north latitudes, so that our course, made good, was always to the west of north. (*He was trying to get east to America.*)

Seventeen months had now elapsed since our departure from England. We had not, upon the whole, been unprofitably employed, but I was sensible that, with regard to the principal object of my instructions, our voyage was only beginning. Therefore my attention was called forth to every circumstance that might contribute to our safety and our ultimate success. With this in view, I ordered a survey to be taken of all the boatswain's and carpenter's stores that were in the ships that I might be fully informed of the quantity, state, and condition of every article, and by that means, know how to use them to the greatest advantage.

Before I sailed from the Society Islands I inquired of the inhabitants if there were any islands in a north or northwest direction from them. They did not know of any. Mendana, in his first voyage in 1568, discovered an island which he named Isle de Jesus in latitude 6° 45′ south and 1,450 leagues from Callao, Peru, which is 200° east longitude from Greenwich. We crossed this latitude near 100 leagues to the eastward of this longitude and saw many birds which are seldom known to go far from land. ঌ

Mendana sailed forty-eight years after Magellan first sailed across the Pacific Ocean. Navigation, especially in matters of longitude, was so inaccurate that islands would be discovered and then lost again, because of error in locating them on charts.

Mendana discovered the Solomon Islands in this voyage but when he tried to return there, twenty-seven years later, he could not find them, and they remained lost until the English navigator Philip Carteret rediscovered them in 1767.

Latitude determinations were more accurate than longitude. The only islands in the region of 6° south latitude and 200° east longitude are the little, uninhabited Starbuck Islands; not much of a place for the "Island of Jesus." It rises only fifteen feet out of the sea.

CHRISTMAS ISLAND ⋖§ On the twenty-fourth, about half an hour after daybreak, land was discovered. It was found to be one of those low islands so common in this ocean—a narrow bank of land enclosing the sea within (an atoll). A few coconut trees were seen in two or three places, but in general the land had a very barren appearance. The wind was at least southeast so that we had to make a few boards to get up to the lee, or west side, of the island, where we found 20 fathoms over a bottom of fine sand. The meeting with soundings determined me to anchor with a view to try to get some turtle, for the island seemed to be a likely place to meet them. We dropped anchor and a boat was dispatched to examine whether it was practical to land, of which I had some doubt, as the sea broke in a dreadful surf all along the shore. When the boat returned, the officer reported that he could see no place to land but there was a great abundance of fish in the shallow water. At daybreak the next morning, I sent two boats to search for a landing place, and two others to fish near the shore. These last returned about eight o'clock with upward of 2 hundredweight of fish. The master of the Resolution reported that about a league to the north was a break in the land and a channel into the lagoon. In consequence of this report, the ships weighed anchor and after two or three trips came to again in 20 fathoms water over a bottom of fine dark sand, before the entrance of the lagoon. The water in the lagoon itself is all very shallow.

In the morning the pinnace and cutter under command of Mr. King were sent to the southeast part of the island to catch turtles. Captain Clerke, having had some of his people on shore all night, had been so fortunate as to turn between forty and fifty on the sand, which were brought on board with all expedition.

The next day I landed on the island, which lies between two channels into the lagoon to prepare the telescope for observing the approaching eclipse of the sun, which was one great inducement to my anchoring here. (*This small island at the mouth of the lagoon is now called Cook Island.*) On the morning of the thirtieth, when the eclipse was to happen, Mr. King, Mr. Bayly, and I went ashore. The sun was clouded at times but was clear when the eclipse ended. These observations I was unable to continue on account of the great heat of the sun, increased by the reflection from the land.

In the afternoon, the boats and turtling party returned on board, except two seamen belonging to the *Discovery* who had been missing two days. Considering how strange a set of beings the generality of seamen are when on shore, instead of being surprised that these two men should lose their way, it is rather to be wondered at that no more of the party were missing. One of the lost men found some salt on the southeast part of the island. Though this was an article of which we were in want, a man who could lose himself as he did, and not know whether he was traveling east, west, north, or south, was not a fit guide to conduct us to the place.

Not a drop of fresh water was found anywhere, though frequently dug for. There were not the smallest traces of any human being having ever been here before us. The few coconut trees upon the island did not exceed thirty in number. I judge the island to be about 45 or 60 miles in circumference. Under the low trees sat infinite numbers of terns that were black above and white below, with a white arch on the forehead. The land from the seacoast to the lagoon was not more than 3 miles across, and flat. We got at this island, to both ships, about three hundred turtles, weighing each about 90 or 100 pounds. They were all of the green kind; and perhaps as good as any in the world. As we kept our Christmas here, I called this discovery Christmas Island. ⧉

HAWAIIAN LANDFALL ⧉ On the second of January, at daybreak, we weighed anchor and resumed our course to the north. On the morning of the eighteenth an island made its appearance, and soon we saw more land entirely detached from the former. Both had the appearance of being high land. Our latitude was 21° 12′ north and longitude 159° 19′ west. We had now light airs and calms, so that at sunset we were not less than 9 or 10 leagues from the nearest land. On the nine-

teenth, at sunrise, we had a fine breeze at east by north, so I steered
for the east end of the second island. At this time we were in some
doubt whether or not the land before us was inhabited, but this doubt
was soon cleared up by seeing some canoes coming off from the shore
toward the ships. I immediately brought to, to give them time to join
us. On their approach we were agreeably surprised to find that they
spoke the language of Tahiti. It required but little address to get them
to come alongside, but no entreaties could prevail upon any of them
to come on board. These people were of a brown color, and though
of the common size, were stoutly made. Some of their visages were
not unlike those of Europeans. In general they wore beards and had
no ornaments. Some were punctured on the hands or near the groin,
though in a small degree. They seemed very mild and had no arms of
any kind.

Seeing no signs of an anchoring place at this eastern extreme of
the island, I bore away to leeward and ranged along the southeast
side at the distance of half a league from the shore. Canoes came off
as we proceeded along the coast, bringing with them roasting pigs
and some very fine potatoes. Several small pigs were purchased for
a sixpenny nail, so that we again found ourselves in a land of plenty—
and just at the time when the turtles we had procured at Christmas
Island were nearly expended.

The inhabitants crowded to the shore and collected themselves on
elevated places to view the ships. The land upon this side of the island
rises in a gentle slope from the sea to the foot of the mountain, which
occupies the center of the country. We continued to sound without
striking ground with a line of 50 fathoms till we came to the northwest end. Night now put a stop to any further researches, and we spent
it standing off and on.

The next morning we stood in for the land and were met with
several canoes filled with people, and some of the people took courage
and ventured on board. In the course of my several voyages, I never
before met with natives of any place so much astonished as these
people were upon entering a ship. Their entire ignorance about everything they saw indicated that till now they had never been visited by
Europeans nor been acquainted with any of our commodities except
iron; which, however, it was plain they had only heard of, or had
known it in some small quantity brought to them at some distant
period.

They were in some respects well-bred, or at least fearful of giving offense: asking where they should sit down, whether they might spit upon the deck, and the like. There was another circumstance in which they also perfectly resembled those of other islanders: they endeavored to steal everything they came near, or rather to take it openly.

Being pretty near the shore, I sent three armed boats under the command of Mr. Williamson to look for a landing place and for fresh water. An order not to permit the crews of the boats to go on shore was issued that I might do everything in my power to prevent the importation of a fatal disease into this land which I knew some of our men labored under, and which, unfortunately, had been already communicated by us to other islands in these seas. With the same view, I ordered all female visitors to be excluded from the ships. I wished to prevent all connection which might convey an irreparable injury to them, and to the whole nation. Another necessary precaution was taken by strictly enjoining that no person known to be capable of propagating the infection should be sent on duty out of the ships.

Whether these regulations, dictated by humanity, had the desired effect, time only can discover. I had been equally attentive to the same object when I first visited the Friendly Islands; yet I afterward found, with real concern, that I had not succeeded. I am much afraid that this will always be the case in such voyages as ours. The opportunity and inducements to an intercourse between the sexes are too numerous to be guarded against. However confident we may be of the health of our men, we are often undeceived too late. Among a number of men there are to be found some so bashful as to conceal their laboring under any symptoms of this disorder, and there are others so profligate as not to care to whom they communicate it.

While the boats were occupied in examining the coast, we stood off and on with the ships, waiting for their return. Mr. Williamson came back and reported that he had seen a large pond behind a beach near one of the villages, which the natives told him contained fresh water, and there was anchoring ground before it. He also reported that he had attempted to land but was prevented by the natives coming down to the boats in great number and attempting to take away the oars, muskets, and in short, everything that they could lay hold of. They pressed so thick upon him that he was obliged to fire, by which one man was killed. It did not appear to Mr. Williamson that the natives had any design to kill, or even hurt, any of his party; but rather, they seemed excited by curiosity. I bore down with the ships and anchored in 25 fathoms, the bottom of fine gray sand. (*Cook's first anchorage in the Hawaiian Islands was on the island of Kauai, on the southwest side of the island, near the village of Waimea.*)

The ships being thus stationed, I went ashore with three armed boats. The very instant I leaped on shore, the collected body of natives all fell flat upon their faces and remained in that very humble posture till by signs I prevailed upon them to rise. They brought a great many small pigs, which they presented to me, using much the same ceremonies we had seen practiced, on such occasions at the Society and other islands. I expressed my acceptance of their proffered friendship by giving them in return such presents as I had brought from the ship for that purpose. Some of the natives conducted me to the water, which proved very good, and in a proper situation for our purpose. Having satisfied myself about this essential point, and about the agreeable disposition of the natives, I returned on board and gave orders that everything should be in readiness for landing and filling the water casks in the morning.

We met with no obstruction in watering; on the contrary, the natives assisted our men in rolling the casks to and from the pool. Everything thus going to my satisfaction, and considering my presence on the spot unnecessary, I left command to Mr. Williamson and made an excursion into the country, up the valley, accompanied by Mr. Anderson and Mr. Webber. A numerous train of natives followed us, and one of them I made choice of as our guide. This man, from time to time, proclaimed our approach, and every one we met with fell prostrate upon the ground and remained in that position until we had passed. This, I understood, is the mode of paying respect to their own great Chiefs. We had observed at every village one or more elevated white objects like pyramids, or rather, obelisks. One of these, which I guessed to be at least 50 feet high, was very conspicuous from the ship's anchoring station. To have a nearer inspection of it was the principal object of my walk. The moment we got to it, we saw that it stood in a burying ground, or marae, resembling in many respects those we were so well acquainted with at other islands in this ocean, and particularly Tahiti. At one end stood what I call the pyramid but in the language of the island is named *henananoo*. It was about 4 feet square at the base; the four sides were composed of small poles interwoven with twigs and branches, forming an indifferent wickerwork, open within from bottom to top; and it had been covered with thin, light gray cloth. Before the henananoo were pieces of wood carved into something like human figures and consecrated to *Tong-arooa,* who is the god of these people. At a little distance, near the middle of the marae, were three square enclosed places with pieces of carved wood at each, and upon them a heap of fern. These we were told were the graves of three Chiefs. Before them was an oblong enclosed space, to which our conductor gave the name of *Tangata-taboo,* telling us so explicitly that we could not mistake his meaning, that three human sacrifices had been buried there, one at the funeral of each Chief. I could trace, on such evidence, the prevalence of these bloody rites throughout this immense ocean, among people disjoined by such a distance, and even ignorant of each other's existence, though so strongly marked as originally of the same nation. Every appearance led us to believe that the barbarous practice was very general here.

Our road to and from the marae lay through the plantations. The greatest part of the ground was flat with ditches full of water intersecting different parts, and roads that seemed artificially raised to some height. The interspaces were planted with taro, which grows here with great strength, as the fields are sunk below the common level so as to contain the water necessary to nourish the roots. On the drier spaces the cloth-mulberry was planted in regular rows, also growing vigorously and kept very clean.

At sunset I brought everybody on board, having procured in the course of the day: nine tons of water, and, by exchanges, chiefly for nails and pieces of iron, about seventy pigs, a few fowl, a quantity of potatoes, a few bananas and taro roots. (*Bougainville's anchor is probably supplying many of the pieces of iron used for trading here.*) These people merited our best commendations in this commercial intercourse, never once attempting to cheat us.

Among the articles which they brought to barter this day was a cloak and cap, which even in countries where dress is more particularly attended to, might be reckoned elegant. The cloaks were nearly the size and shape of the short cloaks worn by the women of England and by the men of Spain, reaching to the middle of the back and tied loosely before. Upon them the most beautiful red and yellow feathers are so closely fixed that the surface might be compared to the thickest and richest velvet. The brilliant colors of the feathers added much to their fine appearance. Some were entirely red and had a broad yellow border which made them appear like a scarlet cloak edged with gold lace. They would not, at first, part with them for anything we offered, asking no less a price than a musket. However, some were purchased for very large nails.

The cap is made almost like a helmet with a middle crest of a hand's breadth. It fits very close upon the head, having notches to admit the ears. It has a frame of twigs covered with a network, into which are wrought feathers in the same manner as upon the cloaks.

One of our visitors was observed to have a very small parcel. Being asked what it was, he pointed to his belly and spoke something of its being dead. On seeing him so anxious to conceal the contents, he was requested to open it, which he did with great reluctance. We found that it contained a thin bit of flesh, which, to appearance, had been dried but was now wet with salt water. The question being put to the person who produced it, he answered that the flesh was part of a man. Another of his countrymen was asked whether it was their custom to eat those killed in battle; he immediately answered in the affirmative. A small wooden instrument beset with shark's teeth had been purchased. From its resemblance to the saw or knife used by the New Zealanders to dissect the bodies of their enemies, it was suspected to have the same use here. One of the natives told us that it was used to cut out the fleshy part of the belly when any person was killed. This man, however, being asked if his countrymen eat the part thus cut out, denied it strongly. An old man then being asked whether they eat the flesh answered in the affirmative and laughed, seemingly at the simplicity of such a question. He also said it was excellent food, or, as he expressed it, "savory eating." I cannot see the least reason to hesitate in pronouncing it to be certain that the horrid banquet of human flesh is as much relished here, amidst plenty, as it is in New Zealand. ε∾

NIIHAU ∾ε In the night, and all the morning on the twenty-second, it rained almost continuously. The wind was at southeast and south, which brought in a short, chopping sea. As there were breakers little more than two cables' length from the stern of our ship, her situation was none of the safest, and the surf broke so high against the shore that we could not land our boats. We had prepared for the worst by dropping the small bower anchor and striking our top-gallant yards.

At seven o'clock the next morning, a breeze of wind springing up at northeast, I took up the anchors with a view of removing the ship farther out. The moment the last anchor was up, the wind veered to the east, which made it necessary to set all the sail we could in order to clear the shore, but before we had tolerable sea-room we were driven some distance to leeward. We made a stretch off with a view to regain the road, but having very little wind and a strong current against us, I found that this was not to be effected. I sent an order to Captain Clerke to put to sea after me. As we drew near the west end of the island, we found the coast to round gradually to the northeast without forming a creek or cove to shelter a vessel from the force of the swell, which rolled in from the north and broke upon the shore in a prodigious surf. All hopes of finding a harbor here having vanished, I steered for Niihau in order to take a nearer view of it and to anchor there if I should find a convenient place. The currents carried us westward within 3 leagues of Niihau, and being tired with plying so unsuccessfully, I gave up all thoughts of getting back to Kauai.

Seeing a village to leeward, and some of the islanders who had come off to the ships informing us that fresh water might be got there, I ran down and came to an anchor before it in 26 fathoms. Another island, called Tahoora (*Kaula*), bore south by west, 7 leagues.

The people resembled those of Kauai and seemed equally well acquainted with the use of iron. I sent Mr. Gore ashore with a guard of marines to trade with the natives for refreshments. I intended to follow soon after, but the surf had increased so much that I was fearful if I got ashore I should not be able to get off again, and this happened to our people who landed with Mr. Gore. The communication between them and the ships by our own boats being soon stopped, the officer and twenty men were left ashore all night, but the violence of the surf, which our own boats would not act against, did not hinder the natives from coming off to the ships in their canoes. The next day the sea ran so high that we had no manner of communication with our party on shore, and even the natives themselves dared not venture out in their canoes. Thus our party had another night to improve their intercourse with the natives.

I sent a boat, as soon as daylight returned, to the southeast point with an order to Mr. Gore to march up to the point. I went myself in the pinnace, taking with me a ram goat, two ewes, a boar and sow, and the seeds of melons, pumpkins, and onions, being desirous of benefiting these poor people by furnishing them with additional articles of food.

I landed with the greatest of ease under the west side of the point and found my party already there with some of the natives in company. While the people were engaged in filling water casks from a small stream occasioned by the late rain, I walked a little way up the country. The Chief began to mutter something which I supposed was a prayer, and two men who carried pigs continued to walk round me all the time, making at least a dozen circuits. The ceremony being performed, we proceeded. Presently, we met people coming from other parts who, on being called to by the attendants, threw themselves prostrate on their faces till I was out of sight.

There was no appearance of any running stream, and though we found some small wells in which fresh water was tolerably good, it seemed scarce. The natives were thinly scattered about, and it was supposed that there could not be more than five hundred people upon the island. The method of living among the natives appeared decent and clean.

After the water casks had been filled, I returned on board with all my people. &

THE SANDWICH ISLANDS ⋅≼ It is worthy of observation that the islands in the Pacific Ocean which our late voyages have added to the geography of the globe have been generally found lying in groups or clusters. Of what number this newly discovered archipelago consists must be left for future investigation. We saw five of them whose names as given by the natives are: Woahoo (*Oahu*), Atooi (*Kauai*), Oneeheow (*Niihau*), Oreehoua (*Lehua*), and Tahoara (*Kaula*). The last, we were told, abounds with birds, which are its only inhabitants. Besides the five which we can distinguish by their names, it appeared that the inhabitants were acquainted with some other islands both to the eastward and westward. I named the whole group the Sandwich Islands in honor of the Earl of Sandwich. Of Oahu, the most easterly of these islands seen by us, we could get no other intelligence but that it is high land and is inhabited.

The inhabitants could be tolerably well understood by those of us who had acquired an acquaintance with the dialects of the South Pacific Islands. It is, however, regretted that we should be obliged, so soon, to leave a place which seemed to be highly worthy of a more accurate examination.

The anchoring place which we occupied on Kauai is on the south-west side, about 6 miles from the west end, before a village which was known by the name of Wymoa. (*The village is still there, the modern spelling is* Waimea.)

The land does not in the least resemble any of the islands we have hitherto visited within the tropic on the south side of the equator. Though it be destitute of the delightful verdure of Tahiti and the luxuriant plains of Tongatapu, covered with trees which afford a friendly shelter from the scorching sun and an enchanting prospect to the eye, and food for the natives which may be truly said to drop from the trees into their mouths without the laborious task of rearing; though, I say, Kauai be destitute of these advantages, its possessing a greater quantity of gently rising land renders it superior to the above favorite islands as being more capable of improvement. From the wooded part to the sea the ground is covered with an excellent sort of grass, about 2 feet high, which grows in tufts. The soil is of brownish-black color, somewhat loose. Upon the high ground it changed to a reddish brown, more stiff and clayish. It produces taro of a much larger size than any we had ever seen, and the sweet potatoes often weigh 10, and sometimes 12 or 14 pounds. (*To this day, Kauai is known as the "Garden Island."*)

Few of those inconveniences which many tropical countries are subject to, either from heat or moisture, seem to be experienced here.

The inhabitants are vigorous, active, and most expert swimmers, leaving their canoes upon the most trifling occasion, diving under them, and swimming to others at a great distance. It was very common to see women with infants at the breast, when the surf was so high that they could not land in the canoes, leap overboard and without endangering their little ones swim to the shore through a sea that looked dreadful. The people seem to be blessed with a frank, cheerful disposition; they live very socially in their intercourse with one another, and they were exceedingly friendly to us. It was a pleasure to observe with how much affection the women managed their infants, and how readily the men lent their assistance to such tender office. From the numbers which we saw collected at every village as we sailed past, it may be supposed that the inhabitants of this island are numerous. Allowing five persons to each house, there would be in every village five hundred, or thirty thousand upon the island. This number is certainly not exaggerated, for we sometimes had three thousand persons, at least, on the beach.

There is no appearance of defense or fortification near any of the villages, and the houses are scattered about without order. Nevertheless, probably wars among themselves are frequent. This might be inferred from the number of weapons which we found them in possession of, and from the excellent order these were kept in. As we understood from their own confession, these wars are between the different districts of their island as well as between it and their neighbors. We need scarcely assign any other cause to account for the appearance of their population bearing no proportion to the extent of their ground capable of cultivation. Notwithstanding this skill in agriculture, the appearance of the island showed that it was capable of much more extensive improvement and of maintaining at least three times the number of inhabitants that are at present upon it.

The greatest part of their vegetable food consists of sweet potatoes, taro, and bananas. The breadfruit and yams are esteemed rarities. Of animal food they can be in no want, as they have an abundance of hogs, which run about the houses, and if they eat dogs, which is not improbable, their stock of these seemed to be considerable. The great number of fishing hooks among them showed that they derive no inconsiderable supply of food from the sea. The taro pudding, though a disagreeable mess from its sourness, was greedily devoured by the natives.

The only iron tools, or rather, bits of iron, seen among them and which they had before our arrival were a piece of iron hoop about 2 inches long fitted into a wooden handle, and another edge tool which our people guessed to be made of the point of a broad sword. Their having the actual possession of these, and their knowing the use of the metal, inclined some on board to think that we had not been the first European visitors of these islands. There are many ways by which such people may get pieces of iron or acquire the knowledge of the existence of such a metal without ever having had an immediate connection with nations that use it. It is well known that Roggewein lost one of his ships on the "Pernicious Islands," which from their situation are probably known, though not frequently visited, to the inhabitants of Tahiti. It is certain these people had a knowledge of iron when Captain Wallis discovered Tahiti; before Captain Wallis' arrival, a Chief of Tahiti had gotten two nails in his possession. Is there not the extensive continent of America to windward, where the Spaniards have been settled for more than two hundred years, during which long period of time shipwrecks must have frequently happened on its coast? It cannot be at all extraordinary that parts of such wrecks, containing iron, should by the easterly trade wind be, from time to time, cast upon islands scattered about the vast ocean. The distance from Kauai to America is no argument against this supposition. This ocean is traversed every year by Spanish ships (*going to and from Guam and Manila*) and it is obvious that besides the accident of losing a mast and its appendages, casks with iron hoops and other things containing iron may be thrown, or fall, overboard during so long a passage. One of my people actually did see some wood in one of the houses at Waimea which he judged to be fir. It was worm-eaten and the natives gave him to understand that it had been driven ashore by the waves of the sea. We had their testimony that they had gotten the specimens of iron found among them from some place to the eastward. Had the Sandwich Islands been discovered at an early period by the Spaniards, there is little doubt that they would have taken advantage of so excellent a situation and have made use of Kauai or some other of the islands as a refreshing place for the ships that sail annually from Acapulco for Manila. &

The evidence is that at least one Spanish ship touched at the Hawaiian Islands before Cook, and there may have been others. There are records that the Spanish navigator Gaetano found the Hawaiian Islands in 1555, only thirty-four years after Magellan crossed the Pacific. The Spanish visits were kept secret, so secret that the knowledge of the islands was lost even to themselves. The bits of iron Cook discovered here may nevertheless have been washed ashore much as Cook conjectured. The finding of a "point of a broad sword" suggests, however, that it may have been left there by an actual Spanish visitor a century or two earlier.

The language of the Sandwich Islands may be said to be almost word for word the same as Tahiti. How shall we account for this nation having spread itself to so many detached islands so widely disjoined from each other in every quarter of the Pacific Ocean? We find these people from New Zealand in the south as far as the Sandwich Islands to the north! And in another direction from Easter Island to the Hebrides! This is over an extent of 60° of latitude (*3,600 miles*) and 83° of longitude (*4,690 miles*) east and west! How much farther in either direction its colonies reach is not known; but what we know already in consequence of this voyage warrants our pronouncing it to be, by far, the most extensive nation upon earth. ও

Anthropologists, archaeologists, and historians have continued to marvel at the spread of the Polynesian people over so vast an ocean on so many tiny and isolated islands. Thor Heyerdahl had a theory that they drifted with the winds and currents from a South American stock of people. The more accepted theory is that they moved to windward, spreading out eastward from Asia.

Indisputably these people at one time had the ability and know-how to make long ocean voyages. The large sailing catamarans, carrying up to seventy people with shelter and cooking fires on deck, which Cook saw in the Tonga Islands, would be capable of voyaging from Tonga or Tahiti to Hawaii. It is not unlikely that in the period when these people were making long voyages that they traveled also to the American continent—Peru and Chile—and some American Indian people may have also moved with the Polynesian voyagers westward into the Pacific Islands. On Easter Island there may have been a blending of the Polynesian and South-American Indian cultures and peoples.

The remarkable resemblance of the language, customs, religion, and arts of the Hawaiians to that of the Tahitians suggests that the cessation of the period of ocean-voyaging was not very many generations before Cook arrived, and that the Hawaiian settlers originally came from Tahiti. But where they came from, not even the Hawaiians knew. Curiously they had retained the knowledge and arts of their Polynesian culture, but had lost the knowledge of their origin. They no longer knew of any other populated lands. Ledyard's statement that the New Zealanders spoke of coming from an island called "Hawyjee" may or may not be an accurate recording of what he heard.

CHAPTER SEVENTEEN

THE COAST OF NORTH AMERICA

February 3, 1778——March 30, 1778

UNPLANNED DEPARTURE FROM THE SANDWICH ISLANDS ✒ I intended
to visit the island the next day, but about seven in the evening, the
anchor of the *Resolution* started and she drove off the bank. As we
had a whole cable out, it was some time before the anchor was at
the bow and then we had the launch to hoist up alongside before we
could make sail. By this unlucky accident we found ourselves at daybreak next morning 3 leagues to the leeward of our last station. Fore-
seeing that it would require more time to recover our position than
I chose to spend, I made the signal for the *Discovery* to weigh and
join us. We were obliged to leave before we had completed our water
and got from them such a quantity of refreshments as their inhabitants
were both able and willing to supply us with. After the *Discovery*
joined us, we stood away to the northward, closehauled, with a gentle
gale from the east. ✑

VOYAGING NORTH ✒ On the seventh of February, being in the latitude
of 29° north, the wind veered to southeast. This enabled us to steer
northeast and east, which course we continued till the twelfth, when
the wind went round by the south and west. I then tacked and stood
to the northward, our latitude being 30° north. Notwithstanding our
advanced latitude and its being the winter season, we had only begun
for a few days past to feel a sensation of cold in the mornings and
evenings.

On the first of March, our latitude being now 49° 49′ north and

191

our longitude 132° west, I stood to the east, closehauled, in order to
make the land. According to the charts it ought not to have been far
from us. From the few signs of the vicinity of land hitherto met with,
we might have concluded that there was none within some thousand
leagues of us. It was remarkable that we should still be attended with
such moderate and mild weather so far to the northward at this time
of year. We can assign no reason why Sir Francis Drake should have
met with such severe cold about this latitude in the month of June.
Viscaino, who was near the same place in the depth of winter, says
little of the cold and speaks of a ridge of snowy mountains somewhere
on the coast. ﻉ

Sebastian Viscaino, in a voyage during the years of 1602–03, carefully explored the West Coast of America when the region was the
Spanish province of California.

NORTH AMERICA ﻉ At daybreak (*the morning of the seventh of
March*) the long-looked-for coast of New Albion (*this portion of
North America was named New Albion by Sir Francis Drake when
he sighted portions of the coast in 1579*) was seen, distance of 10 or
12 leagues. At noon our latitude was 44° 33′ north and our longitude
124° 40′ west. We had 73 fathoms water over a muddy bottom. At
the northern extreme, the land formed a point which I called Cape
Foulweather from the very bad weather that we soon after met with.
(*This cape retains the same name that Cook gave it and can be found
on any ordinary highway map of Oregon.*)
    Our difficulties now began to increase. In the evening the wind came
to the northwest, blowing in squalls with hail and sleet, and the
weather being thick and hazy I stood out to sea. Two days later I
ventured to stand in. At four in the afternoon we saw land again. The
land is of moderate height but in some places it rises higher within,
and many of the hills are covered with tall, straight trees. The whole,
though it might make an agreeable summer prospect, had now an
uncomfortable appearance, as the bare ground was all covered with
snow which seemed to be of a considerable depth. The northern
point was first seen on the seventh, and on that account I called it
Cape Perpetua; it lies in the latitude of 44° 6′ north. The southern
extreme I named Cape Gregory, its latitude is 43° 30′. It is a remarkable point, the land rising almost directly from the sea to a tolerable

height, while that on the east side of it is low. (In our calendar, the seventh of March is distinguished by the name of Perpetua M., and the twelfth by that of Gregory B.)

This is nearly the situation of Cape Blanco discovered by Martin d'Aquilar on the nineteenth of January, 1603. In the very latitude where we now were, geographers have been pleased to place a large entrance or strait, the discovery of which they take upon themselves to ascribe to d'Aquilar. Nothing more is mentioned in the account of his voyage than his having seen, in this situation, a large river, which he would have entered but was prevented by the currents. ⁊

The river that d'Aquilar saw but could not enter must have been the Columbia River. The point d'Aquilar called Cape Blanco is the westernmost promontory in Oregon, it actually lies 100 miles south of Cape Perpetua, and the mouth of the Columbia River lies 140 miles *north* of Cape Perpetua. Cook's latitudes were accurate but those on old charts of early discoveries were not. The existence of the Columbia River was not proven until Captain Robert Gray, of the ship *Columbia,* out of Boston, sailed into the river in 1792 and gave his discovery the name of his ship. Gray's explorations were the beginning basis of United States' claims to the Oregon Territory and the Columbia river basin.

⁊ The wind was very unsettled and blew in squalls with snow showers. At midnight it increased to a very hard gale at northwest, attended with sleet and snow. There was no choice now; we were obliged to stretch to the southward in order to clear the coast. This was done under courses and two close-reefed top-sails—rather more sail than the ships could safely bear—but it was necessary to carry it to avoid the more pressing danger of being forced ashore.

On the morning of the twenty-first a breeze sprung up at southwest. This bringing fair weather, I steered northeasterly in order to fall in with the land beyond that part of it where we had already so unprofitably been tossed about for the last fortnight, and the next morning we saw land. At this time we were in the latitude of 47° 5' north. I continued to stand to the north until we were about 4 leagues from the land. A round hill had the appearance of being an island. Between this island or rock and the extreme of the land, there appeared to be a small opening which flattered us with the hopes of finding a harbor.

These hopes lessened as we drew nearer, for the opening was closed
by low land. On this account I called the point of land to the north
of it Cape Flattery. It lies in the latitude of 48° 15′ north. It is in
this very latitude where we now were that geographers have placed
the pretended strait of Juan de Fucca. We saw nothing like it, nor is
there the least probability that ever any such thing existed. (See
Lache's apocryphal account of Juan de Fucca and his pretended
strait.) ટ✍

As can be seen from above, Cook was approaching the point of
land which he called Cape Flattery from the south. Had he moved
only a few miles to the north so as to pass to the north of this Cape,
he would have sailed right into the Strait of Juan de Fucca. Cook
thereby missed confirming the existence of not only the Columbia
River but this great inlet to Puget Sound as well. Had he sailed in,
the British claims to this territory would have been much more indis-
putable when the conflict concerning the northwest border arose between the United States and Canada in the "Fifty-four-forty or fight"
ruckus of 1844–46.

✍ I stood off to the southward until night, when I tacked and steered
northwest. We were reduced to two courses and, close-reefed top-sails
having a very hard gale, instead of running in for the land I was glad
to get an offing and to keep that which we had already gotten. (*He
was now crossing the mouth of the strait and he could have, though
he did not know it, run in safely.*)
     At length, on the morning of the twenty-ninth, we again saw land.
Our latitude was now 49° 29′ north. The appearance of the country
differed much from that of the parts which we had seen before, being
full of high mountains whose summits were covered with snow. The
ground was covered with high, straight trees that formed a beautiful
prospect of one vast forest. The southeast extreme of land was called
Point Breakers, the other extreme I named Woody Point. Between
these two points the shore forms a large bay, which I called Hope Bay,
hoping to find in it a good harbor and a comfortable station to supply
all our wants, and to make us forget the hardships and delays experienced during a constant succession of adverse winds and boisterous
weather ever since our arrival upon the coast of America. The events
proved that we were not mistaken. ટ✍

CHAPTER EIGHTEEN

NOOTKA SOUND, VANCOUVER ISLAND

March 31, 1778——April 25, 1778

NOOTKA SOUND ✒ We no sooner drew near the inlet than we found the coast to be inhabited, and three canoes came off to the ship. A person, who played the orator, wore the skin of some animal and held in each hand something which rattled as he kept shaking it. After tiring himself with his repeated exhortations, of which we did not understand a word, he was quiet, and then the others by turns said something. After the tumultuous noise had ceased, they lay at a little distance from the ship and canoes began to come off in greater number. We had at one time thirty-two of them near the ship. Though our visitors behaved very peaceably and could not be suspected of any hostile intention, we could not prevail upon any of them to come on board. They showed a great readiness, however, to part with anything they had, and took from us whatever we offered in exchange, but were more desirous of iron than any other article, appearing to be perfectly acquainted with the use of the metal.

I lost no time in endeavoring to find a commodious harbor where we might station ourselves during our continuance in the Sound. Accordingly, I sent three armed boats under the command of Mr. King upon this service, and soon after went myself in a small boat on the same search. Not far from the ships, I met with a convenient snug cove well suited to our purpose. We employed the next day in hauling our ships into the cove, where they were moored, head and stern, fastening our hawsers to the trees on shore.

Our arrival brought a great concourse of natives to our ships; we counted more than a hundred canoes. A trade commenced betwixt us and them, which was carried on with strident honesty on both sides. The articles which they offered to sell were skins of bears, wolves, foxes, deer, raccoons, polecats, martins, and in particular sea otters. They also brought weapons such as bows, arrows, and spears, fishhooks, instruments of various kinds, and wooden visors of many different monstrous figures. The most extraordinary of all articles which they brought to the ships for sale were human skulls and hands not yet quite stripped of the flesh, which they made our people plainly understand they had eaten. They now appeared to have laid fear aside, for they came on board the ships and mixed with our people with the greatest freedom. We soon discovered that they were as light-fingered as any of our friends in the islands we had visited in the course of this voyage. They were far more dangerous thieves; for, possessing sharp iron instruments, they could cut a hook from a tackle, or any other piece of iron from a rope, the instant our backs were turned. One fellow would contrive to amuse the boatkeeper at one end of a boat while another was pulling out the ironwork at the other.

We also got from these people a considerable quantity of very good animal oil, which they saved in bladders. In this traffic some would attempt to cheat us by mixing water with the oil, or carrying their imposition so far as to fill their bladders with mere water without a single drop of oil. It was always better to bear with these tricks than to make them the foundation of a quarrel. Our articles of traffic consisted for the most part of mere trifles, and yet we were put to our shifts to find a constant supply of these. Nothing would go down with our visitors but metal. Brass had by this time supplanted iron, being so eagerly sought after, that before we left this place hardly a bit of it was left in the ships. Whole suits of clothes were stripped of every button, bureaus of their furniture, copper kettles, tin canisters, candlesticks and the like, all went to wreck. Our American friends here got a greater medley and variety of things from us than any other nation whom we had visited in the course of this voyage.

We were visited by some strangers in two or three large canoes, who, by signs, made our people understand that they had come from the southeast, beyond the bay. What was most singular, two silver tablespoons were purchased from them, which, from their peculiar shape, we supposed to be of Spanish manufacture. ᙏ

ROT IN THE RIGGING ⋙ I employed the day in ordering the sails to be unbent, the topmasts to be struck and the fore-mast of the *Resolution* to be unrigged in order to fix a new bib, one of the old ones being decayed. The forge was set up to make the ironwork necessary for the repairs of the fore-mast. Besides one of the bibs being defective, the larboard trestletree and one of the iron trees were sprung. In cutting into the masthead and examining the state of it, both checks were found to be so rotten that there was no possibility of repairing them, and it became necessary to get the mast out. It was fortunate for the voyage that these defects were discovered when we were in a place where the materials requisite were to be procured. We got the fore-mast out and hauled it ashore, and the carpenters were set to work on it. Some parts of the lower-standing rigging having been found to be much decayed, we had time now to put them in order.

According to the old proverb: Misfortunes seldom come single. The mizzen was now the only mast on board the *Resolution* that remained rigged with its top-mast up, and it was so defective that it could not support the latter during the violence of a squall but gave way at the head under the rigging. Our employment, the day after, was to take down the mizzen-mast, the head of which proved to be so rotten that it dropped off while in the slings. In the afternoon I went into the woods with a party of men and cut down a tree for a new mizzen-mast. It was brought to the place where the carpenters were employed upon the fore-mast. The carpenters were also set to work to make a new fore-top-mast to replace the one that had been carried away some time before. After a fortnight of bad weather, the nineteenth proving a fair day, we availed ourselves of it to get up the top-masts, yards, and to fix up the rigging. The mizzen-mast being finished, it was got in and rigged on the twenty-first. ⋙

THE NATURAL HISTORY OF NOOTKA SOUND ⋙ The climate is infinitely milder than that of the East Coast of America under the same parallel of latitude. The thermometer never, even in the night, fell lower than 42°, and very often in the day it rose to 60°. No such thing as frost was perceived in any of the low ground. The trees grow with great vigor and are all of large size.

The sea otter, living mostly in the water, abounds here. It is fully described in the accounts of the Russian adventurers in their expeditions eastward from Kamchatka. The fur of these animals, as men-

tioned in the Russian accounts, is certainly softer and finer than that
of any others we know of. Therefore the discovery of this part of the
continent of North America, where so valuable an article of commerce may be met with, cannot be a matter of indifference. (Old and
middle-aged sea-otter skins are sold by the Russians to the Chinese
for 80 to 100 rubles a skin.) ॐ

THE NOOTKA INDIAN ॐ The persons of the natives are, in general,
under the common stature, being commonly full or plump though
not muscular. Their color we could never positively determine, as
their bodies were incrusted with paint and dirt. When these were
well rubbed off, the whiteness of the skin appeared almost equal to
that of Europeans of our southern nations. Their children, whose
skins had never been stained with paint, equaled ours in whiteness.
A remarkable sameness characterized the countenances of the whole
nation—a dull, phlegmatic want of expression with very little variation. The women are nearly of the same size, color, and form with
the men, from whom it is not easy to distinguish them. They possess
no natural delicacies sufficient to render their person agreeable. Hardly
anyone was seen, even among those in the prime of life, who had
the least pretension to be called handsome. As they rub their bodies
constantly with a red paint of a clayey ocher substance mixed with
oil, their garments contract a rancid, offensive smell and a greasy
nastiness, so that they make a very wretched, dirty appearance. What
is still worse, their heads and their garments swarm with vermin,
which, so depraved is their taste for cleanliness, we used to see them
pick off with great composure and eat.

They faces are often stained with a black, bright red, or white color.
The last of these gives them a ghostly, disgusting aspect. They also
strew mica upon the paint, which makes it glitter. The ears are perforated in the lobe, where they make a large hole, and two others
higher up on the outer edge. In these holes they hang bits of bone,
quills, small shells, tassels, or thin copper. The septum of the nose is
also perforated where they wear small pieces of iron, brass, or copper
shaped like a horseshoe; the ornament thus hangs over the upper lip.

They assume what may be called monstrous decorations. These
consist of an endless variety of carved wooden masks applied to the
face on the upper part of the head. Some resemble human faces,
others the heads of birds, particularly eagles, and many the heads of

animals such as wolves, deer, porpoises, and others. These representations much exceed natural size. They even fix on the head large pieces of carved work, resembling the prow of a canoe and projecting to a considerable distance (*see illustration*). Whether they use these extravagant masquerade ornaments on any particular religious occasion, diversion, or to intimidate their enemies, is uncertain. So fond are they of these disguises that I have seen one of them put his head into a tin kettle he got from us for want of another sort of mask. Though these people cannot be viewed without a kind of horror when equipped in such extravagant dress, yet when divested of them and beheld in their common habit, they have not the least appearance of ferocity, and seem, on the contrary, to be of a quiet, phlegmatic, and inactive disposition, destitute in some measure of animation and vivacity that would render them agreeable social beings. They were thieves in the strictest sense of the word, for they pilfered nothing from us but what had a real value according to their estimation of things. Linen and such things were perfectly secure from their depredations; we could securely leave items hanging out ashore all night without watching. However, their eagerness to possess iron and brass and any metal was so great, that few could resist the temptation to steal it whenever an opportunity offered.

Their houses are built of very long and broad planks, resting on the edges of each other and tied by withes of pink bark, and have only slender poles at considerable distance on the outside, to which they are also tied. They are, upon the whole, miserable dwellings and constructed with little care or ingenuity. On the inside, one may see from one end to the other without interruption. The accommodations of different families are such as to not intercept the sight. The whole might be compared to a long stable with a double range of stalls and a broad passage in the middle. In the middle of the floor is the fireplace, which has neither hearth nor chimney. Their furniture consists chiefly of a great number of chests and boxes of all sizes piled upon each other close to the sides of the house and contain spare garments, skins, masks, and other things they value.

Their fishing implements and other things also lie or hang up in different parts of the house without the least order, so the whole is a complete scene of confusion. The sleeping benches have nothing on them but mats.

The nastiness and stench of their houses are equal to the confu-

NOOTKA INDIAN HEADPIECE

Credit: Courtesy of American Museum of Natural History

sion. They dry their fish indoors, where they also gut them, which, with their bones and fragments thrown down at meals and the addition of other sorts of filth, lie everywhere in heaps and are, I believe, never carried away. In a word, their houses are as filthy as hog sties— everything in and about them stinking of fish, oil, and smoke.

But amidst all the filth and confusion, many are decorated with images. These are the trunks of very large trees, 4 or 5 feet high, set up singly or by pairs, with the front carved into a human face, the arms and hands cut out upon the sides and painted so that the whole is truly a monstrous figure. It was natural for us to think they were representatives of their gods, or symbols of some religious object. But we had proof of the little real estimation they were in, for with a small quantity of iron or brass I could have purchased all the gods in the place.

The young men appeared to be a most indolent and idle set in this community. They were either sitting about in scattered companies to bask themselves in the sun, or lay wallowing in the sand on the beach like a number of hogs for the same purpose, without any covering. This disregard of decency was confined to the men; the women were always properly clothed and behaved with utmost propriety, justly deserving all commendation for a bashfulness and modesty becoming their sex.

They spend a great deal of time in their canoes. We observed that they not only eat and sleep in them, but strip off their clothes and lay themselves along to bask in the sun. Their canoes are sufficiently spacious for the purpose and perfectly dry. Under the shelter of a skin, they are much more comfortable habitations than their houses. Their canoes are of a simple structure—even the largest, which carry twenty people or more, are formed of one tree. Many of them are 40 feet long, 7 feet broad, and about 3 feet deep. Their breadth and flatness enable them to swim firmly without any outrigger, which none of them have. They have great dexterity in managing their paddles, but sails are no part of their art of navigation.

Though we found among them things doubtless of European manufacture, or at least derived from some civilized nation, it by no means appears that they received them immediately from these nations. We never observed the least sign of their having seen ships like ours before, nor of their having traded with such people. Some accounts of a Spanish voyage to their coast in 1774 or 1775 had reached England

A VIEW OF THE
NOOTKA

HABITATIONS OF
SOUND

THE INSIDE OF
NOOTKA

*A HOUSE IN
SOUND*

before I sailed, but the circumstances prove that these ships had not been at Nootka. The most probable way, therefore, by which we can suppose that they get their iron is by trading for it with other Indian tribes who either have communication with European settlements on the continent or receive it through several intermediate nations. Whether these things be introduced by way of Hudson's Bay and Canada from the Indians who deal with traders, and so successively cross from one tribe to another, or whether they be brought from the northwestern part of Mexico in the same manner, cannot be easily determined. ৯৺

CHAPTER NINETEEN

EXPLORATIONS AND DISCOVERIES IN SOUTHERN ALASKA

April 26, 1778——May 25, 1778

OUT TO SEA FROM NOOTKA SOUND   Cook had spent nearly a month in Nootka Sound. Most of the time was spent repairing his ship. The *Resolution,* more than the *Discovery,* seemed to be in bad shape and required considerable repair.

⋙ Everything being now ready, on the morning of the twenty-sixth I intended to put to sea, but the wind and tide being against us, I was obliged to wait till noon. The tide turning in our favor, we cast off the moorings and with our boats towed the ships out of the cove. The mercury in the barometer fell unusually low and we had every other forerunner of an approaching storm, which we expected would be from the southward. This made me hesitate a little whether I should venture to sail. But my anxious impatience to proceed upon the voyage, making a greater impression on my mind that any apprehension of immediate danger, I determined to put to sea at all events.

Our friends the natives attended us till we were almost out of the Sound. One of their chiefs, who had attached himself to me, was among the last who left us. He, and also many others of his countrymen, importuned us much to pay them another visit and by way of encouragement promised to lay in a good stock of skins. I have no doubt that whoever comes after me to this place will find the natives prepared accordingly with no inconsiderable supply of an article for which they could observe we were eager to trade. ⋙

Cook's discovery of the potential fur trade in this region was soon followed up by traders and trappers. In time, many worked their way

overland from Canada and the United States; but the first to return
were members of his present crew. George Dixon, the armorer, and
Nathaniel Portlock, the master's mate, returned here in 1785. They
sailed together in the service of the "King George's Sound Company"
organized for the express purpose of developing the fur trade. Dixon
was in command of the *Queen Charlotte* and Portlock commanded
the *King George*.

Coincident with their commercial interests, Dixon discovered a
large island north of Vancouver and gave it the name of his ship,
Queen Charlotte. The strait north of this island is known as Dixon
Entrance. A younger shipmate of these two men, George Vancouver,
midshipman on the *Discovery*, returned in command of an exploring
expedition in 1793. By sailing around it, he proved the existence of
the island that bears his name, and mapped much of Puget Sound.
Joseph Billings, a seaman also from the *Discovery*, entered the Russian Navy, and in 1788 was sent out by Empress Catherine to explore
Alaska and the North American coast. There were others who no
doubt wanted to return to make their fortunes here, but did not get
the chance. John Ledyard from Connecticut earnestly tried to raise
interest and financial support in America for such a venture, but was
not successful.

*§ We were hardly out of the Sound before the wind shifted to south-
east and increased to a strong gale with squalls and rain, and so dark
a sky that we could not see the length of the ship. Being apprehensive
from the experience I had since our arrival on this coast of the wind
veering more to the south, which would put us in danger of a lee-
shore, we got the tacks on board and stretched off to the southwest
under all the sail the ships could bear, so by daylight the next morning
we were quite clear of the coast. In the afternoon it blew a perfect
hurricane, so that I judged it highly dangerous to run before it, and
therefore brought the ships to, with their heads to the southward
under the fore-sails and mizzen stay-sail. At this time, the *Resolution*
sprang a leak, which alarmed us not a little. It was found to be under
the starboard buttocks, and we could both hear and see the water
rush in. The fish-room was found to be full of water and the casks in
it afloat, but this was in great measure owing to the water not finding
its way to the pump through the coal that lay in the bottom of the
room. The leak was afterward found to be even with the waterline,

if not above it. After the water was bailed out, it appeared that one pump kept it under, which gave us no small satisfaction. I continued the same course until the thirtieth, when I steered north by west in order to make the land. I regretted that I could not do it sooner for the reason that we were now passing the place where geographers have placed the pretended Strait of Admiral de Fonte. (*Cook was now crossing the entrance to Queen Charlotte Sound*). I gave no credit to such vague and improbable stories. Nevertheless, I was desirous of keeping the American coast aboard in order to clear up this point beyond dispute. But it would have been highly imprudent of me to have engaged with the land in weather so exceedingly tempestuous. &

ALASKAN LANDFALL ⋖ On the first of May, seeing nothing of the land, I steered northeasterly, and at seven in the evening we got sight of land. Drawing nearer the land, I steered northwest by north with some showers of hail, snow, and sleet. An arm of the bay seemed to extend in toward the north behind a round, elevated mountain that lies between it and the sea. This mountain I called Mount Edgecumbe and the point of land that shoots out from it, Cape Edgecumbe. (*This inlet is the entrance to the present port of Sitka.*) Mount Edgecumbe far out-tops all the other hills and is wholly covered with snow, but the lower ones bordering the sea are free from it and covered with wood.

As we advanced to the north we found a large bay. In the entrance of that bay are some islands, for which reason I named it the Bay of Islands. It seemed to branch into several arms, one of which turned south and may probably communicate with the bay on the east side of Cape Edgecumbe and make the land of that Cape an island. (*Cook was correct in this conjecture.*)

On the third, a large inlet bore northeast, lying under a very high-peaked mountain, which obtained the name of Mount Fairweather. The inlet was named Cross Sound, as being first seen on that day so marked in our calendar. It too branched into several arms, the largest of which turned to the northward. The southeast point of this sound is a high promontory which obtained the name of Cross Cape. The point under the peaked mountain was called Cape Fairweather.

At five in the afternoon, May 5, the summit of an elevated mountain appeared above the horizon. We supposed it to be Bering's Mount St. Elias, and it stands by that name in our charts. &

One peak in this range was later to bear the name of Mt. Cook, commemorating this voyage, and another Mt. Vancouver, in honor of his discoveries in the Pacific Northwest.

⋞§ In the direction northeast from this station was the appearance of a bay and an island off the south point of it. It is here where I suppose Commodore Bering to have anchored. The latitude, which is 59° 18′, corresponds pretty well with the map of his voyage. The bay I shall distinguish by the name of Bering's Bay, in honor of its discoverer. §⋟

Cook's name did not stick in this instance. The bay kept its Indian name of Yakutat Bay. Vitus Jonassen Bering, Danish by birth, sailed in the service of Empress Anne of Russia in search of the continent of America, east from Siberia. He landed on an island, now known as Kayak Island, 140 miles east of Yakutat Bay, but in about the same latitude.

⋞§ At noon the next day we were in the latitude of 59° 27′ and longitude of 140° 53′. From this station we could see a bay, circular in appearance, under the high land, with low woodland on each side of it (*Icy Bay*). We now found the coast to trend very much to the west, and as we had the wind mostly from the westward, and but little of it, our progress was slow. At noon, on the tenth, to the westward was an island; a point shoots out from the main toward the northeast end of this island. This point I named Cape Suckling. The point of the cape is low, but within it is a high hill, so that at a distance the cape looks like an island. On the north side of Cape Suckling is a bay that appeared to be of some extent and to be covered from most winds. To this bay I had some thoughts of going to stop our leak, as all our endeavors to do it at sea had proved ineffectual, and with this in view I steered for the Cape. As we had only variable light breezes, we approached it slowly. We saw some small islands in the bay, and elevated rocks between the Cape and the northeast end of the island, but still there appeared to be a passage on both sides of the rocks. I continued steering for them all night, having 43 to 27 fathoms over a muddy bottom. At four in the morning the wind shifted to north; it being thus against us, I gave up the design of going into the bay, as it could not be done without loss of time. I therefore bore up for

the west end of the island, but at ten it fell calm. Being not far from
the island, I went in a boat and landed upon it with a view of seeing
what lay on the other side; but finding it farther to the hills than I
had expected, and the way being steep and woody, I was obliged to
drop the design. At the foot of a tree, on a little eminence not far
from the shore, I left a bottle with a paper in it, on which were inscribed the names of the ships and the date of our discovery. Along
with it, I enclosed two silver twopenny pieces of His Majesty's coin
of the date 1772. These were furnished me by the Reverend Dr.
Kaye, and as a mark of my esteem and regard for that gentleman I
named the island Kaye's Island. The southwest point is very remarkable, being a naked rock elevated considerably above the land within.
There is also an elevated rock lying off it which, from some points
of view, appears like a ruined castle. Few trees appear larger than
one might grasp around with his arms and about 40 feet high. The
only purpose they could answer for shipping would be to make top-
gallant-masts and other small things.

In the afternoon we got around the southwest end of the island and
then stood for the westernmost land, now in sight. The bay is distinguished by the name of Controller Bay. From Controller Bay
to a point which I named Cape Hinchinbrook, the direction of the
coast is nearly east and west. ஒ

Unknowingly, Cook landed on the same small island, now called
Kayak Island, where Bering had stopped. Cook's names of Cape
Suckling, Controller Bay, and Hinchinbrook Island remain. The river,
lake, and glacier within the bay honor the name of Bering.

PRINCE WILLIAM SOUND ᛜ The coast seemed to incline to the southward, a direction so contrary to the modern charts founded on the
late Russian discoveries that we had reason to expect that by the inlet
before us we should find a passage to the north, and the land to the
west and southwest was nothing but a group of islands. Add to this:
the wind was now at southeast; we were threatened with fog and
storm; and I wanted to get into some place to stop the leak before we
encountered another gale. These reasons induced me to steer for the
inlet, which we no sooner reached than the weather became so foggy
we could not see a mile before us. I hauled close under Cape Hinchinbrook and anchored before a small cove.

Mr. Gore was sent in a boat in hopes of shooting some edible birds. He had hardly gotten to the island before about twenty natives made their appearance in two large canoes upon which Mr. Gore thought proper to return to the ships while they followed him. One man held out a white garment, which we interpreted as a sign of friendship, and another stood up in the canoe, quite naked, for almost a quarter of an hour with his arms stretched out like a cross and motionless. These canoes were not constructed of wood; the frame, only, was slender laths; and the outside consisted of the skins of seals or of such like animals. They were built and constructed in the same manner as those of the Eskimo. &

The Eskimo canoes that Cook was comparing these to were the canoes of the Eskimo of Labrador and Greenland, whom he knew from his surveying voyages on the Atlantic coast of the continent when a younger man. This similarity perhaps gave him further hope that he had found a water passage to the Atlantic coast.

& Though we returned all their signs of friendship and tried to encourage them to come alongside, we could not prevail. After receiving some presents from us, they retired toward that part of the shore from whence they came.

At ten o'clock next morning, the wind being more moderate and the weather somewhat clearer, we got under sail in order to look for some snug place where we might stop the leak. In the afternoon the bad weather returned with so thick a haze that we could see no land except a point, on the east side of which we discovered a fine bay. To this we plied up, under reefed top-sails and courses. The wind blew strong, in excessively hard squalls. At length, at eight o'clock, the violence of the squalls obliged us to anchor before we had gotten so far into the bay as I intended, but we thought ourselves fortunate that we had sufficiently secured ourselves at this hour, for the night was exceedingly stormy.

The weather, bad as it was, did not hinder the natives from paying us a visit. Many more visited us between one and two in the morning, and some ventured on board. Among these was a good-looking middle-aged man whom we found to be the Chief. He was clothed in a dress of sea-otter's skin, and his cap was ornamented with sky-blue glass beads. Any sort of beads appeared to be in high estimation with these people, and they readily gave fine sea-otter skins in exchange for them. These people were also desirous of iron, but they wanted pieces 8 or 10 inches long, for they absolutely rejected small pieces. Consequently, they got but little from us; iron having, by this time, become a rather scarce article.

After being about three hours alongside the *Resolution,* they all left her and went to the *Discovery.* These men, after looking down all the hatchways and seeing nobody but the officer of the watch and one or two more, no doubt thought they might plunder her with ease. Several of them, without any ceremony, drew their knives and made signs to the officer and people on deck to keep off and began to look for plunder. The first thing they met with was the rudder of one of the boats, which they threw overboard to those of their party who had remained in the canoes. Before they had time to find another article that pleased their fancy, the crew was alarmed and began to come on deck armed with cutlasses. On seeing this, the whole company of plunderers sneaked off, describing to those who had not been on board how much larger our knives were than theirs. I have not the least doubt that their visiting us so early in the morning was with a view to plunder, on a supposition that they would find us all asleep. However, after all these tricks, we had the good fortune to leave them as ignorant of firearms as we found them. They neither saw, nor heard, a musket fired.

I came to a resolution to heel the ship where we were. In heaving the anchor out of the boat, one of the seamen, either through ignorance or carelessness, or both, was carried overboard by the buoy-rope and followed the anchor to the bottom. In this very critical situation he had the presence of mind to disengage himself and come to the surface, where he was taken up with one of his legs fractured in a dangerous manner.

Early the next morning we gave the ship a good heel to port in order to come at the leak. On ripping off the sheathing, we found the leak to be in seams which were very open, both in and under the wale. In several places not a bit of oakum was in them.

On the evening of the sixteenth, the weather cleared up and we found ourselves surrounded on every side by land. Our station on the east side of the Sound is distinguished by the name of Snug Corner Bay, and a very snug place it is. The ground was covered, 2 or 3 feet thick, with snow. The summits of the neighboring hills were covered with wood, but those farther in seemed to be naked rock, buried in snow.

A VIEW OF SNUG CORNER COVE

Credit: Engraving, Author's Private Collection

N PRINCE WILLIAM SOUND

The leak being stopped and the sheathing made good over it, we weighed and steered to the northwestward, thinking, if there should be any passage to the north through this inlet, that it must be in this direction. After we got over to the northwest point we found that the flood tide came into the inlet from the same channel by which we had entered. Although this circumstance did not wholly argue against a passage, it was nothing in its favor. To enable me to form a better judgment, I dispatched Mr. Gore with two armed boats to examine the northern arm, and the master with two boats to examine another arm, which took an easterly direction. Mr. Gore informed me that he had seen the entrance of an arm which he was of the opinion extended a long way to the northeast and that probably by it a passage might be found. On the other hand, Mr. Roberts, one of the mates, was of the opinion they saw the head of this arm. The circumstances rendered the existence of a passage this way very doubtful, so I resolved to spend no more time in searching for a passage in a place that promised so little success. I considered that if the land on the west should prove to be islands agreeable to the late Russian discoveries, we should not fail in getting far enough to the north, and that in good season, provided we did not lose the season searching places where a passage was not only doubtful but improbable. We were now upward of 1,560 miles to the westward of any part of Baffin or Hudson bays. Whatever passage there may be, it must be, or at least part of it must be, north of latitude 72°. Who could expect to find a passage or strait of such extent? 🍃

Cook was correct in his presumption that if any passage to the Atlantic existed at all, then it must be very far to the north. He was perfectly well aware of the very great spread of land that stood between him and the Atlantic and the improbability that any passage would be found. Roald Amundsen was the first to make it by water across the top of the continent, but that was by small boat, and he had to go as far north as 74°. Along the way he was frozen in for three winters. He sailed west from Norway and arrived in Nome, Alaska, in 1906. His ship, the *Gjoa,* is preserved in Golden Gate Park in San Francisco. Cook, however, diligently pursued his commission to explore this coast and looked into every bay extending to the east, even though it is clear he did not expect to find a passage to Baffin or Hudson bays.

*ᵍ The next morning at three o'clock (*the nights were now very short and daylight arrived early, permitting a 3* A.M. *departure*), we weighed and proceeded to the southward down the inlet. Another passage into this inlet was now discovered to the southwest. It is separated from the other by an island to which I gave the name of Montague Island. To the southwest, an island being entirely free of snow and covered with wood and verdure, was called Green Island. When we were again in the open sea, we found the coast trending west by south as far as the eye could reach.

To the inlet which we now left, I gave the name of Prince William Sound. The natives were square, strong-chested, and their heads were large with thick, short necks, and broad, spreading faces. Their teeth were broad, white, equal in size, and evenly set. The hair was black, thick, straight, and strong. Some of the women have agreeable faces which are more delicate, and the complexion of the women and children is white, without any mixture of red. The men had a rather brownish or swarthy cast. Their frocks are made of the skins of different animals, reaching generally to the ankles, and worn with the hairy side outward. When it rains they put over this another frock, ingeniously made from the intestines of whales or some other large animal. It is made to draw tight around the neck, its sleeves reach to the wrists, around which they are tied with a string, and its skirts, when they are in their canoes, are drawn over the rim of the hole in which they sit, so that no water can enter, and it keeps the men entirely dry, for no water can penetrate it. It bears a great resemblance to the dress of the Greenlanders. Mittens for the hands are made of the skins of bear paws.

The most unsightly ornamental fashion adopted by some of both sexes is having the lower lip slit quite through. This incision, which is made even in sucking children, is often more than 2 inches long and assumes the shape of lips and becomes so large as to admit the tongue through. It does not look unlike two mouths. We found many beads of European manufacture among them, and they have a great many iron knives. Everything they have is well and ingeniously made, as if they were furnished with the most complete tool chest. Their sewing, plaiting, and small work on little bags may be put in competition with the most delicate manufactures found in any part of the known world. Considering the otherwise uncivilized or rude state in which these people are, their northern situation amidst a country perpetually covered with snow, and the wretched materials they have to work with, their invention and dexterity in all manual work is equal to that of any nation. Their persons were always clean and decent without grease or dirt. Their wooden vessels were kept in excellent order as well as their boats.

The beads and iron found among these people left no room to doubt that they must have received them from some civilized nation, but we were pretty certain that we were the first Europeans with whom they had ever communicated directly. It remains to be decided from what quarter they got our manufactures. There cannot be the least doubt of their having received these articles through the intervention of the more inland tribes from Hudson Bay or settlements on the Canadian lakes, unless it can be supposed, which is less likely, that the Russian traders from Kamchatka have already extended their traffic thus far. It is remarkable, if the inhabitants of the Sound be supplied with European articles by way of intermediate traffic to the east coast, that they should, in return, never have given the more inland Indians any of their sea-otter skins, which would certainly have been seen, some time or other, in Hudson Bay. As far as I know, this is not the case. The only method of accounting for this must be the very great distance, which though it might not prevent European goods coming so far—being so uncommon—might prevent the skins, which are a common article, from passing through more than two or three tribes. 8~

Cook overlooks the further consideration that a knife, because it is highly valued and carefully kept, can last for generations, so that a knife, bartered in Hudson Bay, might find its way by exchange from tribe to tribe, a hundred years later, in the hands of the Alaskan Eskimo.

COURSE: SOUTHWEST! ~§ After leaving Prince William Sound, I steered to the southwest. We passed a lofty promontory, situated in the latitude of 59° 10′ and the longitude of 152° 15′. As the discovery of it was connected with Princess Elizabeth's birthday, I named it Cape Elizabeth. At first we were in hopes that it was the western extremity of the continent, but not long after we saw our mistake, fresh land appearing in sight. This point of land, by what I can gather from the account of Bering's voyage and the chart that accompanies it, I conclude must be what he called Cape St. Hermogenes. The account of that voyage is so very abridged and the chart so extremely inaccurate that it is hardly possible to find any one place which the navigator either saw or touched at. Were I to form a judgment of Bering's proceedings on this coast, I should suppose that he fell in with the continent near Mt. Fairweather. But I am by no means certain that the bay to which I have given his name is the place where he anchored; nor do I know that what I called Mt. St. Elias is the same conspicuous mountain to which he gave that name. As to his Cape St. Elias, I am entirely at a loss to pronounce where it lies. (*Cape St. Elias has since been identified as the southern tip of Kayak Island* [*Cook's Kayes Island*], *with the outlying rock resembling a castle.*)

On the north side of Cape St. Hermogenes, the coast turned toward the northwest. What we now saw inspired us with hopes of finding here a passage northward without being obliged to proceed any farther to the southwest. (*Cook could see that the trend of the coast was taking him continually farther west, and consequently greatly increasing the distance to the Atlantic.*)

We steered north-northwest along the coast and soon found the land of Cape St. Hermogenes to be an island. The land to the west ended in a low point, which was called Point Banks. (*This name was in honor of the famous naturalist Sir Joseph Banks, a lifelong friend of Cook who sailed with him in his first voyage to the Pacific in the* Endeavour.)

The islands obtained the name of Barren Isles from their very naked appearance. Toward evening the weather cleared up and we saw a very lofty promontory whose elevated summit formed two exceedingly high mountains, seen above the clouds. This promontory I named Cape Douglas in honor of my very good friend Dr. Douglas, canon of Windsor. Between Point Banks and Cape Douglas, the coast seemed to form a large deep bay which, from some smoke that had been seen on Point Banks, obtained the name of Smoky Bay. &

Point Banks was actually the north point of the Kodiak Island group, and Smoky Bay is the strait between Kodiak Island and the mainland, now called Shelikof Strait.

CHAPTER TWENTY

DISCOVERY OF COOK INLET

May 26, 1778——June 5, 1778

COOK INLET ᐊᔥ Having got to the northward of the Barren Islands, we discovered more land extending from Cape Douglas to the north. It formed a chain of mountains of vast height. One, far more conspicuous than the rest, was named Mount St. Augustine. The discovery of this land did not discourage us, as it was supposed to be unconnected with the land of Cape Elizabeth. In a northeast direction the sight was unlimited by anything but the horizon. With these flattering ideas we stood to the northwest till eight o'clock, when we clearly saw summits of mountains everywhere connected by lower land. The land was everywhere covered with snow from the tops of the hills down to the very sea-beach and had every appearance of being part of a great continent. I was now fully persuaded that I should find no passage by this inlet. My persevering in the search of it here was more to satisfy other people than to confirm my own opinion.

Mt. St. Augustine is a conical figure of very considerable height. It remains undetermined whether it be an island or part of the continent. (*It is an island.*) On the north side of Cape Elizabeth, between it and a lofty promontory named Cape Bede, is a bay where there appeared to be two snug harbors. ᐊᔥ

Mt. St. Augustine and Cape Bede, like so many geographical designations Cook made along the coast of North America and Alaska, were taken from the Saint's name for the day that the discovery was made. Not very imaginative, but no doubt he was running short of suitable names by which to call things.

◆§ From Cape Bede the coast trended northeast with a chain of mountains inland extending in the same direction. The land on the coast was woody. What was not much in our favor was the discovery of low land in the middle of the inlet. I steered to the westward of this.

In the morning, having but very little wind and observing the ship to drive to the southward, in order to stop her I dropped a kedge anchor with an 8-inch hawser bent to it; but in bringing the ship up there was such a strong tide setting southward that the hawser parted and we lost both it and the anchor. It was the ebb, and ran between 3 and 4 knots an hour and fell 10 feet 3 inches while we lay at anchor, so there is reason to believe this was not the greatest fall. On the eastern shore we saw two columns of smoke, a sure sign that there were inhabitants here. We weighed with the first of the flood and plied till near seven o'clock, when, the tide being done, we anchored.

Until we got thus far, the water retained the same degree of saltiness at low as at high water, and at both periods was salty as the ocean. But now the water taken up at this ebb, when at the lowest, was found to be very considerably fresher than we had hitherto tasted; insomuch that I was convinced that we were in a large river and not in a strait communicating with northern seas. Through this channel ran a prodigious tide which looked frightful to us. We could not tell whether the agitation of the water was occasioned by the stream or by the breaking of waves against rocks or sands.

I was desirous of having stronger proofs, and therefore weighed with the next flood and drove up with the tide, for we had but little wind. We had now many other proofs of being in a great river, such as: low shores, thick, muddy water, and all manner of dirt, trees, and rubbish floating up and down with the tide. All hopes of finding a passage we now gave up. The water fell, upon a perpendicular, after we had anchored, 21 feet!

As the ebb was almost spent, and we could not return against the flood, I thought I might as well take advantage of the latter to get a nearer view of the eastern branch. With this purpose in view, we weighed with the first of the flood, and stood for the eastern shore. At ten o'clock, finding the ebb begun, I anchored over a gravelly bottom. This eastern branch I shall distinguish by the name of River Turnagain. It is reasonable to suppose that both branches are navigable by ships much farther than we examined them, and that by means of this river and its several branches, a very extensive inland communication lies open. (*Cook's ships were anchored across the bay from the point of land between the eastern and northern branches. On that point of land now lies the city of Anchorage.*)

In the afternoon I sent Mr. King with orders to land on the northern point of the low land on the southeast side of the river; there to display the flag, and to take possession of the country and river in His Majesty's name, and to bury in the ground a bottle containing some pieces of English coin and a paper on which were inscribed the names of our ships and the date of our discovery. The point where Mr. King landed got the name of Point Possession.

If the discovery of this great river, which promises to vie with the most considerable ones already known to be capable of extensive inland navigation, should prove of use either to the present or any future age, the time spent in it ought to be less regretted. But to us, who had a much greater object in view, the delay was an essential loss. The season was advancing apace. We knew not how far we might have to proceed to the south, and were now convinced that the continent of North America extended farther west than from the modern, most reputable charts we had reason to expect. This made the existence of a passage to Baffin or Hudson bays less probable. It was a satisfaction to me to reflect that if I had not examined this very considerable inlet, it would have been assumed, by speculative fabricators of geography, as a fact that it communicates with the sea to the north or Baffin or Hudson bays; and being marked, perhaps, on future maps of the world with greater precision and more certain signs of reality than the invisible—because imaginary—straits of de Fucca and de Fonte.

When Mr. King returned he informed me that as he approached the shore, about twenty natives made their appearance with their arms extended—probably to express their peaceable disposition. They had with them fresh salmon and several dogs. Later, a good many came off when we were in this station. Their company was very acceptable, for they brought with them a large quantity of very fine salmon, which they exchanged for such trifles as we had to give them. Several hundredweight of salmon was procured for the two ships. All the people we met with resembled those who inhabit Prince William Sound. I will be bold to say the Russians have never been among them; for if that had been the case, we should hardly have found them clothed in such valuable skins as those of the sea otter.

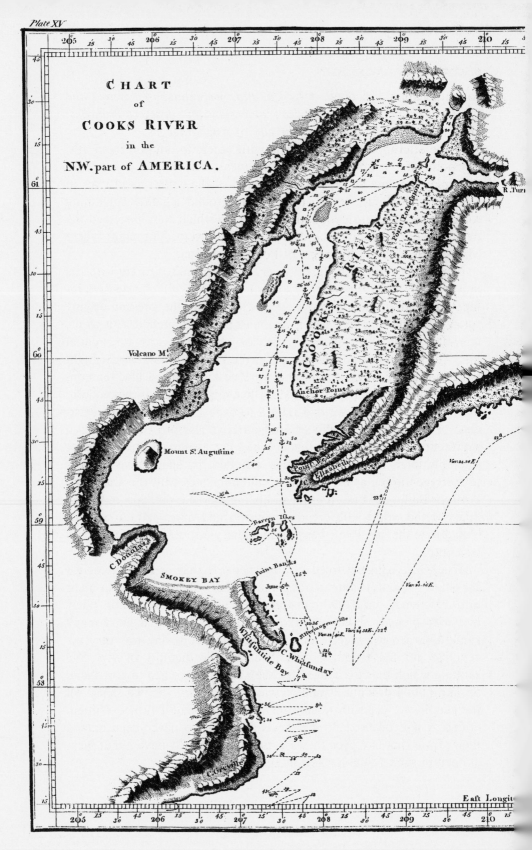

Plate XV

CHART

of

COOKS RIVER

in the

N.W. part of AMERICA.

COOKS RIVER

Point of Confficion

R. Turt

Volcano M.

Anchor Point

Mount S.t Augustine

Point Bede

Point Elizabeth

Van 24.30 E.

Barren Ifles

C. Donolan

SMOKEY BAY

Point Banks

June 6.th

Van 25.30 E.

Whitfuntide Bay

C. Whitfunday

Slebermogene Ifle

Van 22.30 E.   Van 24.32 E.

C. Greene

Eaft Longit

CHART OF COOK INLET ANI

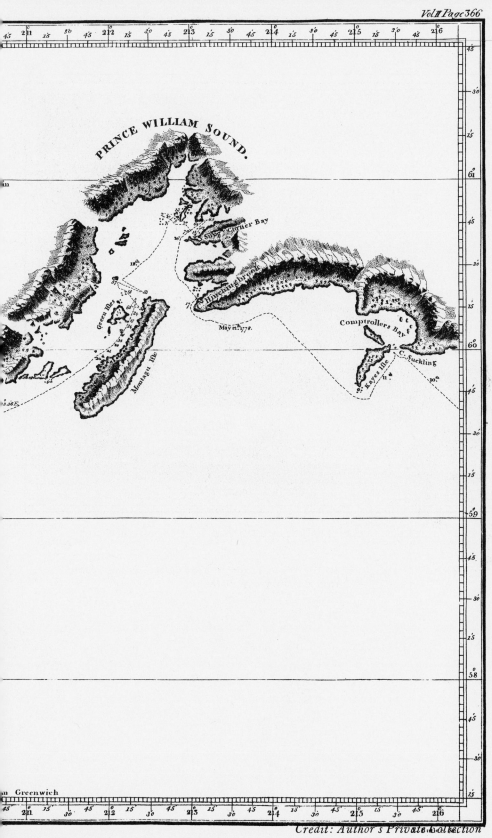

PRINCE WILLIAM SOUND.

Corner Bay

Hinchingbrook

Comptrollers Bay

Green Ille

May 12th 1778.

Kayes Ille

C. Suckling

Montagu Ille

Greenwich

PRINCE WILLIAM SOUND

A SEA OTTER

There is not the least doubt that a very beneficial fur trade might be carried on with the inhabitants of this vast coast. Unless a northern passage should be found practicable, it seems rather too remote for Great Britain to receive any emolument from it. As these poor people make no other use of skins but for clothing themselves, they do not dress more than are necessary for this purpose. It would probably be otherwise were they once habituated to a constant trade with foreigners. This intercourse would increase their wants by introducing them to new luxuries; and in order to purchase these, they would be more assiduous in procuring skins, which they would soon discover to be the commodity most sought for, a plentiful supply of which, I have no doubt, would be had in the country. ॐ

Very soon after this account reached the Western world, the fur trade began, and so "assiduously" was it pursued that in a very few years the sea otter was nearly wiped out. The supply was not "plentiful" enough for the world's demands. For a time it appeared that none of the species remained until a small herd was discovered on the little Aleutian Island of Amchitka, which fortunately was too remote for the trappers to reach and was overlooked in their search for the last sea-otter skin.

ॐ As soon as the ebb tide made in our favor, we weighed and with a light breeze plied down the river until the flood obliged us to anchor. In the afternoon the mountains, for the first time since our entering the river, were clear of clouds; and we discovered a volcano in one of those on the west side. It was emitting only a white smoke, but no fire. (*The ships were now off Anchor Point.*)

At length a fresh breeze sprang up at west with which we got under sail and, at eight, passed the Barren Islands and stretched away for Cape St. Hermogenes (*Marmot Island*). ॐ

Captain Cook left the river without giving it a name. When the account of his explorations reached England, Lord Sandwich directed that it should be called Cook's River. The name has since been altered to Cook Inlet.

CHAPTER TWENTY-ONE

RUSSIAN LETTERS

June 6, 1778——July 1, 1778

KODIAK ✎ At midnight, being past the rocks (*off Marmot Island*), we bore to the southward. At this time the southernmost point of the mainland (*Cook did not know that he was coasting along an island*) lay north, half west. This promontory was named after the day, Cape Whitsunday; a large bay which lies to the west of it obtained the name of Whitsunday Bay (*now called Marmot Bay*). There is some reason to think that the land between Point Banks and Cape Whitsunday was an island (*this is correct*). If this be so, Whitsunday Bay is only a strait or passage that separates it from the mainland (*also correct. The strait is now called Kupreanof Strait*). We saw land all around the bottom of the bay, so that either the land is connected or else the points lock in, one behind the other (*the latter is correct*). I am more inclined to think that the former is the case, and that the land east of the bay is part of the continent (*not so*).

We stood off until noon and then tacked and stood in for the land. The land here forms a point which was named Cape Greville (*now known as Cape Chiniak*). The three following days we had almost constant misty weather with drizzling rain, so that we seldom had a sight of the coast, and the air was raw and cold. The fog clearing up with a change of the wind to the southwest on the evening of the twelfth, we had sight of the land. An elevated point which obtained the name of Cape Barnabas bore northeast, 10 miles distant. The point to the southwest whose elevated summit terminated in two round hills was called Twoheaded Point. This part of the coast is composed of high hills and deep valleys. Not a tree or a bush was to be seen upon it, and in general it had a brownish hue, probably the effect of a mossy covering. From whatever quarter Twoheaded Point was viewed, it had the appearance of an island, or else it is a peninsula (*it actually is an island*).

We were well up with the southermost land next morning and found it to be on an island named Trinity Island. At first we were inclined to think that this was Bering's Foggy Island, but its situation so near the main does not suit his chart. The wind now began to incline to the south, and we had reason to expect that it would soon be at southeast. Experience having taught us that a southeasterly wind was here generally, if not always, accompanied by a thick fog, I was afraid to venture through between the island and the continent. This induced me to stretch out to sea. The gale increasing with thick fog and rain, I steered west-northwest under such sail as we could easily haul the wind, being fully sensible of the danger of running before a strong gale in a thick fog in the vicinity of an unknown coast. It was, however, necessary to run some risk when the wind favored us, for clear weather, we had found, was generally accompanied with winds from the west. ⚭

THE ALASKAN PENINSULA ⚭ Between two and three in the afternoon, land was seen through the fog, not more than 3 miles distant. Upon this we immediately hauled up south, close to the wind. Soon after, the two courses were split (*the courses are the lowest sails on the square-rigged fore- and main-masts*); so we had others to bring to the yards; and several other sails received considerable damage. The next morning, the fog now being dispersed, we found ourselves surrounded by land. The continent, or what was supposed to be the continent, extended from southwest to northeast, and some elevated land bore southeast. The north extreme of the main we named Foggy Cape, but we found it to be an island, and it is distinguished in our chart by the name of Foggy Island, having reason to believe, from its situation, that it is the same island which had that name given to it by Bering. (*The name Foggy Cape remains, but the island is now called Sutwik Island.*)

At the same time, three or four islands lying before a bay formed by the coast of the mainland, bore north by west. A point with three or four pinnacle rocks upon it was called Pinnacle Point. A cluster of small islets lay 9 leagues from the coast south-southeast (*the Semidi Islands*).

There can be no doubt that there is a continuation of the continent between Trinity Island and Foggy Cape which the thick weather prevented us from seeing. For some distance to the southwest of that cape, this country is more broken or rugged than any part we had yet seen. Every part had a very barren aspect and was covered with snow from the summits down to a very small distance from the seacoast.

On the seventeenth the weather was clear, and the air sharp and dry. A large group of islands lying about 7 leagues from the continent extended to the southwest. In the afternoon we got a light breeze of wind which enabled us to steer west for the channel that appeared between the islands and the continent. The largest island in this group was now on our left and is distinguished by the name of Kodiak, according to information we afterward received. I believe them to be the same that Bering calls Schumagin's Islands. Most of these islands are of good height, very barren and rugged, abounding with rocks and steep cliffs, and exhibiting other romantic appearances. There are several snug bays and coves about them, and streams of fresh water run from their elevated parts. Not a tree or a bush was seen to be growing on the land. ষ

Cook, by reason of the large blank spaces and inaccuracies of the Russian charts, understandably had great difficulty reconciling his geography with theirs. When he coasted along the south side of Kodiak Island he thought he was off the mainland and did not know that Shelikof Strait lay between this large land mass and the continent and extended all the way to the mouth of Cook Inlet. (The eastern extremity of Shelikof Strait, which he saw from Cook Inlet, he earlier called Smoky Bay.) The Trinity Islands actually lie just west of Kodiak Island, rather than off the "main" as he believes. This combination of errors led him to mistakenly place Kodiak Island in the Shumagin group.

ষ One of the people shot a very beautiful bird of the auk kind. It is somewhat less than a duck, a black color except for the fore part of the head, which is white. From above and behind each eye arises an elegant yellowish-white crest, revolved backward, as a ram's horn. The bill and feet are red. We generally saw some of them every day, and sometimes large flocks. ষ

THE TUFTED PUFFIN

Credit: Courtesy of American Museum of Natural History

This bird is the tufted puffin, *Lunda eirrhata* (see illustration). The striking tuft of yellow feathers over the eyes is found in a number of birds both in the arctic and antarctic, including the crested auklet and the horned puffin.

A RUSSIAN LETTER ✍ Some time after we got through this channel, the *Discovery,* now 2 miles astern, fired three guns and brought to and made the signal to speak with us. This alarmed me not a little. As no apparent danger had been remarked in the passage through the channel, it was apprehended that some accident, such as springing a leak, must have happened. A boat was immediately sent to her, and in a short time returned with Captain Clerke. I now learned from him that some natives in canoes, who had been following the ship for some time, got under his stern. One of them made many friendly signs, taking off his cap and bowing after the manner of Europeans. A rope being handed down from the ship, to this he fastened a small wooden box; and having delivered this safely, and spoken something and made some signs, the canoes dropped astern and left the *Discovery.* No one on board had any suspicion that the box contained anything till after the departure of the canoes, when it was accidentally opened and a piece of paper was found, folded up carefully, upon which something was written in the Russian language. The date 1778 was prefixed to it, and in the body of the written note there was a reference to the year 1776. I was not learned enough to decipher the alphabet of the writer, but his numerals marked that others had preceded us in visiting this dreary part of the globe. Hopes of soon meeting with some Russian traders could not but give a sensible satisfaction to those who had, for such a length of time, been conversant with the savages of the Pacific Ocean and of the continent of North America.

Captain Clerke was of the opinion that some Russians had been shipwrecked here and that these unfortunate persons, seeing our ships pass, had taken this method to inform us of their situation. Impressed with humane sentiments, he was desirous of our stopping till they might join us. But no such idea occurred to me. It seemed obvious that it would have been the first step taken by such shipwrecked persons to send some of their body off to the ships in the canoes. For this reason I rather thought that the paper contained a note of information, left by some Russian trader who had lately been among these islands, to be delivered to the next of their countrymen who should arrive. The natives, seeing our ships pass, supposing us to be Russians, had resolved to bring off the note, thinking it might induce us to stop. Fully convinced of this, I did not stay to inquire further into the matter, but made sail and stood away to the westward along the coast. 𝓮❧

If Cook truly was so desirous of European company, it is puzzling why he did not follow up this lead. The fact that the note was dated with the current year indicated that it could not have been written long ago, and that very likely the Russian who wrote it was then within these islands. The explanation for proceeding so hastily must be that it was now the nineteenth of June, and the summer solstice was only two days away—thereafter the days would begin to get shorter. The long turn of the coast to the south and west meant that Cook was very much delayed in the purpose of this voyage of finding a passage to the east in the northern latitudes.

According to John Rickman, second-lieutenant on the *Discovery,* who later published an anonymous account of the voyage in 1781 (three years before the official account by Captain Cook), the message came from the "Principal" of a Russian trading post whose residence was on the coast, where the ships were when the note was received. According to Rickman, it contained no urgent message. (See Bibliography, Rickman.)

❧ We continued to run all night with a gentle breeze at northeast. At two o'clock next morning some breakers were seen within us at the distance of 2 miles. Others were seen ahead and on our larboard bow, and between us and the land they were innumerable. We did but just clear them by holding a south course. The breakers were occasioned by rocks, some of which were above the water. They extend several leagues from the land and are very dangerous, especially in thick weather, to which this coast seems much subject. (*This area is now called the Sandman Reefs.*) At noon we had just got on their outside. The nearest land, being an elevated bluff, was called Rock Point; and an island which was called Halibut Island (*now called Sonak Island*) extended from north by east to north by west. Over this and the adjoining islands we could see the mainland, covered with snow. The most southwest hill was discovered to have a volcano which continually threw up vast columns of black smoke. It is a complete cone and the volcano is at the very summit, but we seldom saw it wholly clear of clouds—at times both the base and summit would be clear, when a narrow cloud, sometimes two or three, one above the other, would embrace the middle like a girdle. With the column of smoke issuing perpendicular to a great height out of its top, and spreading before the wind into a tail of vast length, it made a very picturesque appearance. The wind at the height to which the smoke of this volcano reached moved sometimes in a direction contrary to what it did at sea, even when it blew a fresh gale. (*This is the Shishaldin Volcano on Unimak Island—9,387 feet high.*)

In the afternoon, having three hours' calm, our people caught upwards of a hundred halibut, some of which weighed 100 pounds, and none less than 20. This was a very seasonable refreshment to us. In the height of our fishing, which was 3 or 4 miles from shore, a small canoe conducted by one man came to us from the large island. On approaching the ship, he took off his cape and bowed. It was evident that the Russians must have communication and traffic with these people, not only from their acquired politeness, but we had now fresh proof of it—our present visitor wore a pair of green cloth breeches and a jacket of black cloth under the gut-shirt of his own country. He had nothing to barter except a gray fox skin and some fishing implements. With him was a bladder full of something which we supposed to be oil, for he opened it, took a mouthful, and then fastened it again. His canoe was of the same make as we had seen before, but rather smaller, and he used a double-bladed paddle. ६►

THE ALEUTIAN ISLANDS ◄ঙ By eight o'clock we had passed three islands all of a good height (*the Krenitzin Islands*). More of them were now seen to the westward. The weather became gloomy and at length turned to mist, and the wind blew fresh at east. At night I therefore hauled the wind to the southward until daybreak, when we resumed our course to the west.

Daylight availed us little, for the weather was so thick that we could not see a hundred yards before us; but as the wind was now moderate, I ventured to run. At half-past four we were alarmed at hearing the sound of the breakers on our larboard bow. On heaving the lead we found 28 fathoms water and on the next cast, 25. I immediately brought the ship to, with her head to the northward, and anchored, and called the *Discovery* to anchor also.

A few hours after, the fog having cleared away, it appeared that we had escaped very imminent danger. We found ourselves three-quarters of a mile from an island. Two elevated rocks were about half a league from us. There were breakers about them, and yet Providence had, in the dark, conducted the ships through, between these rocks, which I should not have ventured on a clear day, and to an anchoring place that I could not have better chosen. ⟨⟩

The ships, in the darkness and fog, had sailed into a very small bay on the eastern arm of Unalaska Island, probably an indentation on Cape Sedanka.

⟨⟩ In the night the wind blew fresh at south, but was more moderate toward morning, and the fog partially dispersed. Having weighed, we steered to the northward between the island under which we had anchored and another small one near it. The channel is not more than a mile broad, and we now had land in every direction that, extending to the southwest, we afterward found to be one island, known by the name of Oonalaska (*Unalaska*). Between it and the land to the north (*Unalga Island*), which had the appearance of being a group of islands, there seemed to be a channel (*Unalga Pass*). In the afternoon, the tide in our favor, we steered for the channel, in hopes, after we were through, of finding the land trend away to the northward or, at least, a passage out to sea. We supposed ourselves—as it really happened—to be among islands and not in an inlet of the continent.

Being in want of water, and perceiving that we ran some risk of driving about in a rapid tide without wind to govern the ship, I stood for a harbor lying on the south side of the passage; but we were very soon driven past it, and to prevent being forced back through the passage, came to anchor, out of reach of the strong tide; yet even here, we found it to run a full 5½ knots in an hour! At low water we weighed and towed the ships into the harbor.

Soon after we anchored, a native of the island brought on board another note as had been given to Captain Clerke; but it also was written in Russian, which none of us could read. As it could be of no use to me, and might be of consequence to others, I returned it to the bearer and dismissed him with a few presents. &

Cook had dictionaries of the Eskimo language, and he and Mr. Anderson had prepared their own dictionaries of the Polynesian language; but no one had thought to equip himself with a Russian dictionary.

& In walking next day along the shore, I met with a group of natives of both sexes on the grass at a repast of raw fish, which they ate with much relish. The harbor is called by them, Samganoodha (*now called English Bay, for obvious reasons*). It narrows toward the head, where ships can lie landlocked in 7 fathoms. Great plenty of good water may be easily gotten, but not a single stick of wood of any size. &

CHAPTER TWENTY-TWO

PENETRATION OF THE FROZEN NORTH

July 2, 1778——October 25, 1778

⋞§ Having put to sea with a light breeze, we steered to the north, meeting with nothing to obstruct us in this course. The island which forms the northeast side of the passage through which we came is called Oonella (*Unalga*). Another island to the northeast of it is called Accotan (*Akutan*), which is considerably larger than Unalga. It appeared that we might have gone very safely between these two islands and the continent, the southwest point of which is called by the people of these parts Oonemak (*Unimak*). ৯

The opening he saw is Unimak Pass. Unimak is actually an island, but so close to the rest of the Alaskan peninsula as to be considered the terminal point of the long southwest finger of land. Cook does not say from whom he learned these names—presumably from the inhabitants along English Bay—but he very properly used the native words when he could.

⋞§ This coast is on the northwest side of the volcano mountain, so that we must have seen it, if the weather had been tolerably clear. We continued to steer east-northeast—a great hollow swell from the west-southwest assured us that there was no mainland near in that direction. As we advanced to the northeast we found the depth of water gradually decreasing, and the coast tending more and more northerly. The extent of the low land between the foot of the mountain and the seacoast increased, and both the high and low grounds were perfectly destitute of wood. The coast extended as far as northeast, where it seemed to terminate in a point, beyond which we hoped and expected that it would take a more easterly direction. But soon after, we discovered low land extending beyond this point as far as northwest. Thus the fine prospect we had of getting to the north vanished in a moment. Behind this point is a river distinguished by the name of Bristol River, the entrance of which seemed to be a mile broad. We examined some of the water which we had taken up and found it was not half so salty as common sea water, which furnished another proof that we were before a large river. We stood, then, to the southward, with boats ahead sounding, and passed over the south end of a shoal in six fathoms.

The wind having settled again in the southwest quarter, on the morning of the twelfth we stood to the northwest and at ten saw the continent. An elevated hill proved to be an island, which from its figure obtained the name of Round Island (*one of the Walrus Island group*). After edging off the coast a little, our depth gradually increased. The west extreme of the coast is an elevated point which obtained the name of Calm Point from our having calm weather when off it. (*This point is the western tip of Hagemeister Island.*)

During the fourteenth and fifteenth our progress was slow, having little wind, and sometimes so thick a fog that we could not see the length of the ship. On the sixteenth, the fog having cleared up, we found ourselves nearer the land than we expected. I sent Mr. Williamson to this promontory with orders to land and see what direction the coast took beyond it. He reported that he had landed on the point and, having climbed the highest hill, found that the farthest part of the coast in sight bore nearly north. He took possession of the country in His Majesty's name. The promontory he gave the name of Cape Newenham. (*Both here at Cape Newenham and at Cook Inlet, Cook has laid claim to and taken possession of this country in the name of His English Majesty. If Great Britain had followed up Cook's claims in the years following his discoveries, then this land might more properly have become British rather than Russian territory.*) As the coast takes a northerly direction from Cape Newenham, that Cape fixes the northern limit of the great bay or gulf which, in honor of the Admiral Earl of Bristol was named Bristol Bay. Cape Unimak is the south limit of this bay.

We steered north by west till eight the next morning, when our depth of water decreased suddenly to 5 or 6 fathoms. We brought to till a boat from each ship was sent ahead to sound. In bringing our ship up, the cable parted at the clinch, which obliged us to come to with another anchor in 6 fathoms. At low water we made an attempt to get a hawser round the lost anchor, but did not succeed. However, being determined not to leave it behind me as long as there was a probability of recovering it, I persevered in my endeavors, and at last succeeded on the evening of the twentieth. ॐ

According to Ledyard: "We spent the day in sweeping for our anchor, which we finally recovered by the exertions of a madhardy tar, who dived to the freezing bottom and hooked a grappling to the ring."

ॐ While we were thus employed, I ordered Captain Clerke to send his master in a boat to look for a passage in the southwest quarter. He did so, but no channel was to be found in that direction, nor did there appear to be any way to get clear of these shoals but to return by the track which had brought us in. The northernmost part of the coast that we could see, obtained the name of Shoal Ness. I judged it to be in the latitude of 60°. (*The ships had nosed into Kuskokwin Bay, which is very shallow due to the deposits of silt and sand from the large Kuskokwin River.*)

We found more difficulty in returning than we had in advancing, and at last were obliged to anchor to avoid running upon a shoal which had only a depth of 5 feet. While we lay there, twenty-seven men of the country, each in a canoe, came off to the ships. They appeared to be wholly unacquainted with people like us; and they knew not the use of tobacco, nor was any foreign article seen in their possession, unless a knife may be looked on as such. Their canoes were made of skins like all the others we had later seen. Encouraged to venture alongside, a traffic commenced between them and our people, who got dresses of skins, arrows, darts, wooden vessels, etc.; our visitors taking in exchange for these whatever was offered them.

It was the twenty-second, in the evening, before we got clear of these shoals. Fearing that if we continued this course we should find less and less water, I hauled to the southward. I ventured to steer west, when we at last found 26 fathoms. The weather continued for the most part foggy. Continuing our westerly course, the water having deepened to 36 fathoms, we discovered land bearing northwest. We

J. VON STAEHLIN'S MAP OF TH...

THIS MAP WAS PUBLISHED JUST TWO YEARS BEFORE CAPTAIN COOK SET OUT

(ALASKA), LYING WEST OF NORTH AMERICA, BECAME AN OBJECT OF COOK'S SEAR...

Credit: Courtesy of Rare Book Division, New Y...

JEW NORTHERN ARCHIPELAGO"

COVER A "NORTHWEST PASSAGE." THE LARGE ISLAND CALLED ALASCHKA

EN HE ATTEMPTED TO TAKE HIS SHIPS NORTH OF THE AMERICAN CONTINENT.

lic Library: Astor, Lenox and Tilden Foundations

stood toward it, when we tacked, a league from the land. The southeast extremity formed a perpendicular cliff of considerable height, on
which account it was called Point Upright (*the eastern tip of St.
Matthew Island*), and more land was seen to the westward of this
point. Here we met with an incredible number of birds, all of the auk
kind, before described. We supposed it to be one of the many islands
laid down by Mr. Staehlin in his map of the New Northern Archipelago, and we expected every moment to see more of them. ໑ᔇ

The preceding map of the *"New Northern Archipelago,"* published
in 1774 in a book by the same name, was the most reliable and the
most up-to-date information available about this part of the world
when Cook sailed from England in July 1776. J. von Staehlin, the
author, was a member of both the Imperial Academy of Science at
St. Petersburg, Russia, and the Royal Society of London. His appoint-
ment to the Court of Russia and the scientific bodies of St. Petersburg enabled him to receive the reports of Bering and the later Russian voyagers who sailed in the arctic seas east of Asia. This map is
so distorted and inaccurate that nothing is in its proper place. By
referring to the Kurili Island, where the longitude is shown at 175°,
which is about 20° too much, and reducing all longitudes accordingly
in this map by 20°, the "Island of Alaschka" (Alaska) is shown
about where the Seward peninsula lies. Guided by this clumsy map,
it appeared to Cook that to reach the sea that lay north of the American continent he would have to first find a passage between the
"Island" of Alaska and one of the continents—either on the Asian
or North American side. When, in the summer of 1778, he arrived
in the longitude shown on this chart, he found a great land mass. The
only waterway was a blind alley: Cook Inlet. The islands of Unalaska
and Unimak are shown on von Staehlin's chart, but nowhere near
their true position. He had finally found these islands and was now
heading north to search for Alaska.

ᔇᔥ About this time, a light breeze springing up at northwest, we stood
to the northeast. Variable light winds with showers of rain prevailed.
We resumed our course to the northward and at noon, by observation, our latitude was 62° 34', our longitude was 168°.

Mr. Anderson, my surgeon, who had been lingering under a consumption for more than twelve months, expired between three and

four this afternoon, August third. He was a sensible young man, an agreeable companion, well skilled in his own profession and had acquired considerable knowledge of other branches of science. The reader of this *Journal* will have observed how useful an assistant I had found him in the course of the voyage. Had it pleased God to have spared his life, the public, I have no doubt, might have received from him such communications on various parts of the natural history of the several places we visited as would have abundantly shown that he was not unworthy of this commendation. (*Mr. Anderson's journal seems to have been discontinued for about two months before his death. The last date in his manuscript was the third of June.*) Soon after he breathed his last, land was seen to the westward, 12 leagues distant. It was supposed to be an island. To perpetuate the memory of the deceased, for whom I had great regard, I named it Anderson's Island. &

The land Cook saw in the west "12 leagues distant" was probably the southeast cape of St. Lawrence Island. Consequently, Anderson's name is not remembered by having an Alaskan island named for him.

The next day I removed Mr. Law, the surgeon of the *Discovery*, into the *Resolution* and appointed Mr. Samuel, the surgeon's first mate of the *Resolution*, to be surgeon of the *Discovery*.

On the fourth, land was seen extending north-northeast to northwest. We stood for it till four o'clock, when, being 4 miles from it, we tacked. The land before us, which we supposed to be the continent of America, appeared low next the sea, but inland it swelled into hills which rise, one behind another, to a considerable height. At intervals we could see the coast extending from east to northwest, and a pretty high island, 3 leagues distant, so we ran down and anchored between the island and the continent. I then landed upon the island, accompanied by Mr. King and other officers. I hoped to have had from it a view of the coast to the westward, but the fog was so thick that the prospect was not more extensive than from the ship. A low point, Point Rodney, bore north from the island 4 leagues distant. The island was named Sledge Island and is about 4 leagues in circuit. People had lately been on the island, and it is clear that they frequently visit it for some purpose or other. We met with some decayed huts that were partly built below ground, and we found a sledge which occasioned this name be given to the island. It was 10 feet long, 20 inches broad, had a railwork on each side, and was shod with bone. The construction of it was admirable, and all parts were neatly put together with wooden pins, thongs, or lashings of whalebone, which made me think it was entirely the workmanship of the natives.

At three o'clock the next morning we weighed and proceeded to the northwestward. The weather clearing up, we saw high land extending from northeast to northwest. At the same time an island was seen 8 or 10 leagues distant. It appeared to have no great extent and was named King's Island. We spent the night making short boards, the weather being misty and rainy. Being satisfied that the whole was a continued coast, I stood away for its northwest part and came to anchor under it. The next morning it cleared up, so that we could see the land about us. A high, steep rock or island bore west by south, another island to the north of it and much larger, a peaked hill, and a point under, bore southeast. Under this hill lies some low land stretching out to the northwest. This point, which I named Cape Prince of Wales, is the more remarkable by being the western extremity of all America hitherto known. It is situated in the latitude of 65° 46′ and in the longitude of 168° 15′. ॐ

Cook has now anchored just off the American coast in the Bering Strait. He has found the coast of North America, has turned so far *west*, away from his intended goal to get east to Labrador, that he is now *8° 45′ west* of his position in the Hawaiian Islands. The small rock he sees is Fairway Rock, and the large island must be Little Diomede Island.

ॐ In the morning we weighed, but we had scarcely got our sails set when it began to blow and rain very hard with misty weather. The wind, being in contrary direction to the current, raised such a sea that it frequently broke into the ship. Having plied to windward with little effect, I bore up for the island we had seen to the westward proposing to come to an anchor under it till the gale should cease. But we found it composed of two small islands, each not more than 3 or 4 leagues in circuit and, consequently, they could afford us little shelter. Therefore we continued to stretch to the westward, and at eight o'clock land was seen in that direction. I then made a board to the eastward in order to anchor and spend the night. At daybreak we resumed our course to west for the land we had formerly seen. Here the shore forms a large bay in which we anchored about 2 miles from the shore. ৯

EASTERNMOST SIBERIA ৯ As we were standing into this bay we perceived a village and some people whom the sight of the ships seemed to have thrown into confusion or fear. I proposed to land and went with three armed boats. About thirty or forty men, each armed with a spontoon (*a short spear or club*) and a bow and arrows, stood drawn up on a rising ground close by the village. As we drew near, three of them came down toward the shore and were so polite as to take off their caps and to make low bows. We returned the civility, but this did not inspire them with sufficient confidence, for the moment we put the boats ashore, they retired. I followed them alone without anything in my hand, and by signs and gestures prevailed on them to stop and to receive some presents. In return they gave me two fox skins and a couple of sea-horse teeth. (*Walrus teeth*)

They seemed very fearful and cautious. On my laying my hand on the shoulder of one of them, he started back several paces. As I advanced, they retreated, always in the attitude of being ready to use their spears, while those on the rising ground stood ready to support them with their arrows. Myself and two or three of my companions got in among them. A few beads distributed to those about us soon created a confidence, so that by degrees a traffic between us commenced. Nothing we had to offer could induce them to part with a spear or bow. These they held in constant readiness, never once quitting them, except when four or five laid them down while they gave us a song and a dance. Even then they placed them in such a manner that they could lay hold of them in an instant, and for their security they desired us to sit down.

The bows were such as we had seen on the American coast and like those used by the Eskimo. The spears or spontoons were of iron or steel and of Asian workmanship in which pains had been taken to ornament them with inlayings of brass and of a white metal. Other things, and in partcular their clothing, showed that they were possessed of a degree of ingenuity far surpassing what one could expect to find among so northern a people. All the Americans we had seen were low of stature, with round, chubby faces and high cheekbones.

The people we were now among had long visages and were stout and well made. They appeared to be a quite different nation.

Their dogs are of the fox kind, rather large, of different colors, with long soft hair like wool. They are probably used in drawing their sledges in winter. The canoes are of the same sort as those of the North Americans.

At first we supposed this land to be a part of the island of Alaska laid down in Mr. Staehlin's map. But from the figure of the coast, the situation of the opposite shore of America, and from the longitude, we began to think that it was more probably the country of the Tschutski (*Chukchi*) or the eastern extremity of Asia explored by Bering in 1728. To have admitted this I must have pronounced Mr. Staehlin's map and his account of the New Northern Archipelago to be either exceedingly erroneous or else a mere fiction; a judgment which I had no right to pass upon a publication so respectably vouched for without producing the clearest proof. After a stay of between two and three hours with these people, we returned to our ships and weighed anchor. &

THE BERING STRAIT & We stood out of the bay and steered to the northeast. The next day our position was nearly in the middle between the two coasts, each being seven leagues distant. We steered east in order to get nearer the American coast. In this course the water shoaled gradually. I was obliged at last to drop anchor in 6 fathoms—the only remedy we had left to prevent the ships driving into less. While we lay at anchor we found little or no current nor could we perceive that the water either rose or fell.

A breeze springing up at south, I steered northeast, and soon after we saw more land bearing north by east. The coast here forms a point named Point Mulgrave, which lies in the latitude of 67° 45′. The whole was free of snow, and destitute of wood. &

FARTHEST NORTH & I now steered northeast. In this run we met with several sea horses and flights of birds, some like land-larks. Some shags (*cormorants*) were also seen, so that we judged ourselves to be not far from land, but as we had struck fog we could not expect to see any. Some time before noon we perceived a brightness in the northern horizon like that reflected from ice, commonly called the blink. It was little noticed, from a supposition that it was improbable we should meet with ice so soon, yet the sharpness of the air and gloominess of the weather seemed to indicate some sudden change. About an hour after, the sight of a large field of ice left us no longer in doubt. We tacked close to the edge of the ice, being then in the latitude of 70° 41′ and not being able to stand any farther. ৯

Cook did not expect ice so soon, because he was at this point south of the latitudes of northern Norway, the island of Spitsbergen and Baffin Bay, all of which are free of pack ice in the summertime.

৯ The ice was quite impenetrable and extended from west to east as far as the eye could reach. We were close to the edge of the ice, which was as compact as a wall and seemed to be 10 or 12 feet high at least. Farther north it appeared much higher, and its surface was extremely rugged. Here and there we saw upon it pools of water.

We now steered to the southward. The weather, clearing up a little, we saw land. The eastern extreme forms a point which was encumbered with ice, for which reason it obtained the name of Icy Cape. There can be no doubt of its being a continuation of the American continent. Our situation was now more and more critical. We were in shoal water, upon a lee shore, and the main body of the ice to windward was driving down upon us. It was evident that if we remained much longer between it and the land, it would force us ashore, for it seemed nearly to join the land to leeward. The only direction that was open was to the southwest. After making a short board, I made the signal for the *Discovery* to tack, and tacked myself at the same time. The wind proved favorable, so that we lay up southwest.

In the morning of the nineteenth we had a good deal of drift-ice about us—the main ice was about 2 leagues to the north. On the ice lay a prodigious number of sea-horses. As we were in want of fresh provisions, the boats from each ship were sent to get some. By seven in the evening we had received on board nine of these animals, which till now we had supposed to be sea-cows. We were not a little disappointed. The seamen would not have known the difference if we had not happened to have one or two on board who had been in Greenland and declared what animals these were, and that no one ever ate them. Notwithstanding this, we lived upon them as long as they lasted. The lean flesh is coarse, black, and has rather a strong taste; the fat yields a good deal of oil, which burns well in lamps;

THE CREW SHOOTING
ON THE

SEA-HORSES (WALRUSES)
CE FLOES

and their hides, which are very thick, were very useful about our rigging.

They lie in herds of many hundreds upon the ice, huddling one over the other like swine. Their roar is so loud that at night or in foggy weather, they give us notice of the vicinity of ice before we can see it. They are seldom in a hurry to get away till after they have been once fired at; then they tumble one over the other into the sea in the utmost confusion. If we did not at the first discharge kill those fired at we generally lost them. The female will defend the young one to the very last and at the expense of her own life. Nor will the young ones quit the dam though she be dead, so that if you kill one, you are sure of the other. The dam, when in the water, holds the young ones between her fore-fins. (*This animal, which Cook and his seamen call the "sea-horse," is actually the common walrus.*)

By the time we had our sea-horse on board we were, in a manner, surrounded with ice and had no way left to clear it but by standing to the southward. At ten o'clock the next morning, the fog clearing away, we saw the continent of America. As the main ice was at no great distance from us, it is evident that it now covered a part of the sea, which but a few days before had been clear, and that it extended farther to the south than when we first fell in with it. The southern extreme of land seemed to form a point, which was named Cape Lisburne.

As the fog was very thick I steered to the southward to clear the ice. The next morning the fog dispersed and I hauled to the westward. Finding that I could not get to the north near the coast on account of the ice, I resolved to try what could be done at a distance from it. The air was raw, sharp, and cold, and we had fogs, sunshine, showers of snow and sleet by turns.

At ten on the morning of the twenty-sixth, we fell in with the ice, so that it now appeared we had no better prospect of getting north here than nearer the shore. We were, in a manner, embayed by the ice, which appeared high and very close in the northwest and north-east quarters. Having but little wind, I went with the boats to examine the state of the ice. I took particular notice that it was all pure transparent ice, except the upper surface, which was a little porous. It appeared to be entirely composed of frozen snow and to have been all formed at sea. Setting aside the improbability, or rather, impossibility, of such huge masses floating out of rivers in which there is hardly water for a boat, none of the productions of the land we found in-corporated or fixed to it, which must have unavoidably been the case had it been formed in rivers, either great or small. It also appeared to me improbable that this ice could have been the production of the preceding winter alone; I should suppose it rather to have been the production of a great many winters. It was less improbable, accord-ing to my judgment, that the little that remained of the summer could destroy the tenth part of what now subsisted of this mass; for the sun had already exerted upon it the full influence of its rays. I am of the opinion that the sun contributes very little toward reducing these great masses. Although that luminary is a considerable while above the horizon, it seldom shines out for more than a few hours at a time, and is not seen for several days in succession. It is the wind, or rather, the waves raised by the wind, that brings down the bulk of these enormous masses by grinding one piece against another and washing away those parts that lie exposed to the surge of the sea. This was evident from our observing that the upper surface of many pieces had been washed away, while the base, or underpart, remained firm for several fathoms around that which appeared above water. More ice is destroyed in one stormy season than is formed in several winters, and an endless accumulation is prevented. But that there is always a re-maining store, everyone who has been upon the spot will conclude; and none but closet-studying philosophers will dispute. (*The Cap-tain's numerous deductions as to the formation of the ice, the absence of large rivers, the lack of glacier ice from land—arrived at from the study of the ice he has briefly seen here in the fog—are all correct.*) A thick fog, which came while I was thus employed with the boats, hastened me aboard rather sooner than I could have wished, with one sea-horse to each ship. The number of these animals on all the ice that we had seen is almost incredible. By this time, our people began to relish them, and those we had procured before were all consumed. In the afternoon we got on board as much marine beef as was thought necessary. ε∾

NORTH COAST OF SIBERIA ∾§ On the morning of the twenty-ninth we saw the main ice to the northward, and not long after, land bearings southwest and west. As we approached the land, the depth of water decreased very fast so that at noon, when we tacked, we had only 8 fathoms, being 3 miles from the coast. The coast in every respect is like the opposite one of America, that is, low land next to the sea with elevated land farther back. It was perfectly destitute of wood, and even snow, but was covered with a mossy substance that gave it a brownish cast. The point, which is steep and rocky, was named Cape North. The coast beyond it must take a westerly direction, for we could see no land to the northward of it. Being desirous of seeing more of the coast to the westward, we tacked again, thinking we could weather Cape North. But finding we could not, the wind freshening, a thick fog coming on with much snow, and being fearful of the ice coming down upon us, I gave up the design of plying to the westward.

The season was now so far advanced, and the time when the frost is expected to set in so near at hand, that I did not think it consistent with prudence to make any further attempts to find a passage into the Atlantic this year, in any direction, so little was the prospect of succeeding. My attention was now directed toward finding some place where we might supply ourselves with wood and water. The object uppermost in my thoughts was how I should spend the winter, so as to make some improvements in geography and navigation, and, at the same time, be in a condition to return to the north in further search of a passage the ensuing summer.

I bore up to the eastward along this coast, which, by this time, it was pretty certain could only be the continent of Asia. The wind blew fresh with a very heavy fall of snow and a thick mist, and it was necessary to proceed with great caution. I continued to range along the coast at 2 leagues distant. The whole was now covered with snow which had lately fallen, quite down to the sea. The thermometer had been very little above the freezing point, and often below it, so that the water in the vessels upon the deck was frequently covered with a sheet of ice.

An island bore southwest, about 3 leagues from the main, in the latitude of 67° 45′ and was distinguished in the chart by the name of Burney's Island. The coast formed several rocky points connected by a low shore without the least appearance of a harbor. I was now well assured of what I had believed before, that this was the country of the Chukotskiy or the northeast coast of Asia; and thus far Bering proceeded in 1728; that is, to this head, which Muller says is called Serdtse Kamen on account of a rock upon it shaped like a heart.

We had now fair weather and sunshine, and we ranged along the coast at the distance of 4 miles. We saw several of the inhabitants and some of their habitations, which looked like little hillocks of earth. In the evening we passed East Cape, from which the coast changes its direction and trends southwest; it is the same point of land which we passed on the eleventh of August. Those who believed in Mr. Staehlin's map thought it the east point of his island of Alaska, but we had, by this time, satisfied ourselves that it is no other than the eastern promontory of Asia. I must conclude, as Bering did before me, that this is the most eastern point of Asia. It is distant from Cape Prince of Wales on the American coast, 13 leagues in the direction north, 53° west.

After passing the Cape, I steered southwest for the northern point of St. Lawrence Bay, in which we had anchored on the tenth of last month. (*Captain Cook gave the bay this name, having anchored in it on St. Lawrence's day, August 10, 1778. It is remarkable that just fifty years before this date, Bering sailed not far from here on the tenth of August, 1728, on which account the island of St. Lawrence was named in honor of the same saint. A small settlement in the bay preserves Cook's name in its Russian spelling,* Lavrentiya.) We reached the bay by eight o'clock next morning and saw some of the inhabitants at the place where I had seen them before, but none of them attempted to come off to us, which seemed a little extraordinary, as the weather was favorable enough, and those whom we had lately visited had no reason that I know of to dislike our company. These people must be the Chukotskiy, a nation that the Russians had not been able to conquer. I did not wait to examine the bay, although I was very desirous of finding a harbor in these parts to which I might resort next spring. But I wanted one where wood might be gotten, and I knew that none was to be found here. In the afternoon, in the direction of our course, we saw what was first taken for a rock, but it proved to be a dead whale, which some natives had killed and were towing ashore. They concealed themselves behind the fish to avoid being seen by us.

I did not follow the direction of the coast, as I found that it took a westerly direction toward the Gulf of Anadir into which I had no inducement to go, but steered to the southward in order to get a sight of the Island of St. Lawrence, discovered by Bering, which accordingly showed itself. ᐁ᛬

WHERE IS ALASKA? ᐁ᛬ In justice to the memory of Bering, I must say that he has delineated the coast of St. Lawrence Island very well and fixed the latitude and longitude of the points better than could be

OF CHUKOTSKIY
HABITATION

expected from the methods he had to go by. The more I was convinced of my having been upon the coast of Asia, the more I was at a loss to reconcile Mr. Staehlin's map of the New Northern Archipelago with my observation. I had no way to account for the great difference but by supposing that I had mistaken some part of what he calls the island of Alaska for the American continent and missed the channel that separates them. It was with me a matter of some consequence to clear up this point the present season that I might have but one object in view the next. As these northern isles are represented by him as abounding in wood, I was in hopes, if I should find them, of getting a supply of that article, which we now began to be in great want of. With these views I steered over for the American coast.

On the sixth of September, at four in the morning, we got sight of the American coast near Sledge Island (*near the present city of Nome*). If any part of what I had supposed to be the American coast could possibly be the island of Alaska, it was now before us. In that case, I must have missed the channel between it and the main by steering to the west instead of the east after we first fell in with it. I was not therefore at a loss where to go in order to clear up these doubts.

Our course along the coast we found to trend east. In the evening we were abreast of a point beyond which the coast takes a more northerly direction, which obtained the name of Cape Darby. Next morning, at daybreak, we sailed along the coast. Soon after we found ourselves upon a coast covered with wood, an agreeable sight to which, of late, we had not been accustomed, and we saw high land seemingly at a good distance. This was thought to be the continent and the other land the island of Alaska. It was already doubtful whether we should find a passage between them, for the water shoaled as we advanced farther north. We had not more than 3½ fathoms of water, and the *Resolution*, at one time, brought mud up from the bottom. More water was not to be found in any part of the channel, for with the ships and boats we tried it from side to side. I therefore thought it high time to return.

A headland on the west shore was distinguished by the name of Bald Head. On the west side of Bald Head, the shore forms a bay, in the bottom of which is a low beach where we saw a number of huts of the natives. I stretched over to the opposite shore in the expectation of finding wood and anchored under the south end of the point of the peninsula, which obtained the name of Cape Denbigh. Several people were seen upon the peninsula, and one man came off in a small canoe. I gave him a knife and a few beads with which he seemed well pleased. Some of our people thought that he asked for me under the name of *Capitane,* but they were probably mistaken.

Mr. Gore was sent to the peninsula to see if wood and water were there to be gotten. It was soon found to be impossible on account of the shoals, which extended around the bay to the distance of 2 or 3 miles from shore. This being the case, I stood back to the other shore. An island, under the east shore to the southward of Cape Denbigh, was named Besboro Island. At length we came to an anchor half a league from the coast.

Here we took off the driftwood that lay upon the beach. As the wind blew along shore, the boats could sail both ways which enabled us to make great dispatch. I went ashore and walked a little into the country, which, where there was no wood, was covered with plants which produced berries in abundance. Next day a family of natives came near the place where we were taking off wood. I saw the husband, wife, and their child, and a fourth person who bore the human shape and that was all, for he was the most deformed cripple I had ever seen or heard of, and the man was almost blind. Iron was their beloved article. For four knives, which we had made out of an old iron hoop, I got from them near 400 pounds of fish. I gave the child, who was a girl, a few beads, upon which the mother burst into tears, then the father, then the cripple, and, at last, to complete the concert, the girl herself. Their open skin-boat, which was turned on its side, the convex part toward the wind, served for their house.

By night we got the ships amply supplied with wood and had carried on board about 12 tons of water. On the fourteenth, a party of men were sent on shore to cut brooms, which we were in want of, and the branches of spruce trees for brewing beer.

Some doubts being still entertained whether the coast we were now on belonged to an island or the American continent, and the shallowness of the water putting it out of our power to determine this with our ships, I sent Mr. King, with two boats under his command, to make such searches as might leave no room for a variety of opinions on the subject.

Two days later, about seven in the evening, Mr. King returned from his expedition, and reported that he had proceeded 4 leagues farther than the ships had been able to go. He then landed on the west side. From the heights he could see the two coasts join and the inlet to terminate in a small river. In honor of Sir Fletcher Norton, Speaker of the House of Commons, and Mr. King's near relation, I named this inlet Norton's Sound. The bay in which we were at anchor on the southeast side is called by the natives Chacktoole (*the native name still stands, now spelled Shaktolik*).

Having now fully satisfied myself that Mr. Staehlin's map must be erroneous, and having restored the American continent to that place which he had occupied with his imaginary island of Alaska, it was high time to think of leaving these northern regions and to retire to some place during the winter where I might procure refreshments for my people and a supply of provisions. Petropavlovsk, or the harbor of St. Peter and St. Paul in Kamchatka, did not appear likely to furnish either for so large a number of men. I had, besides, other reasons for not repairing thither at this time. The first was the great dislike I had to lie inactive for six or seven months, which would have been the consequence of wintering in any of these northern parts. No place was so conveniently within our reach where we could expect to have our wants supplied as the Sandwich Islands. To them, therefore, I determined to proceed. ટ✻

Always the explorer, Cook, as he has confessed, could not bear not to be sailing in search of new discoveries. He knew from what the Hawaiian natives had told him, that there were other islands in this group that he had not seen. More than that, no doubt, the Polynesian Islands called him back. The lure of the islands was not then, nor is now, easily denied.

MAPPING THE AMERICAN COAST ✻ On the seventeenth, with a light breeze, we steered to the southward and attempted to pass within Besboro Island, but though it lies 7 miles from the continent, we were prevented by meeting with shoal water, so we resumed our course along the coast. The southernmost land in sight proved also to be an island which obtained the name of Stuart's Island. The coast forms a point opposite the island, which was named Cape Stephens. As soon as we were without the island, we steered south by west for the southernmost point of the continent in sight, which was named Point Shallow Water. Shoal water obliged us to haul more to the westward, but at length, we got so far advanced upon the bank that we met sometimes with only 4 fathoms. The wind blowing fresh at northeast, it was high time to look for deep water and to quit a coast upon which we could no longer navigate with any degree of safety.

No land was seen to the southward of Point Shallow Water, which I judge to lie in the latitude of 63°. Between this latitude and Shoal Ness, in the latitude of 60°, the coast is entirely unexplored. Probably it is accessible only to boats or very small vessels. From the masthead, the sea appeared checkered with shoals—the water very much discolored and muddy, and considerably fresher than at any of the places where we had lately anchored. From this I inferred that a considerable river runs into the sea in this unknown part. (*The Captain could not have been more correct, for here is the mouth of the mighty Yukon River.*)

I steered to the westward for the land discovered on the fifth of August, which at noon was 10 leagues distant. I named it Clerke's Island. Near its east part lies a small island remarkable by having upon it three elevated rocks (*now called Punuk Islands*). Not only the greater island, but the small spot was inhabited. 8~

Cook apparently did not realize that the land he called "Clerke's Island" was actually the eastern extremity of the long island of St. Lawrence, whose westernmost portion he had seen on September 4 and correctly identified by the Russian name of St. Lawrence. This island extends across the southern opening of the Bering Strait. It lies only 50 miles from Asia and 120 miles from America. The fact that it was inhabited indicates that the natives of the region were able to cross over to the island, possibly from Asia or America, or both.

~§ We ranged along it in search of a harbor till noon, when seeing no likelihood of succeeding, I left it and steered southwest for the land we had discovered on the twenty-ninth of July. As soon as we opened the channel which separates the two continents, cloudy weather with snow showers immediately commenced; whereas all the time we were in Norton Sound, we had, with the same wind, clear weather. Might not this be occasioned by the mountains to the north of that place attracting the vapors and hindering them to proceed any farther?

At daybreak on the morning of the twenty-third, the land appeared in sight. It proved to be one island 30 miles in extent. I afterward found that it was wholly unknown to the Russians, and therefore considering it as a discovery of our own, I named it Gore Island. It appeared to be barren and without inhabitants. 8~

Plate XVIII

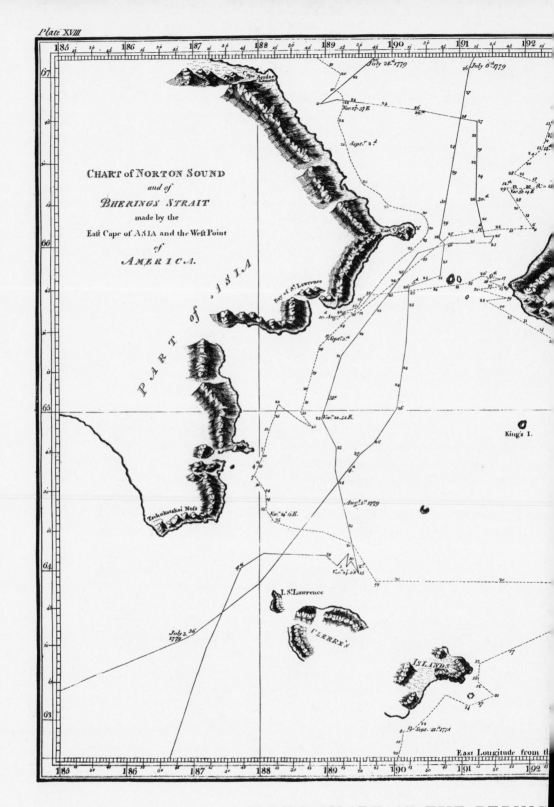

CHART of NORTON SOUND
and of
BHERINGS STRAIT
made by the
East Cape of ASIA and the West Point
of
AMERICA.

PART of ASIA

Cape Serdze Kamen

East Cape

Bay of St Lawrence

Tschukotskoi Noss

King's I.

I. St Lawrence

CLERKE'S

ISLANDS

July 28.º 1779

July 6.º 1779

Var. 27.57 E.

Sept.º 2.d

Var. 22.52 E.

Aug.t 1.st 1779

Var. 34.52 E.

Var. 24.38.

July 3. 56
1779

13. Sept. 21.st 1778

East Longitude from th

COOK'S CHART OF THE BERING

THIS PROVED THAT J. VON STAEHLIN'S

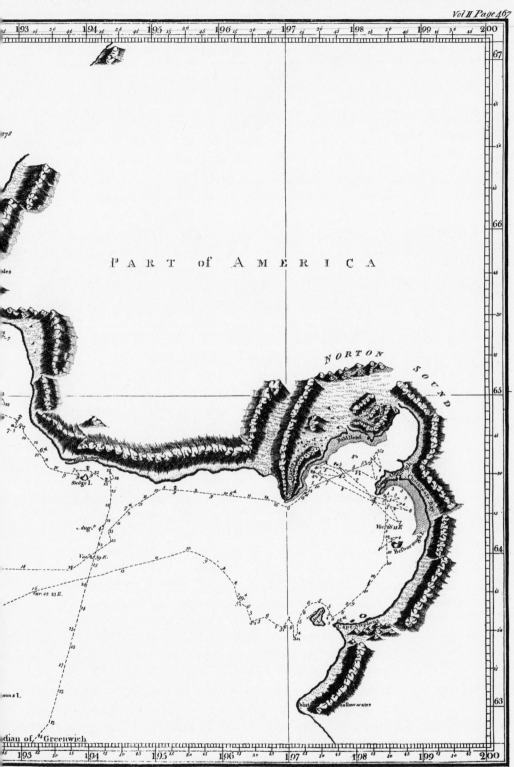

PART of AMERICA

NORTON SOUND

Credit: *Author's Private Collection*

STRAIT AND NORTON SOUND

"ISLAND OF ALASKA" DID NOT EXIST.

This island also had a Russian name, St. Matthew, which it still goes by. Although Cook tried to honor his officers by giving their names to geographical points in this region, he did not succeed very well. The islands of Clerke and Gore now have Russian names—St. Lawrence and St. Matthew. Anderson's Island was also part of St. Lawrence Island. King Island, also called Ukivok, remains on modern charts, but it is an unimpressive spot.

◄§ Four leagues from Cape Upright (*St. Matthew Island*) lies a small island whose elevated summit terminates in several pinnacle rocks. On this account it was named Pinnacle Island. In the afternoon I steered for Samganoodha (*English Bay on the Aleutian Island of Unalaska*), being resolved to spend no more time in searching for a harbor among islands which I now began to suspect had no existence, at least not where modern mapmakers have thought proper to place them. Not long after, the *Resolution* sprang a leak under the starboard buttock which filled the spirit room with water before it was discovered. It was so considerable as to keep one pump constantly employed. We dare not put the ship upon the other tack for fear of getting upon the shoals, but in the evening we wore and stood to the eastward, and then the leak no longer troubled us. This proved that it was above the waterline, which was no small satisfaction. At length, on the second of October we saw the Island of Unalaska. §►

UNALASKA ◄§ I hauled into a bay that lies 10 miles to the westward of English Bay, known by the name of Egoochshac; but we found very deep water, so that we were glad to get out again. The natives visited at different times, bringing dried salmon and other fish which they exchanged with the seamen for tobacco. But a few days before, every ounce of tobacco that was in the ship had been distributed among the seamen and the quantity was not half sufficient to answer their demands. Notwithstanding this, so improvident a creature is an English sailor that they were as profuse in making their bargains as if we had now arrived at a port in Virginia.

On the afternoon of the third of October we anchored in English Bay, and the next morning the carpenters of both ships were set to work to rip off the sheathing under the wale on the starboard side abaft. Many of the seams were found quite open, so that it was no wonder that so much water had found its way into the ship.

A MAN OF UNALASKA

Credit: Engraving, Author's Private Collection

Great quantities of berries everywhere were found ashore; and in order to avail ourselves as much as possible of their useful refreshment, one-third of the people, by turns, had leave to go and pick them. (*Was there ever another ship of the British Navy, before or since, where one-third of the crew was sent on a berry-picking party?*)

If there were any seeds of the scurvy in either ship, these berries and spruce beer, which they drank every other day, effectually eradicated them. 8~

Cook had independently made the correct discovery and deduction that scurvy was caused by some deficiency in the seaman's diet. The berries, being naturally rich in Vitamin C (the lack of which causes scurvy), were indeed an effective treatment for the "seeds of scurvy"—more so than the spruce beer.

~§ We also got plenty of fish, both fresh and dried, which the natives brought us. Some of the fresh salmon was in high perfection. We drew the seine several times at the head of the bay and caught a good many salmon trout, and once a halibut that weighed near 240 lbs. A boat was sent out every morning and seldom returned without eight or ten halibut, which was more than sufficient to serve all our people, and the halibut were excellent. 8~

OTHER EUROPEANS ON THE ISLAND ~§ On the eighth, I received by the hands of an Unalaska man named Derramoushk, a very singular present: a rye loaf, or pie in the form of a loaf, for it enclosed some salmon highly seasoned with pepper; and a note written in a character which none of us could read. It was natural to suppose that this present was from some Russians now in our neighborhood. Therefore we sent by the same hand to our unknown friends a few bottles of rum, wine, and porter (*a kind of beer*). I also sent along with Derramoushk, Corporal Ledyard of the marines, an intelligent man, in order to gain some further information. 8~

In his own journal, Ledyard gives a good account of this trip with Derramoushk to search out the Russians.

I went entirely unarmed by the advice of Captain Cook. The first day we proceeded about 15 miles into the interior part of the island until we approached a village just before night, which consisted of about thirty huts. The huts were composed of a slight frame erected over a square hole sunk about 4 feet into the ground. The whole village was out to see us, and men, women, and children crowded about me. Though they were curious to see me, yet they did not express that extraordinary curiosity that would be expected had they never seen a European before. I was glad to receive it, as it was evidence in favor of what I wished to find true, *viz.*, that there were Europeans now among them. The women were much more tolerable than I expected to have found them; one in particular seemed very busy to please me. As it was now dark, my young chief intimated to me that we must tarry where we were for the night. I very readily conceded, being much fatigued.

At daylight my guide let me know he was ready to go on. I was now so much relieved from the apprehension of any insult or injury from the Indians that my journey would have been agreeable had I not taken lame with swelling feet, which rendered it extremely painful to walk. The country was rough and hilly and the weather wet and cold. About three hours before dark we came to a large bay, where a canoe was sent to bring me across the bay and shorten the journey.

It was a skin canoe after the Eskimo plan, with two holes to accommodate two sitters. The Indians desired I should get into the canoe, which I did not very readily agree to, as there was no place for me but to be thrust into the space between the holes extended at length upon my back and wholly excluded from seeing the way, or the power of extricating myself upon any emergency. As there was no alternative, I submitted myself thus to be stowed away in bulk, and went head foremost very swift through the water about an hour, when I felt the canoe strike a beach. I was drawn out by the shoulders by three or four men. It was now so dark I could not tell who they were. I was conducted to a number of huts like those I left in the morning. To my joy and surprise I discovered that the two men who held me by each arm were two Europeans, fair and comely, and concluded from their appearance they were Russian, which I soon after found to be true.

As I was much fatigued, wet, and cold, I had a change of garments brought me consisting of a blue silk shirt, drawers, fur cap, boots, and gown; all which I put on with the same cheerfulness they were presented with. Hospitality is a virtue peculiar to man, and the obligation is as great to receive as to confer.

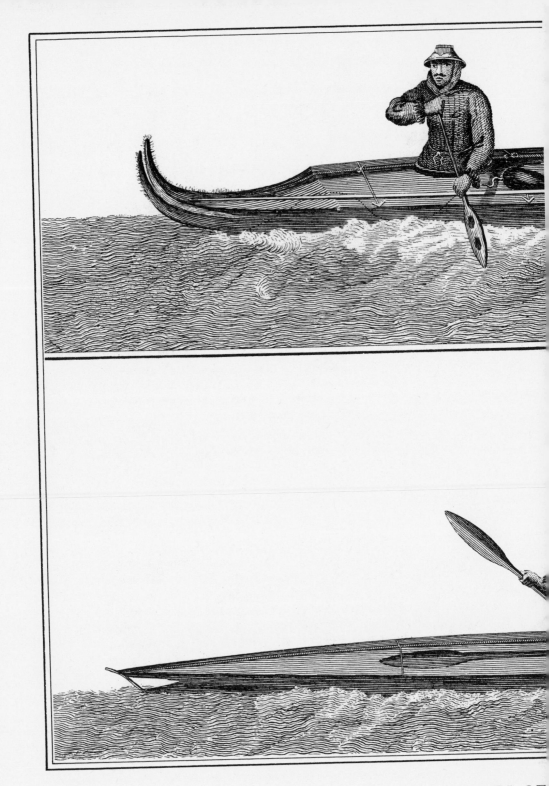

IT WAS IN A TWO-MAN CANOE OF THIS DESIGN THAT JOHN
MADE HIS TRIP TO THE RUSSIA

UNALASKA

EDYARD LAY STRETCHED OUT, BETWEEN TWO NATIVES, WHEN HE

ETTLEMENT ON UNALASKA.

As soon as I was warm and comfortable, a table was set before me with a lamp upon it. All the Russians in the house sat down round me. One of the company gave me to understand that all the white people I saw there were subjects of the Empress Catherine of Russia. I then informed them as well as I could that Commodore Cook wanted to see some of them and had sent me to conduct them to our ships.

I had a very comfortable bed composed of fur skins both under and over me. After I had lain down the Russians assembled the Indians in a very silent manner and said prayers after the manner of the Greek Church, which is much like the Roman. I could not but observe with what particular satisfaction the Indians performed their devotions to God through the medium of their little crucifixes and with what pleasure they went through the multitude of ceremonies attendant on that worship. I think it a religion the best calculated in the world to gain proselytes when the people are either unwilling or unable to speculate, or where they cannot be made acquainted with the history and principles of Christianity without a formal education.

I had a very comfortable night's rest and did not wake the next morning until late. As soon as I was up, I was conducted to a hut at a little distance. There were several Russians already there besides me. Several Indians were heating some water in a large copper caldron over a furnace, the heat of which, and the steam, rendered the hut, which was very tight, extremely hot and suffocating. I soon understood this was a hot bath of which I was asked to make use of in a friendly manner. Before I had finished undressing, I was overcome and fainted away and fell back upon the platform I was sitting on. I was relieved by having some cold water administered to my face and body. I finished undressing and proceeded as I saw the rest do, who were now all naked. The Indians brought us, as we sat or extended ourselves on the platform, water of different temperatures from that which was hot as we could bear to quite cold. The hot water was accompanied with some hard soap and a flesh-brush. After this the water was less warm and by graduations became, at last, cold, which concluded the ceremony.

We again dressed and returned to our lodgings, where breakfast was smoking on the table. Its appearance nearly produced a relapse in my spirits. I am not very subject to fainting, but I could eat none of the breakfast: it was mostly of whale, seahorse, and bear, which though smoked, dried, and boiled, produced a composition of smells very offensive at nine or ten in the morning.

The number of Russians were about thirty, and they had with them about seventy Indians from Kamchatka; these with some American Indians, occupied the village. I found a small sloop of about 30 tons burthen laying in a cove behind the village. This little bark belonged to Kamchatka and came from there with the Asians to this island, which they call Unalaska, in order to establish a fur factory. They had been here about five years and go over to Kamchatka in her once a year to deliver their merchandise.

The next day I set off from this village. I was accompanied by three of the principal Russians. We embarked at the village in a large skin boat much like our whale boats, rowing with twelve oars. As we struck directly across the bay, we shortened our distance, and the next day we arrived by sundown at the bay, where the ships lay. The satisfaction this discovery gave Cook, and the honor redounded to me, may be easily imagined.

On the tenth, Ledyard returned with three Russian furriers. One of these men was either the master or mate of their vessel. For want of an interpreter we had some difficulty in understanding each other. They appeared to have a thorough knowledge of the attempts made by their countrymen to navigate the Frozen Ocean, and the discoveries made by Bering, Tscherikoff, and Spangenberg. They knew no more of Lt. Synd than his name. I laid before them my own chart and found that they were strangers to every part of the American coast except what lies opposite this island. The three Russians remained with me all night, then left us, promising to return in a few days and to bring with them a chart of the islands lying between Unalaska and Kamchatka.

ALASKA FOUND On the fifteenth a Russian landed who, I found, was the principal person among his countrymen in this and the neighboring islands. His name was Erasim Gregorifoff Sin Ismyloff. (*Gerassin Grigorovich Ismailof was stationed at Captain's Harbor, Unalaska Bay.*) He appeared to be a sensible, intelligent man; and I felt no small mortification in not being able to converse with him unless by signs, assisted by figures and other characters. Ismyloff affirmed that they knew nothing of the continent of America to the northward and

PART

OF

ASIA

ARTIC

CIRCLE

KORIAKS

SEA of OKOTSK

KORIAKS

TSCHUTSKI

Anadirsk Guba

Beeting Island

BERINGS STRAIT

CLERKE

BRISTOL

Atako I.

OONALASKA

COOK'S CHART OF
IN THE NORTHERN

THIS WAS THE FIRST MAP TO SHOW WITH ANY ACCURACY THE COAST OF

HIS EXPLORATIONS
PACIFIC OCEAN

NORTH AMERICA AND WHAT WAS TO BECOME THE STATE OF ALASKA.

that neither Lt. Synd nor any other Russian had ever seen it. They call it by the same name which Mr. Staehlin gives to his great island, that is, Alaska. The American continent is called by the Russians as well as the islanders, Alaska, which name is used by them when speaking of the American continent in general. They know perfectly well that it is a great land.

On the nineteenth he made us another visit and brought with him the charts before mentioned, which he allowed me to copy. I shall give some acount of the islands beginning with those that lie nearest to Kamchatka. The first is Bering's Island. Ten leagues from the south end of this lies Maindoi Ostroff (*Ostrov Medny*). The next island is Atakou (*Attu and Akattu*). We next come to a group con- sisting of six or more islands, two of which, Atghka (*Atka*) and Amluk (*Amlia*), are tolerably large. An island called Amoghta (*Amukta*) was 4° west of here. Ismyloff's chart converts about 15 leagues of the coast that I supposed to belong to the continent into an island, distinguished by the name of Ooneemak (*Unimak*).

They all said that no Russians had settled themselves so far to the east as the place where the natives gave the note to Captain Clerke. Mr. Ismyloff said it had been written at Unimak. From him we got the name of Kodiak, the largest of Schumagin's Islands. (*As noted before, when Cook sailed past Kodiak Island he thought it was part of the continent. He incorrectly placed it among the Shumagin Islands.*) This is all the information I got from these people relating to the geography of this part of the world; and I have reason to be- lieve that this was all the information they were able to give. There are Russians settled upon all the principal islands between Unalaska and Kamchatka for the sole purpose of collecting furs. The great object is the sea otter.

Mr. Ismyloff remained with us till the twenty-first, when he took his final leave. To his care I entrusted a letter to the Lord's Commis- sioners of the Admiralty in which was enclosed a chart of all the northern coast I had visited. He said there would be opportunity of sending it to Kamchatka the ensuing spring and that it would be at Petersburg the following winter. Mr. Ismyloff seemed to have abili- ties that might entitle him to a higher station in life than that in which we found him. He was versed in astronomy and in the most useful branches of mathematics. I made him a present of an Hadley's

Octant, and though the first he had ever seen, he made himself acquainted in a short time with most of its uses. ॐ

The letter traveled across the Bering Sea, and across Russia and Europe, much faster than Ismailof expected and reached England in six months.

॰§ It is now time to give some account of the native inhabitants. To all appearances they are the most peaceable, inoffensive people, I ever met with. As to honesty, they might serve as a pattern to the most civilized nation. I doubt whether this was their original disposition, and rather think that it is the consequence of their present state of subjection. At present a great harmony exists between the two nations (*Russian and native*).

Both sexes wear the same fashion; the only difference is in the materials. The women's frock is made of seal skin, and that of the men, of the skins of birds, both reaching below the knee. Over the frock, the men wear another made of gut, which resists water and has a hood which draws around the head. All of them have an oval, snouted cap made of wood. Their food consists of fish, sea-animals, birds, roots, berries, and seaweed. They eat almost everything raw. I was once present when the Chief of Unalaska made his dinner of the raw head of a large halibut just caught.

I saw not a fireplace in any one of their houses, which are lighted as well as heated by lamps. The lamps are made of a flat stone, hollowed on one side like a plate. In the hollow part they put the oil, mixed with a little grass which serves the purpose of a wick. They frequently warm their bodies over one of their lamps by placing it between their legs, under their garments, and sitting over it for a few minutes.

I have frequently mentioned how remarkably the natives of this northwest side of America resemble the Greenlanders and Eskimo in various particulars of person, dress, weapons, canoes, and the like. I was struck with the affinity which we found subsisting between the dialects of the Greenlander and Eskimo and those of Norton Sound and Unalaska. This will appear from a table of corresponding words which I put together (*see Table.*) It must be observed, however, with regard to the words which we collected on this side of America, that

too much stress is not to be laid upon their being accurately represented; for after Mr. Anderson's death, we had few who took much
pains in such matters. Frequently the same words written down by
two or three persons, on being compared, differed not a little. Enough
is certain to warrant the judgment that there is great reason to believe
that all these nations are of the same extraction. If so, there can be
little doubt of there being a northern communication of some sort by
sea between this west side of America and the east side; which communication, however, may be effectually shut against ships by ice or
other impediments. Such, at least, was my opinion at the time. &

TABLE TO SHOW THE AFFINITY BETWEEN
THE LANGUAGE SPOKEN AT NORTON SOUND
(WEST COAST OF AMERICA)
AND THE ESKIMO (ON THE ATLANTIC COAST)

English	Norton Sound	Eskimo
THE CHEEK	OOLLOOAK	OU-LU-UCK-CUR
THE EAR	SHUDEKA	SE-U-TECK
THE HAIR	NOOIT	NEW-ROCK
THE ARM	DALLEK	TELLUCK
THE LEG	KANAIAK	KI-NAW-AUK
THE FOOT	ETSCHEAK	E-TE-KET
IRON	SHAWIK	SHAVECK
ONE	ADOWJAK	ATTOUSET
TWO	AIBA	MARDLUK
THREE	PINGASHOOK	PINGASUT
FOUR	SHETAMIK	SISSAMAT
FIVE	DALLAMIK	TELLIMAT

Much later geographical explorations in the far north of Canada
proved Captain Cook's deductions to be so accurate that it seems he
must have already had a picture in his mind of how the map of
northern Canada would look. The extensiveness of Cook's explorations in Alaska can be gathered from the adjoining table listing
Cook's names for geographical points in the State of Alaska still to
be found on modern maps. Also Cook's chart of the coastline of
North America differs only slightly from a modern one. Modern sur-
veys begin with Cook's; and his require little improvement.

TABLE OF ALASKAN PLACES NAMED BY COOK

Cook's Name	Location
MT. EDGECUMBE	NEAR SITKA
CAPE EDGECUMBE	" "
MT. FAIRWEATHER	GULF OF ALASKA
CAPE FAIRWEATHER	" " "
CROSS SOUND	" " "
CAPE SUCKLING	" " "
CONTROLLER BAY	" " "
CAPE HINCHINBROOK	PRINCE WILLIAM SOUND
SNUG CORNER BAY	" " "
MONTAGUE ISLAND	" " "
GREEN ISLAND	" " "
PRINCE WILLIAM SOUND	" " "
COOK INLET (by Earl of Sandwich)	COOK INLET
CAPE ELIZABETH	" "
BARREN ISLANDS	" "
CAPE DOUGLAS	" "
MT. ST. AUGUSTINE	" "
CAPE BEDE	" "
TURNAGAIN RIVER	" "
POINT POSSESSION	" "
CAPE BARNABAS	KODIAK ISLAND
TWOHEADED ISLAND	" "
TRINITY ISLANDS	" "
FOGGY CAPE	ALASKAN PENINSULA
BRISTOL BAY	BRISTOL BAY
ROUND ISLAND	" "
CAPE NEWENHAM	" "
CAPE UPRIGHT	ST. MATTHEW ISLAND
PINNACLE ISLAND	" " "
CAPE RODNEY	SEWARD PENINSULA
SLEDGE ISLAND	" "
KING ISLAND	" "
CAPE PRINCE OF WALES	" "
CAPE DARBY	" "
MULGRAVE HILLS	CHUKCHI SEA
ICY CAPE	" "
CAPE LISBURNE	" "

TABLE OF ALASKAN PLACES NAMED BY COOK (continued)

Cook's Name	Location
NORTON SOUND	NORTON SOUND
NORTON BAY	" "
BESBORO ISLAND	" "
CAPE DENBIGH	" "
SHAKTOLIK (Chacktoole)	" "
STUART ISLAND	" "
CAPE STEPHENS	

CHAPTER TWENTY-THREE

RETURN TO HAWAII

October 26, 1778——January 16, 1779

⋖ On the morning of the twenty-sixth of October we put to sea from English Harbor. My intention was now to proceed to the Sandwich Islands, there to spend a few of the winter months and then direct our course to Kamchatka so as to be there by the middle of May the ensuing summer. On the second of November, the wind veered to the southward and blew a violent storm, which obliged us to bring to. The *Discovery* fired several guns without us knowing on what occasion they were fired; for we lost sight of her and did not see her until ten the next morning, when she joined us. Captain Clerke came on board and informed me that the main tack gave way, killed one man, and wounded the boatswain and two or three more. His sails and rigging received considerable damage. On the ninth we had eight hours' calm. Availing ourselves of this, as many of our people as could handle a needle were set to work to repair the sails. On the seventeenth the wind again increased to a very strong gale so as to bring us under double-reefed topsails. In lowering down the main-top-sail to reef it, the wind tore it quite out of the foot rope, and it was split in several parts. This sail had only been brought to the yard the day before, after having a repair; but the next morning we got another top-sail to the yard. This gale proved to be the forerunner of the trade wind which in the latitude 25° veered to east and east-southeast. ⋗

AMONG THE HAWAIIAN ISLANDS ⋖ On the morning of the twenty-fifth of November, at which time we were in the latitude of 20° 55′, I spread the ships and steered to the west. ⋗

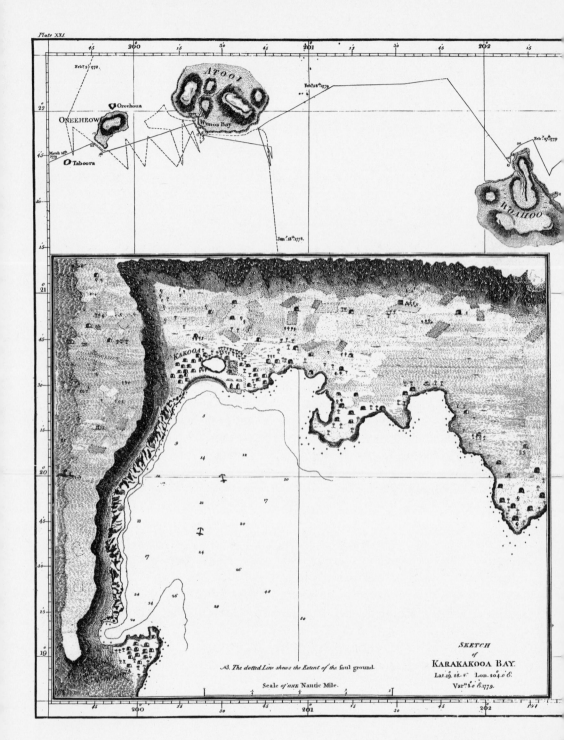

Plate XXI.

ATOOI

Feb.2ᵈ 1778.

Oreehoua

ONEEHEOW

Wynoa Bay

March 1st. 1778.

Taboora

Feb.28th.1778.

WOAHOO

Feb.7ᵗʰ.1779.

Jan.18th.1778.

KAKOOA

N3. The dotted Line shews the Extent of the foul ground.

Scale of ONE Nautic Mile.

SKETCH of
KARAKAKOOA BAY.
Lat.19.28.N. Lon.204.0.6.
Varⁿ8.0.E.1779.

CHART OF THE

OBSERVE THE NUMEROUS TRACKS THE SHIPS MADE AROUND THE ISLAND

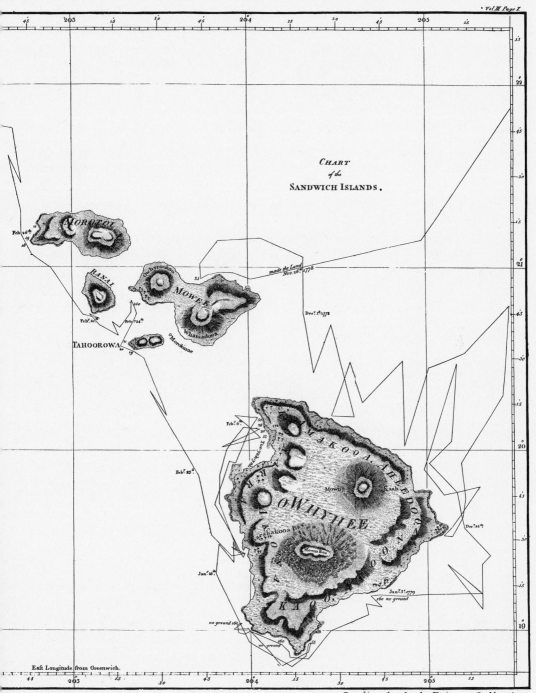

CHART
of the
SANDWICH ISLANDS.

MOROTOI

Feb.ᵗ 26ᵗʰ

RANAI

O-hy-rookoo
MOWEE
Whamadoa

o-Morokinne

TAHOOROWA

made the Land
Nov. 26ᵗ 1778.

Dec.ᵗ 1ˢᵗ 1778.

Feb.ᵗ 6ᵗʰ

Feb.ᵗ 23ᵈ

Jan.ᵗ 16ᵗʰ

WAKOOA ALEEDOO

Mowi
Kaah

OWHYHEE

Kaakooa Bay
Mowna Roa

KAO.

Dec.ᵗ 26ᵗʰ

Jan.ᵗ 31ˢᵗ 1779.
160 no ground

no ground 160

no ground

East Longitude from Greenwich.

HAWAIIAN ISLANDS

F OWHYHEE (HAWAII) WHILE SEEKING A PLACE TO ANCHOR.

When he was at the Island of Kauai last January, Captain Cook learned from the natives that there were other islands to the eastward of Kauai that he could not see. Therefore, in coming south from the Aleutian Islands, he directed his course well to the eastward of where he thought these islands might lie, and after he had reached their approximate latitude turned westward, running before the trade winds, until they would come into view. He knew that once he was on the westward side of the islands—their downwind side—he could never beat against the strong trade winds to reach them. It was necessary to come upon them from the east, or windward, side.

⋖§ At daybreak next morning, land was seen extending from southeast to west. We made sail and stood for it. We were now satisfied that the group of the Sandwich Islands had been only imperfectly discovered, as those of them which we had visited in our progress northward all lie to the leeward of our present station. As it was of the most importance to procure a supply of provisions at these islands, I published an order prohibiting all persons from trading except such as should be appointed by me and Captain Clerke, and these were enjoined to trade only for provisions and refreshments. Women were also forbidden to be admitted onto the ships.

Seeing some canoes coming off to us, I brought to. As soon as they got alongside, many of the occupants came into the ship without the least hesitation. We found them to be of the same nation with the inhabitants of the islands more to leeward, which we had already visited. If we did not mistake them, they knew of our having been there. Indeed, it rather appeared too evident, for these people had among them the venereal disease. I knew of no other way of its reaching them but by an intercourse with their neighbors since our leaving them.

On the afternoon of the thirtieth, being off the northeast end of the island, several canoes came off to the ships. Most of these belonged to a Chief named Terreeoboo, who came in one of them. After a stay of about two hours they left us, except for six or eight who chose to remain on board. A double sailing canoe came to attend upon them, which we towed astern all night. In the evening we discovered another island to windward, which the natives call Hawaii. The name of that, off which we had been for some days, we were told is Maui. Finding that we could fetch Hawaii, I stood for it. In the morning we were surprised to see the summits of the mountains on Hawaii covered with snow. The snow seemed to be of a considerable depth and to have lain there some time. ৈ৶

THE BREWERY ৶ Having procured a quantity of sugarcane, and having found that a strong decoction of it produced a very palatable beer, I ordered it to be brewed for our general use. But when the cask was broached, not one of my crew would even so much as taste it. As I had no motive in preparing this beverage but to save our spirits for a colder climate, I gave myself no trouble either by exerting authority or by persuasion, to prevail upon them to drink it. I knew there was no danger of scurvy so long as we could get a plentiful supply of other vegetables. But that I might not be disappointed in my views, I gave orders that no grog should be served in either ship; and I, myself, and the officers, used this sugarcane beer—a few hops improved it much. It has the taste of new malt beer. I believe no one will doubt its being very wholesome, yet my inconsiderate crew alleged it was injurious to their health.

They had had a resolution which they took on our first arrival in King George's Sound (Vancouver Island) not to drink the spruce beer made there. Whether from a consideration that it was not the first time of their being required to use that liquor, or from some other reasons, they did not attempt to carry their purpose into actual execution. Now they renewed their ignorant opposition to my best endeavors to serve them.

Every innovation whatever on board a ship, though ever so much to the advantage of seamen, is sure to meet with their highest disapprobation. Both portable soup and sauerkraut were, at first, condemned as stuff unfit for human beings. Few commanders have introduced into their ships more novelties, or useful varieties of food and drink, than I have done. Indeed, few commanders have had the same opportunities of trying such experiments, or have been driven to the same necessity of trying them. It has been in a great measure owing to various little deviations from established practice that I have been able to preserve my people from that dreadful distemper, the scurvy, which has destroyed more of our sailors in their peaceful voyages than have fallen by the enemy in military expeditions. ৈ৶

The problem of preventing scurvy was not only one of properly provisioning the ship so that vitamin-rich nourishment was available, but also of overcoming the dietary prejudices that the seamen, like all other people, have. The unfamiliar food was disliked, rejected, and often gave rise to feelings of disgust. Cook knew how to prevent scurvy, but even he could not always effectively teach his crew either by cajoling, or by the practical demonstration of the success of their long voyage, which was free of the ravages of this disease, that fresh food and a varied diet were essential for their health. One of his crew, Joseph Billings, later in the service of Empress Catherine of Russia, returned to the Pacific northwest, where he had been with Cook during this voyage, and many of his crew died of scurvy.

CAPTAIN KING'S JOURNAL
OF THE TRANSACTIONS
ON RETURNING TO
THE SANDWICH ISLANDS

CHAPTER TWENTY-FOUR

HAWAII

January 17, 1779——February 3, 1779

KEALAKEKUA BAY ✍ Kealakekua Bay is situated on the west side of the island of Hawaii; it is about a mile in depth and bounded by two low points of land. On the north point, which is flat and barren, stands the village of Kowrowa; in the bottom of the bay, near a grove of tall coconut trees, there is another village called Kakooa. The shore all around the bay is covered with black coral rock, which makes the landing very dangerous in rough weather, except at the village of Kakooa, where there is fine sandy beach. This bay appearing to Captain Cook a proper place to refit the ships and lay in an additional supply of water and provisions, we moored on the north side, about a quarter of a mile from the shore.

As soon as the inhabitants perceived our intention of anchoring in the bay, they came off from the shore in astonishing numbers and expressed their joy by singing and shouting. The sides, the decks, and the rigging of both ships were soon completely covered with them. A multitude of women and boys who had not been able to get canoes came swimming around us in schools; many of whom, not finding room on board, remained the whole day playing in the water.

Among the Chiefs who came on board the *Resolution* was a young man called Pareea, whom we soon perceived to be a person of great authority. On presenting himself to Captain Cook, he told him the King of the island, who was at that time engaged on a military expedition at Maui, was expected to return within three or four days. A few presents from Captain Cook attached him entirely to our interests, and he became exceedingly useful to us in the management of his

A VIEW OF KEALAKEKUA

Credit: Courtesy of Rare Book Division, New York

BAY HAWAII

countrymen, as we soon had occasion to experience. The *Discovery* had such a number of people hanging on one side as occasioned her to heel considerably, and the men were unable to keep off the crowds, which continued pressing into her. Captain Cook pointed out the danger to Pareea, who immediately went to their assistance, cleared the ship of its incumbrances, and drove away the canoes that surrounded her.

A similar instance happened the same day on board the *Resolution* and we were obliged to have recourse to the assistance of Kaneena, another of their Chiefs, who had attached himself to Captain Cook. Both these Chiefs were men of strong and well-proportioned bodies, and of countenances remarkably pleasing. Kaneena especially, whose portrait Mr. Webber has shown, was one of the finest men I ever saw. He was about six feet high, had regular and expressive features with lively dark eyes; his carriage was easy, firm, and graceful.

Pareea and Kaneena brought on board a third Chief named Koah, who, we were told, was a priest. He was a little old man of an emaciated figure, his eyes exceedingly sore and red, and his body covered with a white leprous scurf. He approached Captain Cook with great veneration and threw over his shoulders a piece of red cloth. Then stepping back, he made an offering of a small pig while he pronounced a discourse that lasted for a considerable time. This ceremony was frequently repeated during our stay at Hawaii and appeared to be a religious adoration. Their idols were always arrayed with red cloth, in the same manner as was done to Captain Cook, and a small pig was their usual offering to the *Eatooas,* or gods.

When we landed at the beach we were received by four men, who carried wands tipped with dog's hair and marched before us, pronouncing with a loud voice a short sentence in which we could only distinguish the word *Orono*. Captain Cook went by this name among the natives of Hawaii, but we could never learn its precise meaning. Sometimes they applied it to an invisible being who lived in the heavens. We also found that it was a title belonging to a personage of great rank and power who resembles the Dalai Lama of the Tartars and the ecclesiastical Emperor of Japan.

Before I proceed to relate the adoration paid to Captain Cook and the peculiar ceremonies with which he was received on this fatal island, it will be necessary to describe the marae situated at the south side of the beach at Kakooa. It was a square, solid pile of stone, about 120 feet long, 60 feet broad, and 42 feet high. The top was flat and well paved and surrounded by a wooden rail on which were fixed the skulls of the captives sacrificed on the death of their Chiefs. In the center stood a ruinous old building of wood connected with a rail on each side by a stone wall, which divided the whole place into two parts. On one side were five poles, upward of 20 feet high, supporting an irregular scaffold.

We were conducted by Koah to the top of this pile. At the entrance we saw two large wooden images with features violently distorted and a long piece of carved wood of a conical form rising from the top of their heads. The rest was without form and wrapped round with red cloth. We were met by a tall young man with a long beard, who presented Captain Cook to the images after chanting a hymn in which he was joined by Koah. They led us to the end of the marae, where the five poles were fixed. At the foot of them were twelve images ranged in a semicircular form; and before the figure stood a high table on which lay a putrid hog and under it pieces of sugarcane, coconuts, breadfruit, bananas, and sweet potatoes. Koah, having placed the Captain under this stand, took down the hog and held it toward him. After having a second time made a long speech pronounced with much vehemence and rapidity, he led him to the scaffolding, which they began to climb together, not without some risk of falling. At this time we saw ten men coming in solemn procession carrying a live hog and a large piece of red cloth. They stopped and prostrated themselves. Kaireekeea, the young man, went to them, and receiving the cloth carried it to Koah, who wrapped it around the Captain and offered him the hog with the same ceremony.

While Captain Cook was aloft in this awkward situation, swathed round with red cloth, and with difficulty keeping his hold among the pieces of rotten scaffolding, Kaireekeea and Koah began their office, chanting sometimes in concert and sometimes alternately. This lasted a considerable time. At length Koah let the hog drop; then he and the Captain descended together. He then led him to the images, and having said something to each in a sneering tone, snapped his fingers at them as he passed. He brought him to the figure in the center, which appeared to be in greater estimation than the rest. Before this figure he prostrated himself and kissed it, desiring Captain Cook, who suffered himself to be directed by Koah throughout the whole of this ceremony, to do the same.

We were now led back to the other division of the marae, where
there was a space 10 or 12 feet square sunk about 3 feet below the
level of the area. Into this we descended and Captain Cook was seated
between two wooden idols. Koah supported one of his arms while
I was desired to support the other. At this time arrived a second procession of natives carrying a baked hog, a pudding, some breadfruit,
coconuts, and other vegetables. Kaireekeea began the same chant as
before, his companions making regular responses. After every response
the parts became gradually shorter. Toward the close, Kaireekeea's
consisted of only two or three words, which the rest answered by the
word *Orono*.

When this offering, which lasted a quarter of an hour, was concluded, the natives sat down and began to cut up the baked hog, to
peel the vegetables, break the coconuts, and brew the kava by chewing it in the same manner as at the Friendly Islands. Kaireekeea then
took part of the kernel of a coconut which he chewed and wrapped
in a piece of cloth. He rubbed the Captain's face, head, arms, and
shoulders with it. Koah and Pareea began to pull the flesh of the hog
in pieces and to put it in our mouths. I had no great objection to
being fed by Pareea, who was very cleanly in his person, but Captain
Cook was served by Koah. Recollecting the putrid hog, he could not
swallow a morsel, and his reluctance was not diminished when the
old man, according to his own mode of civility, had chewed it for him.

When this last ceremony was finished, which Captain Cook put to
an end as soon as he decently could, we quit the marae. After distribut-
ing among the people some pieces of iron and other trifles with which
they seemed highly gratified, the men conducted us to the boats. We
immediately went on board, our minds full of what we had seen; the
meaning of the various ceremonies can only be the subject of conjectures. They were, however, without doubt, expressive of high respect
on the part of the natives. As far as related to the person of Captain
Cook, they seemed to approach adoration.

The next morning I went on shore to erect an observatory. We
fixed on a field of sweet potatoes adjoining the marae, which was
readily granted us. The priests, to prevent the intrusion of the natives,
immediately consecrated the place. This religious interdiction they
call *taboo,* a word we heard often repeated among the islanders and
found to be of very powerful and extensive operation, for no canoes
ever presumed to land near us. The natives sat on the wall, but none

offered to come within the tabooed space until he had obtained our permission. Though the men at our request would come across the field with provisions, all our endeavors could not prevail on the women to approach us; presents were tried, but without effect. We tempted Pareea and Koah to bring them, but in vain. This circumstance afforded no small matter of amusement to our friends on board, where the crowds of women that continued to flock thither obliged them almost every hour to clear the vessel in order to have room to do the necessary duties of the ship. On these occasions, two or three hundred women were frequently made to jump into the water at once, where they continued swimming and playing about until they could again procure admittance.

During the rest of the time we remained in the bay, whenever Captain Cook came on shore he was attended by one of the priests, who went before him giving notice that the Orono had landed and ordering the people to prostrate themselves. The civilities of this society were not, however, confined to mere ceremony and parade. Our party on shore received every day, a constant supply of hogs and vegetables, more than sufficient for our subsistence. Several canoes loaded with provisions were sent to the ships with the same punctuality. No return was ever demanded or even hinted at. Their presents were made more like the discharge of a religious duty than the effect of mere liberality. When we inquired at whose charge all this munificence was displayed, we were told it was at the expense of a great man called Kaoo, the Chief of the priests and grandfather of Kaikeekeea.

We had not always so much reason to be satisfied with the conduct of the warrior Chiefs, or *Earees,* as with that of the priests. We found them sufficiently attentive to their own interests: besides their habit of stealing, which may admit of some excuse from the universality of the practice among the islanders of these seas, they made use of other artifices equally dishonorable.

Things continued in this state until the twenty-fourth, when we were surprised to find that no canoes put off from shore and the natives kept close to their houses. After several hours' suspense, we learned that the bay was tabooed and all intercourse with us interdicted on account of the arrival of Terreeoboo; so the crews of both ships were obliged to pass the day without their usual supply of vegetables. Therefore the next morning they endeavored, both by threats and promises, to induce the natives to come alongside. Some of them were at last venturing to put off, but a Chief was observed attempting to drive them away. A musket was fired over his head to make him desist, which had the desired effect, and refreshments were soon after purchased as usual.

The next day, the King, in a large canoe attended by two others, set out from the village and paddled toward the ships in great state. Their appearance was grand and magnificent. In the first canoe was Terreeoboo and his Chiefs, dressed in rich, feathered cloaks and helmets and armed with long spears and daggers. In the second came the venerable Kaoo, Chief of the priests, and his brethren, with the idols displayed in red cloth. These idols were busts of gigantic size, made of wickerwork and covered with small feathers of various colors. Their eyes were made of pearl oysters with a black nut fixed in the center. Their mouths were set with a double row of the fangs of dogs. The third canoe was filled with hogs and vegetables. As they went along, the priests sang their hymns with great solemnity. After paddling around the ships, instead of going on board as was expected, they made toward the shore, where the observatory was stationed. Captain Cook, perceiving that Terreeoboo was going ashore, followed him and arrived nearly at the same time.

He conducted them into the tent, where they had scarcely been seated when the King rose up and in a very graceful manner threw over the Captain's shoulders the cloak he himself wore, put a feathered helmet on his head, and a curious fan in his hand. He also spread at his feet five or six other cloaks, all exceedingly beautiful and of the greatest value. The King exchanged names with Captain Cook, which among all the islands of the Pacific Ocean is esteemed the strongest pledge of friendship.

A procession of priests with a venerable old personage at their head now appeared. By the looks and gestures of Kaireekeea, I immediately knew the old man to be the Chief of the priests, on whose bounty we had so long subsisted. I was surprised to see in the person of the Chief the same infirm and emaciated old man that came on board the *Resolution* when we were off the northeast side of the island of Maui; and we soon discovered among his attendants, most of the persons who at that time had remained with us all night.

During all this time not a canoe was seen in the bay; and the natives either kept within their huts or lay prostrate on the ground. Captain Cook obtained leave for the natives to come and trade with the ships as usual; but the women, for what reason we could not learn, still continued under the effects of the taboo and were forbidden to stir from home or communicate with us.

The quiet and inoffensive behavior of the natives took away every apprehension of danger. We did not hesitate to trust ourselves among them at all times and in all situations. The officers of both ships went daily up the country in small parties or even singly and frequently remained out the whole night. It would be endless to recount all the instances of kindness and civility we received: boys and girls ran before us; we were invited to accept a draught of coconut milk under the shade of their huts; and young women exerted all their skill and agility to amuse us with songs and dances.

The satisfaction we derived from their gentleness and hospitality was, however, frequently interrupted by that propensity to stealing which they have in common with all the other islanders of these seas. This circumstance was the more distressing, as it sometimes obliged us to have recourse to acts of severity which we would willingly have avoided if the necessity of the case had not absolutely called for them. Some expert swimmers were one day discovered under the ships drawing out the nails of the sheathing, which they performed very dexterously by means of a short stick with a flint stone fixed in the end of it. This practice endangered the very existence of the vessels. We fired small shot at the offenders, but they easily got out of reach by diving under the ship's bottom. It was found necessary to make an example by flogging one of them on board the *Discovery*.

The head of the *Resolution*'s rudder being found exceedingly shaken, and most of the pintles either loose or broken, it was unhung and sent on shore to undergo a thorough repair. At the same time, the carpenters were sent into the country under conduct of some of Kaoo's people to cut planks for the head railwork, which was also entirely decayed and rotten. &

The wooden ships of Captain Cook's day were put together with iron fastenings. Wrought iron lasted well enough until the practice of sheathing the ships with sheet copper was instituted to prevent fouling and infestation of the wood with marine borers. The copper sheathing was effective against barnacles but, unknown to the ship builders of that day, a batterylike chemical action occurs between the ironwork and the copper sheathing, with the result that the ironwork dissolves and disappears. This is what has happened to the ship's pintles, which are metal points on the rudder and fit into sockets on the ship's stern-post, called gudgeons. Dry rot has also infected much of the *Resolution*. At almost every port some rotten part of the vessels has had to be replaced. The "head rail" is the above-deck bulwark in the forepart of the ship.

⋙ January 28, 1779. On this day died William Watman, a seaman of the gunner's crew; an event which I mention the more particularly, as death had hitherto been very rare among us. He was an old man and much respected on account of his attachment to Captain Cook. He had formerly served as a marine twenty-one years, after which he entered as a seaman on board the *Resolution* in 1772 and served with Captain Cook in his voyage toward the South Pole. He had a paralytic stroke, which in two days carried him off. At the request of the King of the island he was buried on the morai and the ceremony was performed with as much solemnity as our situation permitted. Old Kaoo and his brethren were spectators and preserved the most profound interest and attention while the service was read. Afterward they surrounded the grave, sacrificing hogs and performing their usual ceremony of hymns and prayers, which continued until daybreak.

The ships being in great want of fuel, the Captain desired me on the second of February to treat with the priests for the purchase of the rail that surrounded the top of the morai. I must confess I had some doubt about the decency of this proposal, and was apprehensive that even the bare mention of it might be considered by them as a piece of shocking impiety. However, I found myself mistaken. Not the smallest surprise was expressed at the application, and the wood was readily given even without stipulating for anything in return. While the sailors were taking it away, I observed one of them carrying off a carved image and found that they had conveyed to the boats the whole semi-circle of images. Though this was done in the presence of the natives, who had not shown any mark of resentment but had even assisted in the removal, I thought it proper to speak to Kaoo on the subject. He appeared very indifferent about the matter and only desired that we would restore the center image, which he carried into one of the priests' houses.

Terreeoboo and his Chiefs had for some days been very inquisitive about the time of our departure. They imagined we came from some country where provisions had failed and that our visit to them was for the purpose of filling our bellies. The meager appearance of some of our crew, the hearty appetites with which we sat down to their fresh provisions, and our great anxiety to purchase and carry off as much as we were able, led them naturally enough to such a conclusion. A circumstance which puzzled them exceedingly was our having no women with us. It was ridiculous to see them stroking the sides and patting the bellies of the sailors (who were certainly much improved in the sleekness of their looks during our short stay on the island) and telling them by signs and words that it was time for them to go; but if they would come again the next breadfruit season, they would be better able to supply their wants. We had now been sixteen days in the bay, and if our enormous consumption of hogs and vegetables be considered, it need not be wondered that they should wish to see us take our leave.

Terreeoboo had a desire to make sufficient preparation to dismiss us with presents. On telling him we should leave the island on the day after next, a proclamation was made through the village to require the people to bring their hogs and vegetables for the King to present to the Orono. ॐ

CHAPTER TWENTY-FIVE

HAWAIIAN LIFE

᪗ As we are now about to take our leave of the Sandwich Islands, it will not be improper to introduce some general account of their situation, natural history, and customs of the inhabitants.

This group consists of eleven islands called by the natives: Owhyhee, Mowee, Ranai, Morokinnee, Kahowrowee, Morotoi, Woahoo, Attoi (or sometimes Kowi), Oneeheow, Oreehooa, and Tahoora. ᨀ

In modern spelling, which is also an effort to phonetically write the sounds that the natives spoke, the list in the same order becomes: Hawaii, Maui, Lanai, Molokini, Kahoolawe, Molokai, Oahu, Kauai, Nihau, Lehua, and Kaula. (Hereafter the modern spelling will be used.)

᪗ Besides the islands above enumerated, we are told that there is another called Komodoopapapa, lying west-southwest of Kaula and which is low and sandy and visited only for the purpose of catching turtle and sea-fowl. As I could never learn that they knew of any others, it is probable that none exist in their neighborhood. All are inhabited except Molokini and Kaula. ᨀ

The nearest island west of Kaula lies in a *north*westerly direction (there are none to the southwest). This is the island of Nihoa, 125 miles from Kaula. Archaeological evidence indicates that not only tiny Nihoa but also Necker Island, 180 miles farther west, were once inhabited and cultivated.

⋖§ Hawaii, the easternmost, is much the largest of the islands. A mountain called Mauna Loa rises in three peaks, perpetually covered with snow. To the north of the mountain the coast consists of high and abrupt cliffs, down which fall many beautiful cascades of water. Puna, which forms the eastern extremity of the island, is low and flat and the whole country is covered with coconut and breadfruit trees. This as far as we could judge is the finest part of the island, and the King had a place of residence here. The snowy mountain called Mauna Loa was a very conspicuous object all the while we were sailing along the southeast side. It is flat at the top and constantly buried in snow. The coast of the Kau district presents a prospect of the most horrid and dreary kind: the whole country appearing to have undergone a dreadful convulsion. The ground is covered with cinders and intersected with black streaks which mark the course of lava that has flowed, not many ages back, from the mountain to the sea. The southern promontory looks like the dregs of a volcano. Notwithstanding the dismal aspect of this part of the island, there are many villages scattered over it, and it certainly is much more populated than the verdant mountains of Puna. Amidst these ruins are many patches of rich soil carefully laid out in plantations.

In the district of Kona is situated Kealakekua Bay. To the north the country is cultivated with great pains and is extremely populous. Along the coast nothing is seen but large masses of slag and fragments of black scorched rock. Here in a rich ashy soil they cultivate sweet potatoes and the cloth-plant. The fields are enclosed with stone fences and interspersed with groves of coconut trees. Not a single spot of ground that was capable of improvement was left unplanted. Indeed, it appeared hardly possible for the country to be cultivated to greater advantage, or made to yield a larger supply of food. ೩✷

The woodsman from Connecticut, John Ledyard, made the farthest penetration into Hawaii's interior. He reported in his account:

On the twenty-sixth of January, 1779, I sent a billet [1] on board to Cook desiring his permission to make an excursion into the interior parts of the country, proposing, if practicable, to reach the famous peak [2] that terminated the height of land. My pro-

[1] A short note
[2] Mauna Loa

posal was not only granted, but promoted by Cook, who very much wanted some information respecting that part of the island. He desired the gunner of the *Resolution,* the botanist sent out by Mr. Banks (*David Nelson*), and Mr. Simon Woodruff to be of the party. He also procured some attendants among the natives to assist us in carrying our baggage and directing us through the woods. It required some prudence to make a good equipment for this tour, for though we had the full heat of a tropical sun near the margin of the island, we knew we should experience a different temperament in the air the higher we advanced toward the peak. We therefore took each of us a woolen blanket, made some alterations in our dress, and we each took a bottle of brandy.

About two miles without the town the land was level and one plain of little enclosures was separated from the other by low broad walls. These enclosed plantations extended about three miles from town and were succeeded by open plantations. Here the land began to rise with a gentle ascent that continued about one mile, when it became abruptly steep. These were the plantations that contained the breadfruit trees. After leaving the breadfruit forest we continued up the ascent the distance of 1½ miles farther and found the land covered with wild fern. It was now near sundown. Being upon the skirts of those woods that so remarkably surround this island at a uniform distance of 4 and 5 miles from shore we concluded to halt, especially as there was a hut hard by. When we reached the hut we found it inhabited by an elderly man, his wife, and daughter—the emblem of innocent, uninstructed beauty. We sat down together before the door, and from the height of the situation, we had a complete retrospective view of our route—of the town, part of the bay, one of our ships, and an extensive prospect of the ocean and a distant view of three neighboring islands.

We purchased a pig and had him dressed by our host. After supper we had some of brandy diluted with the mountain water. We had so long been confined to the poor brackish water at the bay below that it was a nectar to us.

At night a heavy dew fell and we felt it very chilly and had recourse to our blankets. The next morning when we came to enter the woods we found there had been a heavy rain though none of it had approached us notwithstanding we were within 200 yards of the skirts of the forest. It seemed to be a fact that neither the rain nor the dews descended lower than where the woods terminated. We traversed these woods by a compass, keep-

ing a direct course for the peak, and were happy to find a foot-
path that trended nearly our due course by which means we
traveled by estimation about 15 miles. It was not only excessively
miry and rough, but the way was mostly an ascent, and we had
been unused to walking and especially to carrying such loads as
we had. Our Indian companions were much more fatigued than
we were, though they had nothing to carry and would not carry
anything. The sun had not set when we halted, meeting with a
situation that pleased us. The trunk of a tree that had fallen by
the side of the path lay with one end over another tree that had
fallen before. As it measured 32 feet in circumference and was
4 feet from the ground, it afforded very good shelter except at
the sides, which defect I supplied by large pieces of bark and a
good quantity of boughs which rendered it very commodious. We
slept the night under it much better than we had done the
preceding.

The next morning we set out in good spirits hoping that day
to reach the snowy peak. We had not gone a mile forward before
the path took a direction southwest of west. We consulted our
Indian convoy but to no purpose. At length we concluded to
proceed by the nearest route without any beaten track, and went
in this manner about 4 miles farther finding the way even more
steep and rough but above all impeded by such impenetrable
thickets as would render it impossible for us to proceed farther.
We found the country here, as well as at the seashore, universally
overspread with lava, and every appearance of past eruption and
fire. The woods here are very thick and luxuriant; the largest
trees are nearly 30 feet in girth; and these, with the shrubbery
underneath and the whole intersected with vines, renders it very
umbrageous.

The next day, about two in the afternoon, we cleared the
woods by our old route, and by six o'clock reached the tents, having penetrated about 24 miles, and, we supposed, within 4 miles
of the peak.

Returning to Mr. King's *Journal:*

⋙ The island next in size and nearest in station to Hawaii is Maui;
a low isthmus divides it into two circular peninsulas. The mountains
in both peninsulas rise to an exceedingly great height. To the southward there is a fine spacious bay with a sandy beach, shaded with
coconut trees; it is probable that a good anchorage might be found

here. The country presents a most romantic appearance—the hills rise perpendicularly, and their steep sides, and chasms between, are covered with trees; but the tops of the hills are bare and of reddish-brown color.

Kahoolawe is a small island lying off the southwest part of Maui. The island is destitute of wood and the soil seems to be sandy and barren. Between Kahoolawe and Maui lies the small uninhabited island of Molokini. Molokai lies only 2½ leagues from Maui to the northwest. The southwestern coast, which was the only part near which we approached, is very low, but the land rises to considerable height. It appeared to be entirely without wood. Its produce, we are told, consists chiefly of yams. Lanai lies to the southwest. The country to its south is high and craggy, but other parts appeared to be well inhabited.

Oahu lies to the northwest of Molokai. As far as we could judge from the appearance of the northeast and northwest parts—for we saw nothing of the southern side—it is by far the finest island of the whole group. Nothing can exceed the verdure of the hills, the variety of woods and lawn, and rich, cultivated valleys. (*Seeing "nothing of the southern side" meant that they missed discovering Pearl Harbor, the finest harbor on the "finest island."*)

Kauai lies to the northwest of Oahu. Its productions are the same as of the other islands, but the inhabitants far surpass all the neighboring islands in the management of their plantations. These plantations were divided by regular ditches, the fences were made with neatness approaching elegance, and the roads were finished in a manner that would have done credit to any European engineer.

Nihau lies to the westward of Kauai. The eastern coast is high and rises abruptly from the sea, but the rest of the island consists of low ground. It produces an abundance of yams, and a sweet root called "tee." Lehua and Kaula are two small islands in the neighborhood of Nihau—they are uninhabited.

The climate of the Sandwich Islands differs very little from that of the West Indian Islands, which lie in the same latitude. Upon the whole it may be rather more temperate. The thermometer on shore never rose higher than 88°, and that but one day. Its mean height at noon was 83°. Whether they be subject to violent winds and hurricanes we could not discover. The natives gave us no positive testimony to the fact and no traces of their effects were visible. We generally

saw clouds collecting round the tops of the hills and producing rain
to leeward with fine weather and a clear sky at the seashore. The
winds in general were from the east-southeast to northeast.

The quadrupeds in these, as in all the other islands that have been
discovered in the South Seas, are confined to three sorts: dogs, hogs,
and rats. The dogs, like those of Tahiti, have short crooked legs, long
backs, and pricked ears. They are about the size of a common turnspit,
exceedingly sluggish in their nature, and are fed and left to herd with
the hogs. I do not recollect one instance in which a dog was made a
companion in the manner we do in Europe. Indeed, the custom of
eating them is an insuperable bar to their admission to society. It is
probable that the social qualities of the dog—its fidelity, attachment,
and sagacity—will remain unknown to the natives. ॐ

The "turnspit" was a small nondescript dog used in England on a
treadmill to turn a spit. The Polynesian dog did not survive the subsequent events of the nineteenth and twentieth centuries and none of
the species remain. In the lower left-hand corner of the engraving of
"A View of Huahiné," an illustration of the Polynesian dog can be
seen.

ॐ The supply of hogs we got from them was really astonishing. We
were near four months either cruising the coast or in the harbor at
Hawaii. During all this time a large allowance of fresh pork was
constantly served to both crews. Besides this, and the incredible waste
which in the midst of such plenty was not guarded against, 60 puncheons (*4,200 gallons*) were salted for sea store. Yet we could not
perceive that the supply was at all drained or even that the abundance
had in any way decreased.

The inhabitants of the Sandwich Islands are undoubtedly of the
same race as those of New Zealand, the Society and Friendly Islands,
Easter Island, and the Marquesas. The race possesses all the known
lands between the latitudes 47° south and 20° north and between the
longitudes of 184° east and 100° west. This fact, extraordinary as
it is, might be sufficiently proved by the striking similarity of their
manners and customs, and the general resemblance of their persons
is established beyond all controversy by the absolute identity of their
language. From what continent they originally emigrated and by what
steps they spread through so vast a space, those who are curious in

disquisitions of this nature may perhaps not find it difficult to conjecture. It has been already observed that they bear strong marks of affinity to the tribes of the Ladrones and Caroline islands. The same affinity may be traced among the Battas (*Batavian*) and the Malays. When these events happened is not easy to ascertain. It was probably not lately as they are extremely populous and have no tradition of their origin; on the other hand, the unadulterated state of their language seems to indicate that it could not have been at any very distant period.

It may be thought extremely difficult to form any conjectures respecting the population of the island, many parts with which we were imperfectly acquainted. Two circumstances take away much of this objection: the first that the interior parts are uninhabited, so that if the number along the coast be known this whole will be pretty accurately determined; the other is that there are no towns of any size, the inhabitants being equally dispersed in small villages around the coast. On this ground I will venture a rough calculation of the number of persons in this group of islands. (*Today there are only 114,000 persons of Polynesian ancestry in the Hawaiian Islands*)

		Today's Population 1966 Census
HAWAII	150,000	59,000
MAUI	65,400	38,000
OAHU	60,200	612,000
KAUAI	54,000	25,000
MOLOKAI	36,000	5,600
NIHAU	10,000	280
LANAI	20,400	3,000
LEHUA	4,000	none
TOTAL	400,000	742,880

In their general conduct, these people are of the most mild and affectionate disposition. They appear to live in the utmost harmony and friendship with one another. The women who had children were remarkable for their tender and constant attention to them, and the men would often lend their assistance in those domestic offices. It must, however, be observed that they fall very short in that best test of civilization: the respect paid to women. Here they are not only deprived of the privilege of eating with the men, but the best sorts of food are tabooed. They are not allowed to eat pork, turtle, several kinds of fish, and some species of bananas. In their domestic life they live almost entirely by themselves, and it was evident they had little regard or attention paid to them.

Though the custom of eating the bodies of their enemies be not known by positive evidence to exist in any of the South Sea Islands except New Zealand, yet it is probable that it was originally prevalent in them all. The sacrificing of human victims seems to be a relic of this horrid practice. The inhabitants of the Sandwich Islands bear a nearer resemblance to those of New Zealand both in their person and disposition than to any other people of this family. So it was strongly suspected by Mr. Anderson that they continue to feast on human flesh. The evidence on which he founds this opinion has been stated. I entertained great doubts of the justice of his conclusions and I venture to differ with him. ટ⤳

The resemblance of the New Zealander to the Hawaiian, the two points most distant from each other in Polynesia, may mean that these very distant lands may have been settled by the same subculture of Polynesian people, who had mastered the technique of long sea voyages. The evidence is all on the side of Mr. King that the Hawaiians were not cannibalistic.

⤳ The custom of tattooing the body they have in common with the rest of the natives of the South Sea Islands. The hands and arms of the women are also very neatly marked and they have a singular custom among them: that of tattooing the tip of the tongues of the females.

They have a special dress appropriated to their Chiefs and used on ceremonious occasions consisting of a feathered cloak and helmet. In beauty and magnificence they are perhaps equal to that of any nations in the world. These cloaks are made in different lengths in proportion to the rank of the wearer. Some reach no longer than the middle, others trail the ground. The helmet has a strong lining of wickerwork capable of breaking the blow of any warlike instrument and seems designed for that purpose. The exact resemblance between these and the cloak and helmet formerly worn by the Spaniards was too striking not to excite our curiosity. After exerting every means in our power of obtaining information on the subject, we found that they had no knowledge of any other nation whatever, nor any tradition remaining

A MAN OF THE
SANDWICH ISLANDS DANCING

Credit: Courtesy of Rare Book Division, New York Public Library: Astor,
Lenox and Tilden Foundations

of having ever been visited before. Notwithstanding the results of these inquiries, the uncommon form of dress appears to me a sufficient proof of its European origin and it is a singular deviation from the general resemblance in dress which prevails among these islands. We were driven to a supposition of the shipwreck of some Spanish ship; the course of the Spanish trade from Acapulco to Manila is but a few degrees to the southward in their passage out, and to the northward on their return. ᙂ

Cook's supposition, reported by King, of previous Spanish influ-ence in Hawaii is probably correct but difficult to confirm. His careful observations in themselves must be given great weight in view of his experience with these people. Roderick Cameron, in *The Golden Haze,* states: "It was once thought that a Spanish navigator had touched at Hawaii in the sixteenth century, but this is now generally discredited." Yet there are reports in Spanish archives to the effect that a Spanish navigator named Gaetano stopped at one of the Hawaiian Islands in 1555. The presence of iron objects, as well as the Spanish-appearing helmets and cloaks, may indicate that some shipwrecked survivor may have drifted ashore. This is Michener's thesis in his novel *Hawaii.* Chickering reports that some time between 1528 and 1531 a man and a woman drifted ashore alive on the island of Hawaii. Their ship-wrecked caravel was one of a fleet under command of the Spaniard Don Alvaro de Saavedra. The last word on this controversy has not yet been heard.

ᙂ It is remarkable that the people of these islands are great gamblers. They have a game very much like our draughts (*checkers*). If one may judge from the number of squares, it is much more intricate. The board is about 2 feet long and is divided into 238 squares, of which there are 14 in a row. They make use of black and white pebbles, which they move from square to square.

Swimming is not only a necessary art in which both the men and women are more expert than any people we had hitherto seen, but a favorite diversion among them. One particular mode which they amused themselves in Kealakekua Bay appeared to us most perilous and extraordinary. The surf which breaks on the coast extends to the distance of about 450 feet from the shore. The surges of the sea, accumulating from the shallowness of the water, are dashed against the beach with prodigious violence. Whenever from stormy weather or any extraordinary swell at sea, the impetuosity of the surf is increased to its utmost height, they choose that time for this amusement. The natives, each taking a long narrow board rounded at the ends, set out from shore. The first wave they meet they plunge under, rise again beyond it and make the best of their way by swimming out into the sea. Great difficulty consisted in seizing the proper moment of diving under the wave, which if missed, the person is caught by the surf and driven back again with great violence. All his dexterity is then required to prevent himself from being dashed against the rocks. As soon as they have gained the smooth water beyond the surf, they lay themselves at length on their boards and prepare for their return. As the surf consists of a number of waves of which every third is remarked to be much larger than the others, their first object is to place themselves on the summit of the largest surge, by which they are driven along with amazing rapidity toward the shore. If by mistake they place themselves on one of the smaller waves, which breaks before they reach the land, or should not be able to keep their plank in a proper direction on top of the swell, they are left exposed to the fury of the next and to avoid it are obliged again to dive and regain the place from which they set out. Those who succeed in their object of reaching the shore have still the greatest danger to encounter. The coast being guarded by a chain of rocks with here and there a small opening between them, they are obliged to steer their boards through one of these. In case of failure, to quit it before they reach the rocks and plunging under the wave are the best way back again; this is reckoned very disgraceful and is attended with the loss of the board, which I have often seen, with great terror, dashed to pieces at the very moment the islander quit it. The boldness and address with which we saw them perform these difficult and dangerous maneuvers was altogether astonishing and is scarcely to be credited. ☙

Surfing in canoes was described at Tahiti. Here is the first record in history of surfboards and the technique of their use. The surfboard appears to have been an Hawaiian invention. The first illustration of a Hawaiian surfer and his surfboard can be seen in the figure of a man paddling out on his surfboard in Mr. Webber's "View of Kealakekua Bay, Hawaii."

❧ An accident of which I was a spectator shows at how early a period they are familiarized to the water and lose all fear of it and set its danger at defiance. A canoe overset in which was a woman with her children, one of them an infant not more than four years old who seemed highly delighted with what had happened, swimming about at ease, and playing a hundred tricks, until the canoe was put to right again.

Besides the amusements I have mentioned, the young children have one which showed no small degree of dexterity. They take a short stick with a peg sharpened at both ends running through one extremity of it and extending about an inch on each side. Throwing up a ball made of green leaves molded together and secured with twine, they catch it on the point of the peg and immediately throw it up again from the peg and turn the stick around and then keep catching on each peg alternately without missing it for a considerable time. They are also no less expert at tossing in the air and catching in their turn a number of these balls. We frequently saw little children thus keep in motion five at a time.

The great resemblance which prevails in the mode of agriculture and navigation among all the inhabitants of the South Sea Islands leaves little to add. The largest canoe we saw was a double canoe belonging to Terreeoboo, which measured 70 feet in length, 3½ in depth, and 12 in breadth; and each was hollowed out of one tree. They make cordage for the rigging of their canoes from the fibrous coating of the coconut. Some of this we purchased for our own use and found it well adapted to the smaller running rigging.

The gourds grow to so enormous a size that some are capable of containing 10 to 12 gallons and are applied to all manner of domestic purposes. In order to fit them better to their respective uses, they have the ingenuity to give them different forms by tying bandages around them during their growth.

Among their arts we must not forget that of making salt, with which we were amply supplied during our stay. Their salt pans are made of earth lined with clay, being generally about 8 feet square and 8 inches deep. They are raised on a bank of stones near the high-water mark from whence the salt water is conducted to them in small trenches. The sun quickly performs the necessary process of evaporation.

The people of these islands are divided into three classes. The first are the *Erees,* or chiefs of each district, one of whom is superior to the rest and is called the *Eree-Taboo* and *Eree-Moee.* By the first of these words they express his absolute authority, and by the latter that all are obliged to prostrate themselves (or, as the word signifies, put themselves to sleep) in his presence. The second class are those who appear to enjoy right of property without authority. The third are the tow-tows, or servants, who have neither rank nor property.

The great power and high rank of Terreeoboo, the Eree-Taboo of Hawaii, was very evident. On his first arrival at Kealakekua all the natives were seen prostrated at the entrance of their houses, and the canoes for two days were "tabooed," or forbidden, to go out until he took off the restraint. He was at this time just returning from Maui, for the possession of which he was contending in favor of his son, Teewano, who had married the daughter and only child of the late King of that island, against Taheetenee, his surviving brother. The two most powerful Chiefs of these islands are Terreeoboo of Hawaii and Perreeorannee of Oahu, the rest of the smaller isles being subject to one or other of these.

The power of the Erees over the inferior classes of people appears to be absolute. The people, on the other hand, pay them the most implicit obedience. It is, however, remarkable that the Chiefs were never guilty, as far at least as came within my knowledge, of any acts of cruelty or injustice, or even of insolent behavior toward them; though at the same time, they exercised their power over one another in the most haughty and oppressive manner. How far the property of the lower class is secured against the rapacity and despotism of the great Chiefs, I cannot say; but it is sufficiently protected against private theft or mutual depredation. Not only their plantations, which are spread over the whole country, but also their houses, their hogs, and their cloth were left unguarded without the smallest apprehension.

The religion of the people resembles that of the Society and Friendly islands; yet we had never met with a regular society of priests until we discovered the cloisters of Kakooa in Kealakekua Bay. The head of this order was called Orono, a title implying something highly sacred and which in the person of Omeeah, was honored almost to adoration. It has been mentioned that the title of Orono, with all its honors, was given to Captain Cook. It is also certain that they regarded us generally as a race of people superior to themselves and often used to say that the great *Eatooa* dwelled in our country. ও

Eatooa in Hawaiian and "God" in English express nearly the same concept. The *Orono* is nearer to God than what we might mean by "priest"; he is more like a saint, or God's chosen being on earth—

very similar, as Mr. King points out, to the Emperor of Japan, whom
the Japanese viewed as being so near to God that he was a god on
earth. Certainly the Hawaiians looked upon Cook as a saintly person,
close to God, and perhaps as an emissary from the great *Eatooa.*
Centuries before Cook's arrival in the Islands, the Hawaiians had lost
contact with all other Polynesian peoples. Their legends, however,
preserved the tradition that one day the great *Orono,* who had departed their islands many generations earlier, would return again. Cook
and his ships unwittingly fitted into their legend. Furthermore, Cook's
immediate friendliness with the Hawaiians, his dignity, his effortless
command over his men, his knowledge of the Polynesian language and
customs—in short his entire manner and person—were everything
that the *Orono* should be.

The godliness of Cook remained a Hawaiian tradition long after
his visit. His memory was revered and stories of him were passed to
the next generation, so that Cook's stay became part of the Hawaiian
religious legends. Later, in the 1800's, whalers from New England
and the Christian missionaries, also from New England, viewed the
reverence of Cook as sacrilegious; and besides: Cook was an Englishman and American feelings against the English ran high after the War
of 1812. These New Englanders suppressed the Cook tradition; the
naked Hawaiian was forced into clothes; white man's diseases appeared; and soon the land was no longer Polynesian. To this day,
Hawaiian and American alike, little know what Cook did in Hawaii
or for what he stood. The least that can be said is that Cook was
more replete with saintly virtues than the American missionary, and
he was certainly closer to the ways of God than many of us. The existence of the Hawaiian people could not long have remained unknown
to the Western world. If they could have had a Savior, it could only
have been Captain Cook.

The Tonga Islands, where Cook stayed the longest and made repeated visits, were the only group of Polynesian Islands to reach the
twentieth century more or less intact. The presence of this nation
among us was called to the attention of the world at the Coronation
of Queen Elizabeth of England in the handsome royal figure of Queen
Salote of Tonga.

◄§ An infinite variety of images are found, both in the maraes and
within their houses. It became obvious to us in how little estimation

they were held from their frequent expressions of contempt for them, and from their offering them for sale for trifles. At the same time, there was one particular figure in favor to which all their adoration was addressed. In a bay to the southward of Kealakekua, our gentlemen were conducted to a large house in which they found the black figure of a man, resting on his fingers and toes, with his head inclined backward, the limbs well formed and exactly proportioned, and the whole beautifully polished. This figure was called *Maee;* round it were thirteen others of rude and distorted shapes which they said were the Eatooees of deceased Chiefs, whose names they recounted. Likewise there were many ludicrous and some obscene idols, like the Priapus of the ancients.

Human sacrifices are more frequent here, according to the account of the natives themselves, than in any other islands we visited. These horrible rites are not only had recourse to upon the commencement of war, but the death of any considerable Chief calls for a sacrifice of one or more tow-tows. We were told that ten men were destined to suffer on the death of Terreeoboo. What may (if anything possibly can) lessen in some small degree the horror of this practice is that the unhappy victims have not the most distant intimation of their fate. Those who are fixed upon to fall are set upon with clubs, and after being dispatched, are brought dead to the place where the remainder of the rites are completed.

To the class of religious customs may be added that of knocking out their fore-teeth. Scarcely any of the lower people, and very few of the Chiefs, had not lost one or more of them. We understood that the voluntary punishment was designed as a propitiatory sacrifice to the Eatooa.

Concerning their marriages, I can inform the reader that such a relation or compact exists among them. From what I had an opportunity of observing of the domestic concerns of the lowest class, the house seemed to be under the direction of one man and woman, and the children in the like state of subordinates as in civilized countries. ॐ

CHAPTER TWENTY-SIX

DEPARTURE FROM HAWAII

February 3, 1779——February 11, 1779

GOOD-BYES ✅ Wednesday, February 3, 1779: the next day being fixed for our departure, Terreeoboo invited Captain Cook to attend him at the place where Kaoo resided. On our arrival we found the ground covered with parcels of cloth, a vast quantity of red and yellow feathers tied to the fibers of coconut husks, and a great number of hatchets and other pieces of ironware that had been gotten in barter from us. A little distance from these lay an immense quantity of vegetables of every kind, and near them was a large herd of hogs. Kaireekeea informed me that it was a gift or tribute from the people of that district to the King, and the King seemed much pleased with this mark of their duty. Having selected about a third part of the ironware and feathers, and a few pieces of cloth, he afterward presented the remainder of the cloth, together with all the hogs and vegetables, to Captain Cook. We were astonished at the value and magnitude of this present, which far exceeded everything of the kind we had seen either at the Friendly or Society islands. Boats were immediately sent to carry them on board. Large hogs were picked out to be salted for sea-store; the smaller pigs and vegetables were divided between the two crews.

The same day we quit the marae and got the tents and astronomical instruments on board. The charm of the taboo was now removed, and we no sooner left the place than the natives rushed in and searched eagerly for something of value we might have left behind.

I (*Mr. King*) happened to remain the last on shore. As I waited for the return of the boat, several natives came crowding about me and made me sit down by them. They began to lament our separation, and it was, indeed, not without difficulty that I was able to quit them. Having had the command of the party on shore during the whole time we were in the bay, I had an opportunity to become better acquainted with the natives than those whose duty required them to be generally on board. I cannot too often, nor too particularly mention, their unbounded and constant friendship. I was strongly solicited to remain behind with offers of the most flattering kind. When I excused myself by saying that Captain Cook would not give his consent, they proposed that I should retire into the mountains, where they would conceal me until after the departure of the ships. On my further assuring them that the Captain would not leave the bay without me, Terreeoboo and Kaoo waited upon Captain Cook, whose son they supposed I was, with a formal request that I might be left behind. The Captain, to avoid giving a positive refusal to an offer so kindly intended, told them he could not part with me at that time, but he would return to the island next year and would endeavor to settle the matter to their satisfaction.

Early on the morning of the fourth, we unmoored and sailed out of the bay with the *Discovery* in company, and were followed by a great number of canoes. Captain Cook's design was to finish the survey of Hawaii before he visited the other islands, in hopes of meeting with a road better sheltered than the one we had just left. Then he proposed to take a view of the southeast part of Maui, where the natives informed us we would find an excellent harbor (*Maalaea Bay*). ᛞ

GALES ᛞ Having a light breeze off the land, we made some way to the northward and passed the westernmost point of Hawaii, where we found ourselves abreast of a deep bay. We had hopes that this bay would furnish us with a safe harbor. Koah accompanied us and had changed his name out of compliment to us into "Britannee." With Britannee for a guide, the pinnace was hoisted out and he and the master were sent to examine the bay while the ships worked up after them.

In the afternoon the weather became gloomy and the gusts of wind that blew off the land were so violent as to make it necessary to take in all sails and bring to under mizzen stay-sail. All the canoes left us at the beginning of the gale, but Mr. Bligh, on his return, had the satisfaction of saving an old woman and two men whose canoe had been overset by the violence of the wind. And besides these distressed people, we had a great many women on board whom the natives had left behind in their hurry to shift for themselves.

The master reported he was directed to some wells of water, but found they would by no means answer our purpose. Instead of meeting with a safe anchorage, he found the shores low and rocky, and a flat bed of coral rocks running along the coast and extending upwards of a mile from land.

In the evening we again made sail, but about midnight it blew so violently as to split both the fore- and main-top-sails. In the morning we were 4 or 5 leagues from shore and the weather very unsettled, so that none of the canoes would venture out. Our guests were obliged to remain with us, much to their dissatisfaction, for they were all seasick.

In the afternoon we saw a canoe with two men paddling toward us who had been driven off the shore by the boisterous weather. We therefore stopped the ship's way in order to take them in. These poor wretches were entirely exhausted with fatigue. It was with difficulty that we got them up the ship's side, together with a child about four years old, whom they had tied under the thwarts of the canoe, where it had lain with only its head above water. The child being committed to the care of one of the women, we found it next morning perfectly recovered.

In the night, a gale of wind came on which obliged us to double-reef the top-sails and get down the top-gallant yards. At daybreak we found that the fore-mast had again given way. The fishes, which were put on the head of the mast in Nootka Sound on the coast of America, were sprung and the parts so very defective as to make it absolutely necessary to replace them and, of course, to unstep the mast.

In this difficulty, the Captain was for some time in doubt whether he should run the chance of meeting with a harbor in the islands to leeward, or return to Kealakekua Bay. It was imagined that the neighborhood of Kealakekua had been pretty well drained of refreshments. On the other hand, it was considered as too great a risk to leave a place that was tolerably sheltered and which once left could not be regained for the mere hopes of meeting with a better. We therefore continued standing on toward the land. It began to blow hard from the southeast, and at two in the morning, in a heavy squall, we found ourselves close in with the breakers. We had just room to haul off and avoid them. During the remainder of the day we kept beating, and before night we were within a mile of the bay. We stood off and on till daylight, and the next morning dropped anchor nearly in the same place as before. ৪৯

CHAPTER TWENTY-SEVEN

DISASTROUS MISUNDERSTANDINGS

February 12, 1779——February 22, 1779

REPAIRS COMMENCED ✍ We were employed the whole of the eleventh and twelfth in getting out the fore-mast and sending it, with the carpenter, on shore. Besides the damage which the head had sustained, we found the keel exceedingly rotten, having a large hole up the middle of it capable of holding four or five coconuts. Fortunately, the logs of red toa-wood, which had been cut at Mooréa for anchorstocks, were found fit to replace the sprung parts. As these repairs were likely to take several days, Mr. Bayly got the astronomical apparatus on shore and pitched our tents on the marae. We renewed our friendly correspondence with the priests, who, to the greater security of the workmen, tabooed the place where the masts lay. The sailmakers were also sent on shore to repair the damage which had taken place in their department. They were lodged in the house adjoining the marae, which was lent us by the priests.

We were surprised to find our reception very different from what it had been on our first arrival—no shouts, no bustle, no confusion— a solitary bay, with only here and there a canoe stealing close along the shore. The impulse of curiosity which had before operated to so great a degree might now indeed be supposed to have ceased, but the hospitable treatment we had met with and the friendly footing on which we parted, gave us reason to expect that they would again flock about us with great joy on our return. Our anxiety was at length relieved by word that Terreeoboo was absent and had left the bay under taboo. Though this account appeared satisfactory to most of us, others

319

were of the opinion that there was something very suspicious in the behavior of the natives, and that the interdiction of all intercourse with us was only to give them time to consult with the Chiefs in what manner to treat us. Probably our sudden return for which they could see no apparent cause, and the necessity of which we found it difficult to make them comprehend, might occasion some alarm. Yet the un-suspicious conduct of Terreeoboo, who on his arrival the next morn-ing came immediately to visit Captain Cook, and the consequent re-turn of the natives to their former friendly intercourse with us, are strong proofs that they meant no change of conduct. But it is very difficult to draw any certain conclusion from the actions of people with whose customs, as well as language, we are so imperfectly acquainted. Some idea may be formed of the difficulties, perhaps not very apparent, which those in their transactions with these strangers encounter who have to steer their course amidst much uncertainty; and where a trifling error may be attended by the most fatal conse-quences. ৪৯

TEMPERS FLARE ৽৳ Saturday, February 13: Toward the evening, the officer who commanded the watering party came to inform me that several Chiefs had assembled at the well near the beach, driving away the natives whom he had hired to assist the sailors in rolling down the casks to the shore. He told me that he thought their behavior ex-tremely suspicious and that the islanders had armed themselves with stones and were growing very tumultuous. I went myself to the spot, attended by a marine with his musket. Seeing us approach, they threw away their stones, and on my speaking to some of the Chiefs the mob was driven away. Having left things quiet here, I went to meet Cap-tain Cook, whom I saw coming on shore. I related to him what had just passed and he ordered me, in case of their beginning to throw stones, to fire a ball at the offenders.

Soon after, we were alarmed by a continued fire of muskets from the *Discovery*, which we observed to be directed at a canoe that we saw paddling toward the shore. We concluded that the firing was in consequence of some theft. Accordingly we ran to the place where we supposed the canoe would land, but were too late. We were at this time ignorant that the goods had already been restored, so having inquired of the natives which way the people had fled, we followed them till it was near dusk. Suspecting that the natives, who frequently encouraged us in the pursuit, were amusing us with fake information, we thought it in vain to continue the search any longer and returned to the beach.

During our absence a difference of a more serious and unpleasant nature had happened. The officer, observing Captain Cook and me engaged in the pursuit of the offenders, thought it his duty to seize the canoe which was left drawn up on the shore. Unfortunately, this canoe belonged to Pareea, who, arriving the same moment from the *Discovery*, claimed his property with many protestations of innocence. The officer refused to give it up and was joined by the crew of the pinnace; a scuffle ensued in which Pareea was knocked down by a violent blow on the head with an oar. The natives, who had hitherto been peaceable spectators, immediately attacked our people with a shower of stones, which forced them to retreat and swim off to a rock some distance from the shore. The pinnace was immediately ransacked by the islanders, and but for the timely interposition of Pareea, who recovered from the blow and forgot it, would have been entirely demolished. Having driven away the crowd, he made signs to our people that they might come and take possession of the pinnace and that he would endeavor to get back the things which had been taken out of it. He followed in his canoe, with a midshipman's cap and other trifling articles of plunder and with much concern at what had happened. He asked if the *Orono* would kill him and whether he would permit him to come on board the next day. On being assured that he would be well received, he joined noses with the officers in token of friendship and paddled over to the village.

When Captain Cook was informed of what had passed he expressed much uneasiness at it. "I am afraid," said he, "that these people will oblige me to use some violent measures, for they must not be left to imagine that they have gained an advantage over us." He gave orders that every man and woman on board should be immediately turned out of the ship. On shore, our former confidence in the natives being now much abated, I posted a double guard on the marae. At about eleven that night five islanders were observed creeping round the bottom of the marae; but finding themselves discovered, they retired out of sight. About midnight, one of them ventured up close to the observatory. The sentinel fired over him, on which the man fled, and we passed the remainder of the night without further disturbance. ৪৶

SUNDAY, FEBRUARY 14, 1779: THE FATAL MORNING ⌒ Next morning, at daylight, I was hailed by the *Discovery* and informed that their
cutter had been stolen during the night from the buoy where it was
moored.

When I arrived on board, I found the marines arming, and Captain
Cook loading his double-barreled gun. It had been his usual practice
whenever anything of consequence was lost at any of the islands in
the ocean to get the King or one of the principal Erees on board and
to keep him as hostage till it was restored. This method, which had
always been attended with success, he meant to pursue on the present
occasion. At the same time he had given orders to stop all canoes that
should attempt to leave the bay, with an intention of seizing and
destroying them if he could not recover the cutter by peaceable means.
Accordingly, the boats of both ships, well-manned and armed, were
stationed across the bay. Before I left the ship, some great guns had
been fired at two large canoes that were attempting to make their
escape.

Between seven and eight o'clock, we quit the ships together; Captain Cook, in the pinnace, having Mr. Phillips and nine marines with
him; and myself in the small boat. The last orders I received from
him were to quiet the minds of the natives on our side of the bay by
assuring them they would not be hurt; to keep my people together,
and to be on my guard. We then parted. The Captain went toward
Kowrowa, where the King resided. I proceeded to the beach and took
a walk to the huts of old Kaoo and the priests, and explained to them,
as well as I could, the object of the hostile preparation, which had
exceedingly alarmed them. They had already heard of the cutter's
being stolen. I assured them that though Captain Cook was resolved
to recover it and to punish the authors of the theft, yet they need not
be under the smallest apprehension of suffering any evil from us. Kaoo
asked me with great earnestness, "Is Terreeoboo to be hurt?" I assured
him he was not. Both he and the rest of his brethren seemed much
satisfied with this assurance.

In the meantime, Captain Cook, having called over the launch,
which was stationed at the north point of the bay, and taken it along
with him, proceeded to Kowrowa, and landed with the lieutenant and
nine marines. He immediately marched into the village, where he was
received with the usual marks of respect, the people prostrating themselves before him and bringing their customary offerings of small hogs.

His next step was to inquire for Terreeoboo and his sons, who had been his constant guests on board the *Resolution*. The natives immediately led Captain Cook to the house where the King had slept. They found the old man just awake from sleep. After a short conversation about the loss of the cutter, from which Captain Cook was convinced that he was in no way privy to it, he invited him to spend the day on board the *Resolution*. To this proposal the King readily consented and immediately got up to accompany him.

Things were in this prosperous train, the two boys being already in the pinnace, and the rest of the party having advanced near the waterside, when an elderly woman called Kaneekabareea, the mother of the boys, and one of the King's favorite wives, came after him and with many tears and entreaties besought him not to go on board. At the same time, two Chiefs who came along with her laid hold of him and, insisting that he should go no farther, forced him to sit down. The natives were collecting in prodigious numbers along the shore. They had probably been alarmed by the firing of the great guns and the appearances of hostility in the bay and began to throng around Captain Cook and their King.

In this situation the lieutenant of marines, observing that his men were huddled close together in the crowd and thus incapable of using their arms, proposed to the Captain to draw them up along the rocks close to the water's edge. The crowd readily made way for them to pass, and they were drawn up on a line about 30 yards from where the King was sitting.

The old King remained on the ground with the strongest marks of terror and dejection in his countenance. Captain Cook, not willing to abandon the object for which he had come on shore, continued to urge him in the most pressing manner to proceed. While on the other hand, whenever the King appeared to follow him, the Chiefs, who stood round him, interposed—at first with prayers and entreaties but afterward with force—and insisted on his staying where he was. Captain Cook, finding that the alarm had spread too generally and that it was in vain to think any longer of getting him off without bloodshed, at last gave up the point. He observed to Mr. Phillips that it would be impossible to compel him to go on board without the risk of killing a great number of the inhabitants.

Though the enterprise had now failed and was abandoned, yet his person did not appear to have been in the least danger, until an acci-

dent happened which gave a fatal turn to the affair. Boats, which had
been stationed across the bay, fired at some canoes that were attempting to get out. Unfortunately, they had killed a Chief of the first rank.
The news of his death arrived at the village just as Captain Cook had
left the King and was walking slowly toward the shore. The ferment
it occasioned was very conspicuous. The men put on their war-mats
and armed themselves with spears and stones. One of the natives came
up to the Captain flourishing a long iron spike by way of defiance and
threatening to throw a stone. The Captain desired him to desist; but
the man, persisting in his insolence, he was at length provoked to fire
a load of small-shot. Since the man had his mat on, this had no other
effect than to irritate and encourage them. Several stones were thrown
by the natives, and one of the Erees attempted to stab Mr. Phillips but
failed in the attempt and received from him a blow with the butt end
of his musket. Captain Cook now fired his second barrel, loaded with
ball, and killed one of the foremost of the natives. A general attack
with stones immediately followed, which was answered by a discharge
of muskets from the marines—and the people in the boats. The
islanders, contrary to the expectations of everyone, stood the fire with
great firmness. Before the marines had time to reload, they broke in
upon them with dreadful shouts and yells. What followed was a scene
of the utmost horror and confusion.

Four of the marines were cut off among the rocks in their retreat
and fell to the fury of the enemy; three more were dangerously
wounded, and the lieutenant received a stab between the shoulders, but
having fortunately reserved his fire, shot the man who had wounded
him just as he was going to repeat the blow. The last time our unfortunate commander was seen distinctly, he was standing at the water's
edge and calling out to the boats to cease firing and to pull in. If it be
true, as some of those who were present have imagined, that the
marines and boatmen had fired without his orders and that he was
desirous of preventing further bloodshed, it is probable that his humanity on this occasion proved fatal to him. While he faced the natives,
none of them had shown him any violence, but having turned about
to give his orders to the boats, he was stabbed in the back and fell
with his face in the water. On seeing him fall, the islanders set up a
great shout, and his body was immediately dragged on shore and
surrounded by the enemy, who, snatching the dagger out of each

other's hand, showed a savage eagerness to have a share in his destruction. Thus fell our great and excellent commander! ᥱ᭞

THE FIGHT ENDS ᥱ᭞ It has been related that four of the marines were killed on the spot; the rest, with Mr. Phillips, threw themselves into the water and escaped under a cover of a smart fire from the boats. Our people continued for some time to keep a constant fire from the boats, which were not more than 20 yards from the land, in order to afford their companions an opportunity of escaping.

Our party at the marae, where the masts and sails were on shore, had a guard of only six marines. Being at the distance of only a short mile from the village, we could see distinctly an immense crowd on the spot where Captain Cook had landed, and heard the firing of the muskets, and could perceive some extraordinary battle and agitation in the multitude. It is impossible for me to describe the emotions of my mind during the time of these transactions on the other side of the bay. Where a life so dear and valuable was concerned, it was impossible not to be alarmed by appearances both new and threatening. I knew that a long and uninterrupted course of success in his transactions with the natives of these seas had given the Captain a degree of confidence that I was always fearful might at some unlucky moment put him too much off his guard.

My first care on hearing the muskets fire was to assure the people assembled round the wall of our field and seemingly equally at a loss with ourselves as to how to account for what they had seen and heard, that they would not be molested. Captain Clerke, observing through his telescope that we were surrounded by natives and apprehending they meant to attack us, ordered two 4-pounders to be fired. Fortunately, these guns, though well aimed, did no mischief. One of the balls broke a coconut tree in the middle, and the other shivered a rock. As I had just before given them the strongest assurance of their safety, I was exceedingly mortified at this act of hostility. To prevent a repetition, I dispatched a boat to acquaint Captain Clerke that at present I was on the most friendly terms with the natives. At the same moment our friend Kaireekeea, having also received intelligence of the death of Captain Cook, came to me with great sorrow and dejection to inquire if it was true.

Our situation was extremely critical; not only our own lives but the

THE DEATH OF

CAPTAIN COOK

return of at least one of the ships was involved in the same common danger. We had the masts of the *Resolution* and the greatest part of our sails on shore. Their loss would have been irreparable. Though the natives had not as yet shown the smallest disposition to molest us, yet it was impossible to answer for the altercation which the news might produce.

Having placed the marines on top of the marae, which formed a strong and advantageous spot, and left the command with Mr. Bligh, I went on board the *Discovery* in order to represent to Captain Clerke the dangerous situation of our affair. As soon as I quit the spot, the natives began to annoy our people with stones. I had scarcely reached the ship before I heard the firing of the marines. I therefore returned instantly on shore, where I found things growing more alarming. The natives were arming and putting on their mats, and their number was increasing very fast. I could also perceive several large bodies marching toward us from the north village. They began at first to attack us with stones from behind the walls of their enclosures. Finding no resistance on our part, they soon grew more daring. A few resolute fellows made their appearance at the foot of the marae with a design of storming it from the side next to the sea, which was its only accessible part. They were not dislodged till after they had stood a considerable number of shot and had seen one of their party fall. The bravery of these assailants well deserves to be mentioned.

About this time, a strong reinforcement from both ships landed and the natives retreated behind their walls. This gave me access to our friendly priests, and I sent one of them to endeavor to bring their countrymen to terms and to propose to them that if they would desist from throwing stones, I would not permit our men to fire. This truce was agreed to, and we were suffered to launch the masts and carry off the sails, and our astronomical apparatus was unmolested. As soon as we quit the marae, they took possession of it. ✑

DELIBERATIONS ✑ When I got on board the *Discovery,* I found no decisive plan had been adopted for our future proceedings. The restitution of the boat and the recovery of the body of Captain Cook were the objects which, on all hands, we agreed to insist on.

It was my opinion that some vigorous steps should be taken. The confidence which their success in killing our Chief and forcing us to quit the shore must have inspired, would, I had no doubt, encourage them to make some further dangerous attempts—the more especially as contrary to our expectations, they had little reason to dread the effects of our firearms, for this weapon had produced no signs of terror in them. On our side, such was the condition of the ships and the state of discipline among us, that had a vigorous attack been made in the night, it would have been impossible to answer for the consequences. I was supported by the opinion of most of the officers on board. Nothing seemed so likely to encourage the natives to make the attempt as the appearance of our being inclined to an accommodation which they could only attribute to weakness or fear.

In favor of more conciliatory measures, it was justly urged that the mischief was done and irreparable; that the natives had a strong claim to our regard on account of their former friendship and kindness; and the late melancholy accident did not appear to have arisen from any premeditated design. On the part of Terreeoboo, his ignorance of the theft, his readiness to accompany Captain Cook on board, and his having actually sent his two sons in the boat, must free him from the smallest degree of suspicion. The conduct of his women and the Erees might easily be accounted for: from the apprehensions occasioned by the armed force with which Captain Cook came on shore, and from the hostile preparations in the bay—so different from the terms of friendship and confidence in which both parties had hitherto lived—they had some reason to imagine the attempt would be made to carry off their King by force. The arming of the natives was evidently to resist, and was naturally to be expected from a people full of affection and attachment to their Chief.

To these motives of humanity others of a prudent nature were added: we were in want of water and other refreshments; our foremast would require six to eight days' work before it could be stepped; spring was advancing apace and the speedy prosecution of our next northern expedition ought now to be our sole object. Therefore to engage in a vindictive contest with the inhabitants might not only lay us under the imputation of unnecessary cruelty, but would occasion a delay in the equipment of the ships.

During the time we were engaged in concerting some plan for our future conduct, the natives kept possession of the shore and some of them had the boldness to approach within pistol-shot range and to insult us by marks of contempt and defiance. It was with difficulty we could restrain the sailors from the use of arms. In pursuance of our plan, it was determined that I should proceed toward the shore with the boats of both ships, well-manned and armed, to bring the natives to a parley; and, if possible, obtain a conference with some of the Chiefs. I was to demand the dead bodies, particularly that of Captain Cook, to threaten them with our vengeance in case of refusal, but by no means to fire unless attacked.

I left the ships about four in the afternoon. As we approached the shore I perceived every indication of a hostile reception. The whole crowd of natives was in motion; the women and children retiring; the men putting on their war mats and arming themselves with long spears and daggers. Concluding that all attempts to bring them to parley would be in vain unless I first gave them some ground for mutual confidence, I ordered the armed boats to stop and went on in a small boat, alone, with a white flag in my hand. By a general cry of joy from the natives, I had the satisfaction to find it was instantly understood. The women returned from the side of the hill; the men threw off their mats; and all sat down by the water-side, extending their arms and inviting me to come ashore. I saw Koah, with a boldness and assurance altogether unaccountable, swimming off to the boat with a white flag in his hand. I thought it necessary to return the mark of confidence and therefore received him into the boat. I must confess I had long harbored an unfavorable opinion of this man. The priests told us he was of malicious disposition and no friend of ours. The repeated detection of his fraud and treachery convinced us of the truth of the representation. The shocking transaction of the morning, in which he was seen acting a principal part, made me feel the utmost horror at finding myself so near him. I told him that I had come to demand the body of Captain Cook and to declare war against them unless it was instantly restored. He assured me this would be done as soon as possible. With much assurance, as if nothing extraordinary had happened, he leaped into the sea, swam ashore, and called to his countrymen that we were all friends again.

We waited an hour with great anxiety. When they found they could not prevail on me to land, they attempted, under pretense of wishing to converse with more ease, to decoy our boat among some rocks, where they could cut us off from the rest. I began now to express some impatience at Koah's delay and was strongly inclined to break off further communication when a Chief came to us who was the particular friend of Captain Clerke and had sailed on the *Discovery* when we last left the bay, intending to take his passage to Maui. He told us he came from Terreeoboo to acquaint us that the body was carried up country, that it would be brought to us the next morning. There appeared to be a great deal of sincerity in his manner. On being asked if he told a falsehood, he hooked his two forefingers together, which is understood among these islanders as the sign of truth, in the use of which they are very scrupulous.

As I was now at a loss in what manner to proceed, I sent Mr. Vancouver to acquaint Captain Clerke with all that had happened. Mr. Vancouver came back with orders for me to return on board, having first given the natives to understand that if the body was not brought next morning, the town would be destroyed. When they saw that we were going off they endeavored to provoke us by the most insulting gestures. Some of our people said they saw the natives parading about in the clothes of our unfortunate comrades and a Chief brandishing Captain Cook's dagger, and a woman holding the scabbard. No doubt our behavior had given them a mean opinion of our courage, for they could have little notion of the humanity that directed it.

Measures were taken to guard against any attack they might make in the night. The boats were moored with top chains, additional sentinels were posted, and guard boats were stationed to row around the ships to prevent the natives from cutting the cables. We observed a prodigious number of lights in the hills, and I believed them to have been the sacrifices they were performing on account of the war in which they imagined themselves about to be engaged. We remained the whole night undisturbed, except by the howlings and lamentations which were heard from the shore.

In the morning we heard conchs blowing in different parts of the coast, and large parties were seen marching over the hills. Appearances were so alarming that we carried out a stream anchor to enable us to haul the ships abreast of the town in case of an attack. As it was determined that nothing should interfere with the repair of the mast and the preparations for our departure, the greatest part of the day was taken up in getting the fore-mast in proper situation on deck for the carpenters to work on it.

The necessary alterations in the commissions of the officers were made. The command of the expedition having devolved on Captain Clerke, he removed on board the *Resolution*. He appointed Mr. Gore to be Captain of the *Discovery* and promoted Mr. Harvey, a midship-

man who had been with Captain Cook in his two last voyages, to the
vacant lieutenancy. (*Our narrator, Mr. King, became first lieutenant
on the* Resolution.) &

FRIENDLY OVERTURES ◆§ About eight o'clock, it being very dark, a
canoe was heard paddling toward the ship. There were two persons
in the canoe and they roared out "Tinnee," which was the way in
which they pronounced my name. When they came on board, they
threw themselves at our feet. One of them was the person who constantly attended Captain Cook, and who, though a man of rank in
the island, could scarcely be hindered from performing for him the
lowest effects of a menial servant. After lamenting with an abundance
of tears the loss of the Orono, he told us he had brought a part of his
body. He then presented us with a small bundle wrapped up in a cloth,
which he brought under his arm. It is impossible to describe the horror
which seized upon us on finding in it a piece of human flesh about
10 pounds weight. This, he said, was all that remained. The rest was
cut to pieces and burned; but the head and all the bones, except what
belonged to the trunk, were in the possession of Terreeoboo and the
other Erees. This afforded an opportunity of informing ourselves
whether they were cannibals—we put the question whether they had
not eaten some of it. They showed as much horror at the idea as a
European and asked, very naturally, if that was the custom among us.
They afterward asked us with great earnestness, "When will the Orono
come again?" The same inquiry was frequently made afterward by
others, which showed they considered him a being of a superior nature.

Our two friendly visitors informed us further that the Chiefs were
eager to revenge the death of their countrymen and particularly cautioned us against Koah, who they said was our mortal and implacable
enemy and desired nothing more ardently than an opportunity of fighting us, and that the blowing of the conch we heard this morning was
meant as a challenge. We learned that seventeen of their countrymen
were killed in the first action at Kowrowa, of whom five were Chiefs.
Eight, they said, were killed at the observatory.

Our situation was becoming extremely awkward and unpromising;
none of the purposes for which this pacific course of proceeding had
been adopted having been in the least forwarded by it. We did not
seem to be at all advanced toward a reconciliation with the islanders.
They still kept in force on the shore as if determined to resist any

attempts we might make to land, and yet the attempt was becoming absolutely necessary, as the completing of our supply of water would not admit of any longer delay.

An attack could not have been made without some danger; for the loss of a very few men might have been severely felt by us during the remaining course of our voyage. Delaying the execution of our threats, though on the one hand lessening their opinion of our prowess, had the effect of causing them to disperse on the other. About noon the next day, finding us to persist in our inactivity, great bodies of them marched off over the hills and never appeared afterward. Those, however, who remained were not the less daring and insolent.

The next morning the boats of both ships were sent ashore for water, and the *Discovery* was warped close to the beach in order to cover that service. The natives kept perpetually harassing our waterers with stones, nor could the small force we had on shore with the advantage of muskets compel them to retreat. It was now found absolutely necessary to burn down some straggling houses near the wall behind which they had taken shelter. In executing these orders, I am sorry to add, our people were hurried into acts of unnecessary cruelty and devastation. Something ought to be allowed to their resentment of the repeated insults and contemptuous behavior of the islanders and to the natural desire of revenging the loss of their commander. But their conduct served strongly to convince me that the utmost precaution is necessary in trusting the discretionary use of arms in the hands of seamen or soldiers. Orders had been given to burn only a few straggling huts; we were therefore a good deal surprised to see the whole village on fire. Before a boat that was sent to stop the progress of the mischief could reach the shore, the houses of our old and constant friends, the priests, were all in flame. It is very extraordinary that amidst all these disturbances the women of the island who were on board never offered to leave us nor showed the smallest apprehensions either for themselves or their friends ashore. Some of them who were on deck when the town was in flames seemed to admire the sight and cried that it was *"maitai,"* or very fine.

The natives, being at last convinced that it was not the want of ability to punish them which had hitherto made us tolerate their provocations, desisted from giving us any further molestations. In the evening, a Chief called Eappo, whom we knew to be a man of the very first consequence, came with presents from Terreeaboo to sue for peace. He was dismissed with the same answer that until the remains of Captain Cook were restored, no peace would be granted. ॐ

PEACE RETURNS ॐ Early in the morning of the twentieth we had the satisfaction of getting the fore-mast stepped. It was an operation attended with great difficulty and some danger, our ropes being so exceedingly rotten that the purchase gave way several times. At the beach the waterers did not meet with the least opposition, and the natives came among us again without the smallest appearance of diffidence or apprehension.

Between ten and eleven o'clock we saw a great number of people descending the hill in a procession, each man carrying a sugarcane on his shoulders and breadfruit, taro, and bananas in his hand. They were proceeded by two drummers, who, when they came to the water-side, sat down by a white flag and began to beat their drums. Captain Clerke, conjecturing that they had brought the bones of Captain Cook, went himself in the pinnace to receive them. When we arrived at the beach, Eappo delivered to the Captain the bones, wrapped up in a large quantity of fine new cloth and covered with a spotted cloak of black and white feathers. We found in it both the hands of Captain Cook; the metacarpal bones; the skull, but with the scalp separated from it and the bones of the face wanting; the bones of both arms with the skin of the forearms hanging to them; and the thigh and leg bones joined together, but without the feet. The whole bore evident marks of having been in the fire, except the hands, which were crammed with salt, apparently with an intention of preserving them.

The next morning Eappo and the King's son came on board and brought with them the remaining bones of Captain Cook, the barrels of his guns, his shoes, and some other trifles that belonged to him. Eappo took great pains to convince us that Terreeoboo, Maihamaiha, and himself were most desirous of peace. He lamented with great sorrow the death of six Chiefs we had killed, some of whom, he said, were among our best friends. The cutter, he told us, was taken away by Pareea's people, very probably in revenge for the blow that had been given him, and that it had been broken up the next day.

Nothing now remained but to perform the last offices to our great and unfortunate commander. Eappo was dismissed with orders to taboo all the bay. In the afternoon the bones, having been put into a coffin and the service read over them, they were committed to the deep with the usual military honors. What our feelings were on this occasion, I leave the world to conceive; those who were present know that it is not in my power to express them.

During the forenoon of the twenty-second, not a canoe was seen in the bay, the taboo which Eappo had laid before at our request not yet being taken off. At length Eappo came off to us. We assured him that we were now entirely satisfied; and that as the Orono was buried, all remembrance of what had passed was buried with him. We desired him to take off the taboo and make it known that the people might bring us provisions as usual. The ships were soon surrounded with canoes; and many of the Chiefs came on board, expressing great sorrow at what happened and their satisfaction at our reconciliation. Among the rest came the old treacherous Koah, but he was refused admittance.

As we had now everything ready for sea, Captain Clerke gave orders to unmoor. About eight in the evening we dismissed all the natives, and Eappo and the friendly Kaireekeea took an affectionate leave of us. We immediately weighed and stood out of the bay. The natives were collected on the shore in great numbers; and, as we passed along, we received our last farewells with every mark of affection and good will. ⩦

CHAPTER TWENTY-EIGHT

MR. COOK, CAPTAIN OF SHIPS AND MEN, NAVIGATOR OF THE WORLD

Historians and biographers have had difficulty in creating any clear or significant picture of Cook's personality, or even a description of what sort of man he was. This difficulty is partly a consequence of a regrettable lack of personal information about the man, for none of his biographers knew him, and his contemporaries left us with only a few sketches. Mrs. Cook did not preserve any of his letters to her; nor do we have any of hers to him. He was a man of incontrovertible genius, but unlike so many other men of genius, there was nothing colorful or flamboyant about his personality: no points of contrast to help us along; no amusing anecdotes; no place where he oversteps the bounds of less-gifted but sensible persons—his genius was largely one of extraordinary sensibleness.

Any who have captained small vessels in cruises of any length would not, I think, have trouble in knowing something of the nature and capacity of this man. A successful cruise—the really great cruise —is when nothing adventuresome occurs. Adventures arise out of poor planning, lack of knowledge, inadequate experience, pigheaded-ness, impatience, failure to heed the danger signs, carrying on when it's time to wait, and a whole long list of human foibles—which most of us possess—and which can change a pleasure cruise into a situation of alarming hazards. Men who have been justly praised for small-boat cruises, competently undertaken, often in trying and dangerous seas and climates, would know the character of Captain Cook; for they must have possessed some of the same characteristics in order to have succeeded.

The true genius in this business of voyaging leaves nothing to chance. His powers of observation, his keenness of mind, his knowledge and experience, his patience and caution, his control over his ambition, egotism, fear, and emotion, all serve to exclude chance, and make the voyage an apparently routine affair. In our space-age voyaging, we have a team of experts to eliminate chance; but on Cook's ships, he alone was responsible for the whole effort. There were times when Cook had to take a chance, and go ahead when he was not sure of the outcome; but he always felt that the chancy situation ought not to have occurred and was a mark against his professional competence.

An extraordinary attribute of human nature is that on rare occasions in the course of history, a man will arise from humble circumstances—from an environment that gives him nothing and where all others in that environment live and die with history noting nothing of their arrival or departure—and go on to greatness, seemingly in no way deterred by his disadvantageous beginning. Cook, a farmboy, had little formal schooling, and that only because his father's landowner thought he seemed brighter than most boys. All of Cook's family never left the locality nor rose above the servile customs of their time. What Cook learned, he taught himself, studying in the glow of the swinging lamps in the cabins of numerous sailing ships. Yet this seaman from the fore-deck of the British Navy, serving with men impressed against their will into that service, was able (by the time he was forty) to converse with the most learned men of England.

Cook learned his seamanship in the rigorous school provided by the lee shore of the western coast of England. From the age of seventeen until he was twenty-eight, through all the grades of command from apprentice seaman to first mate, he learned to sail with the unlighted and unmarked coast of England on his lee—in and out of estuaries, bays, rivers, and harbors. Until the invention of inboard power and propellers, most sailing ships ended their days piled up on a lee shore because their captain and crew could not get the ship to windward, off the shore, in the fury of a gale. Consequently, most captains set their courses, if they could possibly manage it, so as never to have the shore under their lee. But the successful explorer must learn how to come to an unknown land, coast along it, and find harbors to anchor his ships. Cook's schooling in the Irish Sea provided him with these credentials, and by his choice, he selected just such a ship as he learned to sail in when he went exploring in the Pacific.

Cook taught himself mathematics, astronomy, navigation, and surveying while serving in ships of the British Navy on the coast of Canada and Newfoundland. He learned these subjects from such books as the ship's officers had carried out with them, and from the instruction of the officers, more educated than he, who took interest enough in him to teach him what they knew. Something about seaman Cook must even then have set him apart from ordinary men in the noncommissioned grades to allow him into the officers' company and to use their limited libraries. He did not receive a commission and join the ranks of gentlemen until the age of forty, when he was given command of the *Endeavour*. All of his knowledge and ability, so ably demonstrated in that famous first voyage of his around the world, had already been acquired before this time—all of it while in the noncommissioned service. Cook not only learned his subjects well, but soon surpassed his teachers, yet never showed signs that he felt that he was doing anything more than his ordinary duty.

Cook's three voyages were the longest and most extensive sailing voyages in the history of the world, and Cook's personal greatness is demonstrated in his accounts of these voyages. He was at sea, all told, eight and one-half years, taking his ships into all the blank spaces on the maps that existed in his day. In the second voyage he sailed all the way around the world in the Antarctic Ocean, where occur the most violent winds and seas of any part of the world, but lost only one man by sickness, and never a report of undue hazard or hardship experienced by his men. His care of his men, accomplished almost against their will, because they were accustomed to the usual naval neglect of their welfare, revealed his tolerance of his men's emotions, his wisdom in his men's care, and his overriding humanity; but, more than that, showed the world that with the proper skill and attention to detail, a ship could sail for years and come back home again, with all aboard safe and sound, instead of, as was usual, depleted of their crews.

Cook's remarkable perseverance shows in all his undertakings, whether it was hanging on a coast in a gale to fix the coast's position, or continuing until his keels stirred up mud on the coast of Alaska, or penetrating below the Antarctic Circle. In the second voyage he was sent out to prove or disprove a geographical theory—the presence of a southern continent. He penetrated the ice all the way to 71° south to disprove it; but even then he sees a duty to go on when he cannot. He wrote in his *Journal* at that point:

⋞ I will not say that it was impossible anywhere to get in among this ice, but I will assert that the bare attempting of it would be a very dangerous enterprise and what I believe no man in my situation would have thought of. I, whose ambition leads me not only farther than any other has been before me, but as far as I think it possible for man to go, was not sorry at meeting with this interruption. Since therefore we could not proceed one inch farther south, no other reason need be assigned for our tacking and stretching to the north. ⋟

In the hands of any ordinary commander, the point at which the voyage would have become "a very dangerous enterprise" had long since been passed. Only Cook's genius allowed them to survive this long. I doubt that a modern engineless sailing ship, equipped with the best gear obtainable, could retrace Cook's track.

Because of the need for long sojourns in the islands of the milder climates to refit and to wait out the arctic and antarctic winters before making another penetration, Cook, of necessity, needed to establish commerce and communication with the inhabitants of these islands. He needed to let the inhabitants participate in the success of his voyage (even though they could not comprehend what it was all about) by providing him with support bases. To do this, he learned the language, customs, arts, dietary habits, and industries of these people. He made them his friends and helpmates even when they were, by natural traits, inclined to be warlike. He moored for many months in New Zealand, Tonga, Tahiti, Nootka, and Hawaii, carrying on commerce and generally avoiding the conflict which so easily develops between people who cannot understand each other's ways and which the circumstances of his death demonstrate can occur so rapidly and tragically. The success of the voyage required him to be both a cultural anthropologist and a diplomat. The Maori chief, Te Horeta, who was a boy when Cook landed in New Zealand and grew up to be a bloody warrior against the white settlers, recalled his boyhood impressions in this way: [1]

We thought the English sailors were goblins, although they were friendly goblins. There was one supreme man in the ship. We knew that he was the loard of the whole by his perfectly gentlemanly and noble manner. He seldom spoke, but some of the

[1] White, John. *Ancient History of the Maori*, vol. 5, page 121.

goblins spoke much; but this man did not utter many words. He liked to feel the Maori cloaks and handle their weapons. He took the small boys out to the ship and gave them biscuit, and he gave me a nail of which I was very fond and mourned greatly when it was lost. He was a very good man and came to us—the children—and patted our cheeks and gently touched our heads. (*Te Horeta recalled the old Maori proverb*) A *rangatira*—a nobleman—cannot be lost in a crowd.

Rangatira among the hostile Maori, or *Orono* among the friendly Hawaiians, Cook's personal greatness was evident to all who saw him. When Cook's ships returned to the Arctic-Asian coast under the command of Captain Clerke, the Russian commander at Kamchatka told Mr. King a most remarkable story, which Mr. King recorded in his *Journal:*

⋙ The length of time we had been out since we had touched at any known port appeared to them (*the Russians*) so very incredible that it required the testimony of our maps to gain their belief. Major Behm (*the Russian commander*) then related to us a very curious fact that but for our arrival he would have been totally at a loss to account for.

It is well known that the Chukotskiy are the only people of the north of Asia who have maintained their independence and resisted all the attempts that have been made by the Russians to reduce them. The last expedition against them was undertaken in the year 1750 and terminated in the retreat of the Russian forces and the loss of the commanding officer. Since that time, the Russians had removed their frontier fortress from the Anadyr to the Indigirka River. From this fort Major Behm had received dispatches that a party of the Chukotskiy had arrived with propositions of friendship and a voluntary offer of tribute. On inquiry into the cause of this unexpected alteration of their sentiments, they had said that toward the end of last summer they had been visited by two very large Russian boats, that they had been treated by the people who were in them with the greatest kindness, and had entered into a league of friendship and amnity with them; and that, relying on their friendly disposition, they had now come to the fort in order to settle a treaty on such terms as might be acceptable to both nations.

This extraordinary history had occasioned much speculation; had we not furnished them with a key to it, it must have remained perfectly unintelligible. (*The Chukotskiy were recalling Cook's visit to them the preceding year.*) We felt no small satisfaction in having, though accidentally, shown the Russians the only true way of collecting tribute and extending their dominions. We hope that the good understanding which this event has given rise to, may rescue a brave people from the future invasions of such a powerful neighbor. ᐧᐁ

Cook's ability to win over these people, who had expected only to meet with hostility from all Europeans, accomplished more in the span of a few hours than had years of Russian arms. His tact, patience, and ability to establish a feeling of brotherhood with foreign and primitive people seemed more remarkable to the primitive people themselves than to Cook, who accepted humanity as a matter of course. His interest and desire to know the people he visited was genuine and not merely because he needed a place to gather provisions and repair his ships. In this voyage, his descriptions of the people of Tasmania, New Zealand, Cook Archipelago, Tongo, Tahiti, Hawaii, Vancouver Island, Alaska, Aleutian Islands, Chukotski, and of the arctic, are as complete as he could make them. In every instance we are permitted to know their appearance, dress, food, customs, religion, social organization, industry, language, and even an understanding of the inner personalities of these people. He was, in most instances, the first to observe, and the first to record, the characteristics of the people he visited. All later anthropological studies must begin with the accurate records that he made.

Among his men, he was their unquestioned leader. They perhaps thought his regulations regarding cleanliness, airing of bedding and quarters, heat below decks, and fresh food at all times, even when the diet was very unfamiliar fare, was a mite old-womanly for an officer in the British Navy; but at the conclusion of his second voyage Cook knew that his accomplishments in public health, or more especially in health on board ship, would justly make him famous. He wrote:

ᐧᐁ Whatever may be the public judgment about other matters, it is with real satisfaction, and without claiming any merit but that of attention to my duty, that I conclude with an observation which facts enable me to make, that our having discovered the possibility of preserving health among a numerous ship's company, for such a length of time, in such varieties of climate, and amidst such continued hardships and fatigue, will make this voyage remarkable in the opinion of every benevolent person, when the disputes about the southern continent shall have ceased to engage the attention and to divide the judgment of philosophers. &

For this contribution to public medicine, Cook won the Sir Godfrey Copley gold medal for the best paper presented to the Royal Society. When the medal was presented to Mrs. Cook—the Captain had already left on his third voyage when the award was made— Sir John Pringle, President of the Society, in making the presentation remarked: "Here are no vain boastings of the empiric, nor ingenious and delusive theories of the dogmatist: but a concise, and artless, and an uncontested relation, of the means by which, under divine favor, Captain Cook with a company of a hundred and eighteen men, performed a voyage of three years and eighteen days, throughout all the climates, from 52 degrees north to 71 degrees south, with a loss of only one man by sickness. I would inquire of the most conversant in the study of bills of mortality, whether, in the most healthful climate and in the best condition of life, they have ever found so small a number of deaths within that space of time? How great and agreeable then, must our surprise be, after perusing the histories of long navigations in former days, when so many perished by marine diseases, to find the air of the sea acquitted of all malignity; and, in fine, that a voyage round the world may be undertaken with less danger, perhaps, to health, than a common tour in Europe!"

Cook's accomplishments, however, by no means put an end to scurvy on ships. Some of Cook's own men who later commanded ships in this same ocean did not learn the lesson that Cook taught them. They were not able to overcome their dietary prejudices, nor those of their men, and many perished of this disease.

Cook's contributions to anthropology, linguistics, and public health were remarkable achievements in themselves, but they were not the primary purpose of his voyages. He was sent to clear up matters of obscure geography and to open unexplored parts of the world to navigation, and this meant that he was to prepare charts where none existed before. A ship would not leave on a voyage without as complete a collection of charts as it was possible to obtain. The ship's navigator requires these charts to show him the location of lands, harbors, reefs, shoals, rocks, and islands; and he requires tables of the expected winds, currents, and tides. Cook's monumental accomplishment was not only to sail his ships where none had sailed before, but to prepare accurate charts as he proceeded. Of necessity, he must discover the land, shoals, rocks, and reefs before the ships, in effect, discovered them by piling up on some such obstruction. Cook's charts of Hawaii and Alaska put these places on the map and initiated their subsequent development. These charts, like all others he prepared, needed little improvement. The meticulousness he showed was characteristic of the attentive care with which he approached all his assignments and which made his contributions seem so unromantic and almost easy while they were so far-reaching and changed the subsequent history of the world.

CHAPTER TWENTY-NINE

EPILOGUE

March 15, 1779——October 4, 1780

When the nasty business at Kealakekua Bay had been settled and the ships' crew and the natives had reestablished friendly relations sufficient for the crew to get the masts and rigging off the shore and onto the *Resolution* again, the expedition sailed north and west visiting and exploring the other islands of the Sandwich group. They sailed past the barren island of Kahoolawe and along the west coast of Maui, Lanai, and Molokai. Going across Kaiwi Channel they sailed to the windward, or east side, of Oahu, thereby overlooking the finest harbor in the Hawaiian Islands, Pearl Harbor. Rounding the north point of Oahu they anchored in Waimea Bay, now famous among surfers for its high and challenging surf. Not finding conditions here suitable for taking on more supplies, they stayed only a day on Oahu before proceeding to the anchoring ground on Kauai, where they had been the year before when they first discovered the Hawaiian Islands. Here they were remorseful to find many of the natives now infected with venereal disease. The casks received a final filling with fresh water in preparation for the long voyage back to the arctic. They stopped again briefly at Niihau and then sailed directly for the Russian village of Petropavlovsk (St. Peter and St. Paul), near the southern tip of the Kamchatka peninsula. From here, dispatches were sent across Siberia and Russia to St. Petersburg, and on to London, informing the world of Captain Cook's death.

It was the middle of May before the floating ice left the harbor, and the middle of June before there was enough warmth to proceed

345

farther to the north. They passed through Bering Strait again, where, during a brief spell of clear weather, they could see the coast of America and Asia at the same time. North of Bering Strait, in the latitudes between 68° and 69°, progress was again blocked by ice. Even in July the temperature was often below freezing and visibility was severely reduced by frequent snowstorms. The rest of the summer was spent in the Arctic Ocean while they tried to work their ships in among the floating ice until at last Mr. King concluded:

⋅§ A connected, solid field of ice rendering every effort we could make to a nearer approach to the land fruitless, we took a last farewell of a northwest passage to Old England. §⋅

On their way south, Captain Clerke (who had shown evidences of the disease since he left England) died of tuberculosis. At the time of his death, he was only thirty-eight years of age and was near to completing his fourth voyage around the world. He went around the world first as a midshipman on board the *Dolphin,* in command of Commodore John Byron. He shipped out as a master's mate on the *Endeavour;* and after so many deaths at Batavia, he returned a lieutenant. He was the second lieutenant on board the *Resolution* on Cook's second voyage, and Captain of the *Discovery,* and later commander of the expedition in this third voyage. He had sailed more watery miles on the globe than even Captain Cook.

Captain Gore succeeded to command of the expedition; and our narrator of events preceding and subsequent to Cook's death, Mr. King, became Captain King in command of the *Discovery.* The ships returned to the harbor of Petropavlovsk, where Captain Clerke was buried. Here they repaired the bow of the *Discovery,* which had several broken planks from being driven upon the ice. In the course of making the repairs, much of the ship was found to be rotten.

⋅§ Being now about to visit nations, our reception among whom might a good deal depend on the respectability of our appearance, two guns were taken out of the hold and mounted on deck. Our visit here had drawn the attention of the Russian commanders in Siberia to the defenseless situation of the place. I was told by an honest sergeant, with many significant shrugs, that, as we had found our way into it, other nations might do the same, some of whom might not be altogether welcome. §⋅

From the twenty-fourth of August to the ninth of October the ships stayed in the harbor while their crews visited with their Russian friends, repaired their ships, which were now showing considerable weakness and rot, and took on provisions.

On their way south along the western limit of the Pacific Ocean, they viewed—but did not land upon—the northern Kuril Island and the east coast of Japan. Contrary winds drove them off the coast of Japan, so they continued nearly due south until they discovered a new group of islands, which, like the Hawaiian Islands and the Aleutian Islands, were later to have a prominent place in American History: Iwo Jima. From here, heading west again, they passed the small island of Pratas between Formosa and the China mainland and made their way to Portuguese Macao.

At Macao and Canton, the sea-otter skins, which the crew had collected along the coast of Alaska and used for bedclothes and to add warmth to their seamen's clothes, were found to be highly valued by the Chinese. They sold their old and poorly preserved collection of furs for over 2,000 pounds sterling, a small fortune in its day. Captain King recorded:

⁐ The rage with which our seamen were possessed to return to Cook Inlet and buy another cargo of skins to make their fortunes, at one time was not far short of mutiny. And, I must own, I could not help indulging myself with the thought of the project. ⁐

Although King was never able to return to the northwest coast of America, as mentioned earlier, four of his shipmates did return. His armorer, George Dixon, and his master's mate, Nathaniel Portlock, in command of the *Queen Charlotte* and the *King George,* returned to start a fur trade between America and China. These fur-trading ships were the very next vessels to visit Hawaii, Vancouver Island, and Alaska after Cook's exploration. (His midshipman, George Vancouver, returned to survey the Pacific Northwest and establish British claims over that of the Spanish.) The Russians extended their operation south along the American coast all the way to California, and Joseph Billings, seaman on the *Discovery,* entered into the service of the Empress of Russia and explored the Alaskan country from 1785 to 1794. Very soon both the sea otter and the fur seal were nearly extinct.

On their way home from Macao the ships stopped at the islands of Poulo Condore off the coast of South Vietnam, where the men visited with the people and obtained more fresh food. They passed by Singapore and continued south to the passage between Sumatra and Java at Batavia. Knowing the unhealthiness of Batavia, both by reputation and by the near decimation of Cook's crew on the *Endeavour,* the expedition stopped only on the island of Krakatau in the Sunda Strait to take on more water. They felt themselves fortunate to escape through the strait without the death of a single man. The ships were sailed nonstop across the Indian Ocean to Cape Town. The officers had received information in Macao and from Dutch ships at Java to the effect that England was now at war with France, Spain, and the United States. Not knowing how the fortunes of war might have changed the political scene, or what enemy ships might be lurking in the traveled routes of the sea, it had been Captain Gore's intention to sail directly from Java to England; but the ships continued to fall apart, and it became apparent in the Indian Ocean that they could proceed no farther than Cape Town, where repairs would have to be made. When the ships were ready for sea again, they sailed from here, nonstop again, passing north of Ireland to avoid the French and then after stopping in North Scotland, returned to the Nore

◄§ . . . after an absence of four years, two months, and twenty-two days. In the course of our voyage, the *Resolution* lost but five men by sickness, three of whom were in a precarious state of health at our departure from England; the *Discovery* did not lose a man. Another circumstance attending this voyage, which if we consider its duration, and the nature of the service in which we were engaged, will appear scarcely less singular than the extraordinary healthiness of the crews, was that the two ships never lost sight of each other for a day together, except twice: which was owing the first time to an accident that happened to the *Discovery* off the coast of Hawaii; and the second to the fogs we met at the entrance to Avacha Bay. §►

Captain King might have added that this was the longest single exploring voyage in all history. And from that time on, there was never another scientific expedition under sail that was at sea for so many years.

BIBLIOGRAPHY

Publications Used in the Preparation of This Account

Andrews, Clarence L., *The Story of Alaska*. Caxton, Caldwell, Idaho, 1938.

Bancroft, Hubert H., *History of Alaska*.

Beaglehole, J. C., *The Journals of Captain James Cook on His Voyages of Discovery*. I. *The Voyage of the* Endeavour. II. *The Voyage of the* Resolution *and the* Adventure. III. *The Voyage of the* Resolution *and the* Discovery. Hakluyt Society, Cambridge University Press, I, 1955; II, 1961; III, 1967.

Beaglehole, J. C., *On the Character of Captain Cook*. Geographical Journal. Volume CXXII, 4, 1956.

Buck, Peter H., *Cook's Discovery of the Hawaiian Islands*. Bulletin of Bernie Pauabie, Bishop Museum of Polynesian Ethics and Natural History #186, 26, Honolulu, 1945.

Cameron, Roderick, *The Golden Haze*. World, New York, 1964.

Chickering, William H., *Within the Sound of These Waves*. Harcourt, N.Y., 1941.

Cook, James and King, James, *A Voyage to the Pacific Ocean*. Dublin, 1784.

Douglas, H. P., *Cook as an Hydrographical Surveyor*. Geographical Journal. Volume LXXIII, 110, London, 1929.

Dyson, Frank, *Captain Cook as an Astronomer*. Geographical Journal. Volume LXIII, 117, London, 1929.

Emory, Kenneth P., *Polynesian Stone Remains*. Papers of the Peabody Museum of Am. Arch. & Ethn., Studies in the Anthropology of Oceania and Asia. Harvard University. Volume XX, 9; 1943.

Kippis, A., *A Narrative of the Voyages Round the World Performed by Captain James Cook*. Derby & Jackson, New York, 1860.

Martin, John, *An Account of the Natives of the Tonga Islands in the South Pacific Ocean—compiled and arranged from the extensive communications of Mr. William Mariner*. London, 1816.

Michener, James A., *Hawaii*. Random House, New York, 1959.

Moorehead, Alan, *The Fatal Impact*. Harper & Row, New York, 1966.

Munford, James K., *John Ledyard's Journal of Captain Cook's Last Voyage*. Oregon University Press, Corvallis, Oregon, 1963.

Newbolt, Henry, *Captain James Cook and the Sandwich Islands*. Geographical Journal. Volume LXXIII, 97, 1929.

Oliver, Douglas L., *The Pacific Islands*. Harvard University Press, Cambridge, Mass., 1962.

Rickman, John, *Journal of Captain Cook's Last Voyage to the Pacific Ocean on Discovery*. London, 1781.

Rose, J. H., *Captain Cook and the Founding of British Power in the Pacific*. Geographical Journal. Volume LXXIII, No. 2, 108, London, 1929.

Suggs, Robert C., *The Island Civilizations of Polynesia*. New American Library, New York, 1960.

Wallis, Helen, *Carteret's Voyage Round the World*. Hakluyt Society, Cambridge University Press, 1965.

Warner, O., *Captain Cook and the South Pacific*. American Heritage Pub. Co., New York, 1963.

Recent Publications of Cook's Journals Between the Years 1900–1966.

JAMES COOK IN NEW ZEALAND, extracts from the Journals of Capt. James Cook, giving full account in his own words of his adventures and discoveries in New Zealand.

Edited by A. H. and A. W. Reed, Wellington.

Published by A. H. and A. W. Reed, 1951.

THE EXPLORATIONS OF CAPT. JAMES COOK IN THE PACIFIC as told by selections from his own Journals, 1768–1779.

Edited by A. Grenfell Price, New York.

Published by Limited Editions Club, 1957.

THE JOURNALS AND DISCOVERIES OF CAPT. JAMES COOK on his voyages of discovery. Edited from original manuscripts by

J. C. Beaglehole, ass't. of J. A. Williamson, Cambridge.

Published for Hakluyt Society at University Press, 1955, 1961, 1967.

VOYAGES OF DISCOVERY, James Cook.

Published for "Everyman's 99" by Dutton–no date.

THE VOYAGES OF CAPT. JAMES COOK ROUND THE WORLD. Selections from his Journals.

Edited by Christopher Lloyd.

Published by Chanticleer Press, 1949.

Recent Publications About Cook, 1946–1966

1. Williamson, J. A., COOK AND THE OPENING OF THE PACIFIC. Hodder and Stoughton, London, 1946.
2. Vander Cook, Jr., GREAT SAILOR. Dial Press, New York, 1951.
3. Guyther, Jr., CAPTAIN COOK AND THE SOUTH PACIFIC, VOYAGE OF THE ENDEAVOUR. Houghton Mifflin, Boston, 1955 (first voyage only).
4. Cameron, R., THE GOLDEN HAZE. World Publishing Co., New York, 1964.
5. Moorehead, Alan, THE FATAL IMPACT. Harper & Row, New York, 1966.

Recent Biographies of Cook, 1900–1965.

Author:

James Bonwick–1901.

Arthur Kitson–1907.

Sir Joseph Carruthers–1930.

R. T. Gould–1935.

Gordon Campbell–1936.

Hugh Carrington–1939.

H. P. Kendall–1951.

Christopher Lloyd–1952.

Ledyard's Account

Munford, J. E., editor, JOHN LEDYARD'S JOURNAL OF CAP-
TAIN COOK'S LAST VOYAGE. University of Oregon Press,
1964.

Ledyard, John, A JOURNAL OF CAPTAIN COOK'S LAST
VOYAGE. Republished by Quadrangle Books, Chicago, 1963.

Index ೪